Contents

Illustrations

Preface

This book is about Transformational Politics—a newly emerging field in political science concerned with major challenges facing us in the Post-Modern or Post–Cold War world. Transformationalists are concerned with developing new theories, bold visions of preferred futures, and transition strategies for getting there from here. This book will focus specifically on two processes that are linked to transformation—citizen empowerment and community mediation.

Empowerment is a major theme of Transformational Politics. The term "empowerment" is widely used by transformationalists, educators, and political activists. Although empowerment has positive connotations in popular American culture, there is a great deal of confusion about its meaning. The purpose of this study is to provide greater conceptual clarity and to develop a theoretical framework for empowerment that will enhance its value for transformationalists and others.

Mediation is a form of alternative dispute resolution or "popular justice," which is viewed as a supplement to, or alternative to, the formal legal system. Community mediation is a noncoercive, voluntary mode of conflict resolution that is facilitated by a neutral third party, the mediator, who assists people in conflict to negotiate, problem-solve, and craft a mutually agreeable solution to their dispute. The use of mediation has grown rapidly in the United States in recent years, and has been applied to a wide range of interpersonal as well as international problems.

This study explores possible linkages between the community mediation and citizen empowerment processes. Many advocates of community mediation claim that it is preferable to formal adjudication procedures because mediation is empowering for participants and perhaps even for the community. Advocates also claim that community mediation may be an important vehicle for personal and political transformation, and that it can contribute to democratic participation and community building as well.

My interest in empowerment and community mediation began in the early 1980s. The unemployment rate was at an all-time high, and researchers began to discover that long-term unemployment created serious personal and social impacts in addition to financial problems. Many workers confronting long-term structural unemployment developed major physical and mental health problems. Researchers found that unemployment increases personal stress and lowers self-esteem. In short, they found that unemployment is disempowering. The evidence for this relationship became so clear that President Reagan declared unemployment to be the nation's number one public health problem.

At the time I was the Executive Director of an action research program that designed and tested empowerment strategies for those attempting to cope with long-term unemployment. We developed an integrated empowerment model that combined training in job search and coping skills with support groups and the provision of material and non-material resources. I soon discovered what others have also learned: that helping others is personally empowering work.

Our program offices were located in an office building with the Honolulu Neighborhood Justice Center and other United Way agencies. I learned about community mediation and became a volunteer mediator and a mediation trainer. Like many other citizens, I was initially attracted to mediation work by ideological claims that community mediation was preferable to using the formal court system. Advocates of mediation argued that unlike the courts, it was empowering for its participants. I realized that although mediation ideology was a powerful symbolic resource for the community mediation movement, its claims were still untested and were taken on faith by mediators, program staff, and advocates. Although my initial interest in community mediation had been as a practitioner, I became aware that as a new field, and an emerging social movement, there were many questions that required research if we were to understand mediation's impact on social and political as well as legal issues.

Hawaii provided a uniquely supportive environment for doing this research. Informal dispute resolution is deeply rooted in Polynesian societies, and in Hawaii the indigenous form of conflict resolution called Ho'oponono is being revived. There are community mediation programs on all five of the major islands, and strong cooperation between the university conflict resolution researchers and community practitioners. Many of the University of Hawaii faculty, staff, and students serve as volunteer mediators, and some community mediation practitioners teach and conduct research at the university. The University of Hawaii Political Science Department's Graduate Program in

Conflict Resolution, the research- and policy-oriented Program on Conflict Resolution, the Spark Matsunaga Peace Institute, and the Richardson Law School support and coordinate these conflict resolution activities.

Many people have helped with this book. The Honolulu Neighborhood Justice staff and volunteer mediators gave generously of their time and were genuinely interested in helping to learn more about community mediation. Executive Director, Leland Chang, and Training Director, Jean Fargo, were especially supportive of this project and provided access to program documents, training workshops, and mediators. Much of the data collection was supported by a Hewlett Foundation grant administered through the Program on Conflict Resolution. I received ongoing support and assistance from the Program on Conflict Resolution Staff, especially from Associate Director Karen Cross, and the staff of the University of Hawaii Peace Institute. Follow-up research was supported by a Florida Atlantic University Foundation research grant. Several research assistants contributed to various aspects of this research including: Tom Feeney, Peggy Brandwen, Sharon Richards, Jennifer Simmons, Bill Thomas, and Linda Socolow. I appreciate their efforts and enthusiasm.

My involvement since 1988 with the Transformational Politics group of the American Political Science Association has provided me with a number of close friendships and a stimulating intellectual environment while I worked on this project. Many of these people, as well as colleagues at Florida Atlantic University and the University of Hawaii, have read all or parts of this manuscript and offered helpful comments. They include: Andrew Arno, John Barkai, Barry Bozeman, Jeanne Hendricks, Thomas Keene, George Kent, Anthony Marsella, Neal Milner, Ira Rohter, and William Warters.

I would like to thank Ted Becker, editor of the Praeger Series on Transformational Politics and Political Science, Dan Eades, acquisitions editor, Terri M. Jennings, production editor, and the Praeger staff for encouragement, patience, and valuable assistance.

Finally, and most importantly, Jan has been with me from the beginning of this project and has contributed immeasurably to it in many ways. Her love, unrelenting support, infinite patience, and computer expertise made this project viable. I dedicate this book to her.

Mediation,
Citizen Empowerment,
and Transformational Politics

1

Transformational Politics, Empowerment, and Conflict Resolution

May you live in interesting times.

old curse (anonymous)

TURBULENCE AND TRANSFORMATION

We do live in exciting times, and while some may regard this as a curse, others regard it as a blessing, or at least an opportunity. We live in a highly turbulent world and in transformational times. We are in the twilight of the twentieth century, and the world stands on the threshold of a new era, the beginning of the third millennium. The old order has ended, but the shape of the new world order is difficult to discern amongst the turmoil and chaos. Economic, social, political, and intellectual revolutions are occurring throughout the world.

Many scholars believe that we are at a major turning point in history comparable to what happened at the end of World War I and again at the end of World War II when fundamental breaks with the past set in motion major world transformations. These major sociopolitical transformations are similar to the dynamics of an earthquake in which massive tectonic plates collide and grind against each other for years as unbelievable tension and pressure builds. For a long time only slight tremors may be detected, until inevitably one day a tremendous shift occurs that generates chaos, conflict, and perhaps cataclysmic destruction. As a result, the underlying pressures are temporarily eased, the landscape is reshaped and a new order is eventually established.

After nearly fifty years of a terrifying, yet relatively stable period of Cold War hostility that developed shortly after World War II, major tremors began to occur in 1989. The Berlin Wall, a powerful symbol of Cold War animosity, was torn down. Our former enemy and communist super power, the Soviet Union, fragmented and was replaced by the Commonwealth of Independent States (CIS) in January 1992. East and West Germany have been reunited, and the forces of global democracy appear to be gaining strength throughout the world. At the same time, the resurgence of nationalism and ethnic conflict and weapons proliferation may presage new political disorders.

While most observers would agree that we are now in the Post–Cold War era, there is little agreement on what is actually happening, the significance of the political convulsions that engulf us, and what we can or should do about it. This turbulent world is difficult to comprehend for several reasons. First, the changes that are occurring are sometimes visible, dramatic, and revolutionary, and at other times subtle, gradual, and evolutionary. Second, these changes are occurring at many levels: individual, local, national, and global, and they are interrelated in complex ways. Sometimes they are complementary and synergistic, and at other times conflicting. We don't understand these interactions very well. Third, changes that may prove advantageous in the short term or at one level may later appear to be disastrous in the long term or at another level. Fourth, the occurrence of so many apparently conflicting trends and conflicting values makes it difficult to discern any clear trends or directions. For example, some of the most important and interesting conflicting trends and values in the world today would include: integration versus disintegration, universalism versus tribalism, centralization versus decentralization, globalism versus localism, individualism versus communitarianism, materialism versus spiritualism, democracy versus authoritarianism, modernization versus traditionalism, and change versus continuity.

Given the complexity of these conflicting trends and values, it is difficult to discern what is happening in the world and how these changes will shape the future. Consequently, there is a vigorous debate between the optimists who believe that this may be the "best of times" and the pessimists who argue that this may be the "worst of times." For example, optimists have proclaimed the "end of history" and a victory of liberal democracy over communism (Fukuyama 1989), while pessimists contend that "we will soon learn to miss the Cold War" because we are likely to be returning "back to the future" and to a resumption of the historical balance of power warfare that prevailed for hundreds of years in Europe (Mearsheimer 1990). Optimists suggest that we are at a "democratic moment" in history when the United States might successfully promote global democracy and world peace (Diamond 1994), while pessimists point to evidence of the rise of tribalism, nationalism, and racism as new sources of fragmentation and authoritarianism (Huntington 1993). Optimists contend that major war is "obsolete," and like many other outmoded institutions and customs such as slavery, bearbaiting, and dueling, major war will be increasingly less likely (Mueller 1989; Ray 1989). Pessimists contend that many bitter Post–Cold War conflicts will be generated by the emerging "clash of civilizations" (Huntington 1993). Optimists stress the great economic and democratic political benefits that will flow from technological advances, such as the "telecommunication revolution" and the information super highway (Naisbitt 1994), while pessimists stress the overwhelming dangers (some generated by technology) of the "world problematique," including global warming, environmental pollution, and the "population explosion" (Ehrlich and Ehrlich 1990). Some scholars believe that "teledemocracy" can revitalize democracy and increase citizen participation in political decision making (Slaton 1992), while critics are concerned about the dangers of "the tyranny of the majority" or charismatic dictators using electronic town meeting forums to manipulate public opinion (Arterton 1987). Finally, some optimistic policy analysts and political decision makers believe that we can "reinvent" local, state, and national government (Osborne and Gaebler 1992; Gore 1993), while others focus on the intractability of government gridlock and government corruption (Hellinger and Judd 1994).

TRANSFORMATIONAL POLITICS

These debates and issues are the stuff of Transformational Politics, a new interdisciplinary field of inquiry that includes a diverse group of scholars, policy analysts, policy-makers, practitioners, and other concerned citizens who share common values and concerns but often differ with regard to issue areas, theoretical focus, and methodological approach. Transformational Politics has been an organized section of the American Political Science Association (APSA) since 1991. The petition submitted to the APSA to establish an organized section on Transformational Politics provides one of the few public attempts to set forth the concerns and parameters of Transformational Politics. It states, "Our purpose is to explore those trends in contemporary life that are challenging the viability of traditional divisions in political science and political life (normative/empirical; personal/professional; theory/practice; Liberal/Conservative; Left/Right; global/local; secular/spiritual, to name a few). *We are committed to examining alternatives that seek a new synthesis*" (no author, no date).

The petition suggests the need to promote a new approach to political science and to develop a political community consistent with a number of ethical imperatives. These ethical imperatives are set forth as the basis for beginning a common dialogue but are clearly not intended to bind or exclude those individuals who do not share each specific concern or who may disagree. According to the petition, the ethical imperatives that concern transformationalists include:

1. A politics of participation that provides every member of society with full opportunities to influence the political, social, and economic institutions

affecting their lives, that fosters collective and personal responsibility to fulfill that task;

2. A politics of social justice and hope that seeks to reduce the material inequities within and between nations, and that treats the problems and scarcities before us as opportunities to clarify our sense of what truly is important in life;

3. A politics of conflict resolution and healing that acknowledges and respects differences and goes beyond "us against them," or "right versus wrong," in promoting cooperation and community in all matters;

4. A politics of human growth that fosters the full development of each person's potential;

5. A politics of ecology and unitive consciousness, which understands that we are only one part of a seamless web of life, that we are responsible to all life on earth, and that our journey can have sacred meaning—as we comprehend that term (no author, no date).

In a more recent effort at formulating political transformation theory, Theodore Becker and Christa Slaton attempted to differentiate transformation from other kinds of social and political change. They argue, "All theories of drastic political change and/or revolution are not necessarily theories of political transformation. In order to qualify as such, they must seek to come to terms with major socioeconomic-technological developments—and attendant dislocations and turmoil—by helping envision novel, adaptive, evolutionary ways of public and private life. Recreating past systems through violent means, or piecemeal reform of them is not the stuff of transformational politics and theories thereof" (1991, 1).

Most transformationalists would agree that the existing economic, social, and political systems and structures are flawed, ineffective, and dysfunctional and therefore that structural changes are necessary and desirable in order to bring about greater social justice, human growth, and effectiveness. Most would also agree that these transformations should be evolutionary, not revolutionary, and they should ideally be nonviolent and noncoercive. In practice, however, differentiating between approaches that are reformist and transformational can be more problematic. Some reform measures may be clearly designed and intended to maintain the existing status quo and to control disruptive social conflict, but other measures such as efforts to "reinvent" government or facilitate human growth may have transformational outcomes in the longer term. I will return to this important issue of distinguishing between reform and transformation in greater detail in the final chapter.

Another approach to understanding or at least differentiating Transformational Politics from other movements or perspectives is to focus on the major concepts or values that concern transformational theorists and practitioners. Given the diversity of Transformational Politics it is impossible and perhaps undesirable to be definitive, but Becker and Slaton have suggested that central values and concepts would include "(1) personal empowerment of individual citizens; (2) grassroots, direct democracy; (3) deep ecology, or an awareness and sensitivity to the interdependence of humankind and all aspects of its environment on Earth's ecosphere; (4) respect, if not appreciation for, the vast diversity of races, sexes, lifestyles within any society and/or around the globe; (5) collaboration and cooperation being a superior way of human interaction to that of competitiveness" (1991, 1).

While this list of concepts and values is not exhaustive, it does comprise a core set of values to which many transformationalists would subscribe. Despite these broad communalities, transformationalists have different ways of thinking about Transformational Politics, and they focus on diverse interests and issues. Among the multiple perspectives or orientations that might be included within the rubric of Transformational Politics are: (1) green politics (see Spretnak and Capra 1986; Rensenbrink 1992; Slaton and Becker 1990), (2) environmental politics (see Walbek 1988; Milbrath 1989), (3) feminist politics (see Kelly 1989; Starhawk 1987), (4) spiritual politics (see Spretnak 1986; McLaughlin and Davidson 1994), (5) new age politics (see Bookchin 1986; Satin 1979; Spangler 1988), and (6) neo-populist politics (Boyte 1980; Boyte and Reissman 1986; Bellah et al. 1985; Reissman 1986). While some of the theorists cited here might not specifically identify themselves as belonging to a Transformational Politics movement, their theories and perspectives are central to transformational concerns.

Transformationalists are also interested in a variety of social and political movements and phenomenon, including (1) peace movements and other social movements (see Zisk 1992), (2) democratic movements (Diamond 1994), (3) new models of strong or mass participatory democracy (Barber 1984; Mansbridge 1983), (4) tools for enhancing democratic participation, such as teledemocracy (see Etzioni 1993a; Becker and Slaton 1991), (6) communitarianism (see Bellah et al. 1985; Etzioni 1993b; Barber 1992), (7) individual transformation (see Halpern 1991; Abalos 1993), (8) transforming leadership (see Burns 1978; Fishell 1992; Couto 1993), (9) transformational teaching (see Couto 1994; Schwerin 1992), (10) models of transformational research (see Gaventa 1985; Yeich and Levine 1992), (11) new transformational paradigms and quantum theories (see Becker 1991). Thus, Transformational Politics as a field of inquiry, is as diverse and dynamic as its phenomenon of interest for theory, research, and teaching.

EMPOWERMENT AND CONFLICT RESOLUTION

This book focuses on two processes or social movements central to Transformational Politics, the theory and process of empowerment, and the social movement and process of conflict resolution known as community mediation.

The primary empirical analysis focuses on the postulated linkage between the mediation process and citizen empowerment.

I contend that empowerment is the core concept or value of Transformational Politics. Empowerment is central to the theoretical and ideological concerns of most transformationalist groups and movements including green politics, feminist politics, participatory democracy, transforming leadership, communitarianism, neo-populism, and community mediation, as well as the other areas of interest to transformationalists. Empowerment is the leitmotif of the Transformational Politics movement. Indeed, the term "empowerment" appears so frequently in the Transformational Politics literature as well as other areas, such as education and even business literature, that it has become almost a buzzword. Despite its frequent use, however, and its strong appeal to people with diverse interests and perspectives, there is a good deal of confusion about the meaning of empowerment. It is a fuzzy concept. But like the concept of power, empowerment is of such great importance that it warrants the labor required to gain a better grasp of its complex meanings. Therefore my primary purpose is to provide greater conceptual clarity and theoretical development of the empowerment concept. Given its widespread appeal to a wide diversity of people, it has great potential as a paradigm for Transformational Politics. Empowerment is associated with the positive transformation of individuals, groups, and structures.

Conflict resolution is also of central concern to Transformational Politics and to the Post–Cold War world and Information Age we are entering. Conflict resolution is important to this study for at least three reasons. First, the process of transformation and conflict are inextricably linked. Second, some models of conflict resolution are believed to be particularly empowering or transformational. Third, a type of conflict resolution called "alternative dispute resolution" has been growing rapidly in the United States and more recently has been exported to Eastern Europe and Russia, where it is promoted as a noncoercive tool for facilitating the transition from authoritarianism to democracy.

The occurrence of conflict is natural and inevitable. Conflicts occur in all organizations, communities, societies, and relationships. They involve a struggle between two or more people over values, or competition for status, power, and scarce resources (Coser 1967). But conflict is far more likely to occur and perhaps to intensify during conditions of turmoil, turbulence, and transformation. On one hand, conflict can lead to transformation by demonstrating the dysfunctionality of existing structures and institutions. On the other hand, the process of transformation often generates conflict by its very nature as institutions, structures, and power elites at all levels of society and government resist efforts to change the status quo.

While conflict is natural and inevitable, many people are quite uncomfortable with it and may seek to avoid conflict situations whenever possible. If it is mishandled, conflict can develop negative dynamics and cause psychological or physical damage. But conflict is not necessarily bad or dysfunctional. If handled correctly, conflict can be functional and result in positive growth for individuals, groups, and organizations (Coser 1967). Therefore, the type of conflict resolution employed is a key to whether the outcome of a conflict situation is beneficial or damaging. There are many alternatives for resolving conflicts, including conflict avoidance, problem solving, negotiation, mediation, arbitration, adjudication, legislation, or violent means such as murder or war. Some of these methods of conflict resolution, such as war or adjudication, are by their nature violent and oppressive, while other methods of conflict resolution, such as problem solving and mediation, can be highly cooperative and collaborative. As mentioned above, most transformationalists prefer the nonviolent, noncoercive modes of conflict resolution such as facilitation or mediation, which is the focus of this study.

Mediation can take different forms, but it can be simply defined "as an effort by a neutral third party to resolve a dispute through the conduct of a face-to-face meeting between the disputing parties" (McGillis 1986, 32). In recent years the practice of mediation has grown rapidly in the United States and in other countries. It is used in a wide variety of disputes, such as neighbor-neighbor, divorce, commercial, environmental, and public policy conflicts. American mediation consultants are now teaching these techniques in Eastern Europe and Russia as a positive way of dealing with the many conflicts that are emerging as a result of making the difficult transformation from authoritarian to more democratic rule in these formerly communist nations (Shonholtz 1993b; Ondrusek 1993; Stulberg 1993; Wildau, Moore, and Mayer 1993).

One of the major reasons for the appeal of community mediation to transformationalists as well as others is because of the linkage that is believed to exist between participation in the mediation process and the empowerment of individuals and communities. According to advocates of mediation, some forms of conflict management such as the formal court system are disempowering for the disputing parties because of the domination and control of judges and lawyers that is inherent in the court system. In contrast, other types of conflict resolution, such as mediation and facilitation are considered to be empowering because they are voluntary and noncoercive, and they enable the parties in conflict to own their own conflict, control the conflict resolution process, and craft resolutions that are mutually agreeable.

Empowerment is a core value in mediation ideology, and community mediation is viewed by many of its advocates as a transformational social movement that has the potential to empower not only disputants but also the mediators as well as the community. In this study I will examine many of these claims and compare the ideological rhetoric about empowerment to the reality of community mediation.

The purpose of this study is to develop empowerment theory in the context of community mediation. I use a case study of a large urban community mediation program to ground the theory. I operationalize the empowerment concept and assess some of the most widely believed hypotheses about the linkage between citizen empowerment and community mediation. In order to do justice to the complexity of the empowerment concept, I use a mix of both qualitative and quantitative methods, including participant observation; interviews with community mediation staff, volunteer mediators, and disputants; content analysis of documents and literature; conceptual analysis of the empowerment concept; data collection using surveys and psychological instruments; and an extensive empirical data analysis. The primary contributions of this study to Transformational Politics and the community mediation movement include the development and elaboration of empowerment theory, an analysis of mediation ideology, mediation training, the mediation process, and organizational leadership, and the exploration of the linkage between community mediation and personal and social transformation.

OVERVIEW OF THE CHAPTERS

Chapter 2 provides a general introduction to the American community mediation movement. Mediation is not a new conflict resolution process. It has existed for hundreds of years, and it has been practiced in Europe, colonial America, and many non-Western cultures. Many types of conflict resolution, or conflict management, fall under the rubric of mediation, including labor mediation, environmental mediation, and international commercial mediation. But the focus of this study is on community mediation, and especially on the citizen volunteer mediators who mediate a variety of disputes as a community service usually without financial compensation. Community mediation is known by many other names, such as alternative dispute resolution (ADR), informal justice, neighborhood justice, and popular justice.

I discuss the ideology that has developed around community mediation, its functions for the mediation movement, and the centrality of empowerment in mediation ideology. The ideology of community mediation claims that mediation resolves conflicts in ways that are empowering for both the participants and the community. Thus, it may serve as a vehicle for personal and political transformation. To assess the validity of these claims, I investigate the empowerment process in a community mediation setting. The research objectives include (1) theory building through clarification and development of the empowerment concept, (2) empirical analysis to measure empowerment and to test propositions about participation and empowerment, and (3) increased understanding of the social and political implications of community mediation and empowerment.

The proposition that *mediation participation empowers mediators* provides the research focus. Volunteer mediators were chosen as the research participants for several reasons. First, given their training and ongoing experience with the mediation process, they are more likely to be empowered than are the disputants. Second, mediators play a key role in the mediation process but have been overlooked by researchers, so there is a research gap. Third, there are now over 25,000 active mediators in the United States, with thousands more being trained every year. Understanding how mediators are affected by their experiences as conflict resolvers has important implications for conflict management theory and public policy.

I describe the mediation process and various models and styles of mediation. I discuss the variety of roles and characteristics associated with mediators, as well as their use of power in managing the conflict process. All of these elements—the mediation ideology, mediators' roles and styles, and their use of power—may be linked to mediator empowerment. In the next chapter I ground this general discussion of mediation ideology and the mediation process in a case study of one of the most successful community mediation programs operating today.

Chapter 3 examines the development of community mediation in Hawaii and in particular the history, operation, and ideology of the Honolulu Neighborhood Justice Center (HNJC). The values of empowerment and volunteerism are strongly held in this organization, and I discuss how they are reflected and played out in the recruitment of volunteer citizen mediators, their training as mediators, and their mediation and organizational leadership activities. Many of the applicants for mediator training are motivated by the belief that it will add to their personal growth in empowering ways. The training is designed to teach mediation skills and to inculcate the value of empowerment.

An extensive analysis was done of the organization operation and culture using participant observation of training, mediation sessions, staff activities, and leadership activities, interviews, and content analysis of program documents. Interviews and surveys were used to collect personal and demographic data on disputants and mediators, and empowerment data on mediators.

Empowerment is a core value in mediation ideology and it is often discussed by mediation theorists, program staff, and volunteer mediators, but its meanings are unclear. The occurrence of empowerment as a result of the community mediation process is taken on faith. Therefore, I focus on clarifying the empowerment concept and developing a theoretical framework for empowerment in chapter 4. This project is vital for at least two reasons. First, the development of the empowerment theory is the major focus of this study. It is of primary concern to Transformational Politics as well as many other fields, but it is difficult to grasp because of its complexity and resistance to empirical measurement. Second, the development of empowerment theory in this chapter provides the foundations for the research design and empirical analysis that follow. It enables the development of a mediator-empowerment model that links mediation participation and empowerment, and suggests a number of indicators that are used to operationalize the empowerment concept.

To clarify the empowerment concept I follow a method of conceptual analysis developed by Giovanni Sartori (1984). I apply this methodology to a comparative analysis of the writings of social science and mediation theorists on empowerment as well as to survey data on volunteer mediators. Using this approach I delineate eight primary empowerment components, including self-esteem, self-efficacy, knowledge and skills, political awareness, social participation, political participation, rights and responsibilities, and access to psychological, social, and material resources. These components are used to reconstruct a definition for empowerment and to develop a theoretical framework for the empowerment process. The conceptual analysis yields numerous useful insights about the nature of empowerment and how it can be developed in individuals and groups, and how it can be measured and studied. I then set forth the mediator-empowerment model, which suggests how the major forms of mediation participation—training, mediation practice, and leadership—might be linked to mediator empowerment.

The research design in chapter 5 flows from this model. I discuss the critical research decisions involved in creating the design and describe the instrument design and construction. I use eleven measures of psychological empowerment, including self-esteem, general self-efficacy, political efficacy, political awareness, group cooperation, perceived competence, desirability of control, and three locus of control measures. I also use three measures of disempowerment, including powerlessness, normlessness, and social isolation. Three groups—mediator *Trainees*, *Mediators*, and *Leaders*—were compared across all fourteen measures of empowerment and disempowerment.

The empirical analysis that follows in chapter 6 has several phases and purposes. One question that occurs in the mediation literature pertains to the kind of people who volunteer to be community mediators. Mediation ideology suggests that mediators are similar to the people who bring their disputes to the mediation center and that community mediation is a situation of "neighbor helping neighbor." In support of this view, some disputants who are favorably impressed with their mediation experience apply to become mediators themselves. In addition, some of the volunteer mediators bring their own conflicts to be resolved at their mediation center. To assess this view I compare the mediators' characteristics to the disputants' characteristics and to some of the characteristics of the general Hawaiian population. The mediators' characteristics are also considered later in the analysis to evaluate the results of the main empirical analysis and to interpret the findings. This data is useful because other studies of community empowerment have linked data such as level of education to individual levels of empowerment.

Another phase of the empirical analysis focuses on the empowerment components. A factor analysis of the empowerment indices reveals three clear empowerment dimensions, which I named mastery, political awareness/participation, and leadership. The results of this empirical analysis support the findings of the conceptual analysis of empowerment reported in chapter 4.

The main phase of the empirical analysis focuses on the linkage between mediation participation and citizen empowerment. The research question that provides the empirical focus for this study is: *Does mediation participation empower mediators?* I look first at the effects of mediation training on mediator empowerment, then at the effects of mediating disputes, and finally at the empowering effects associated with organizational leadership. The findings for mediation training are uniformly clear and strong. The findings for experienced mediators and organizational leaders are more complex. I discuss and interpret these findings and compare them to research data on other community mediation programs and other community settings.

In chapter 7 I discuss what is now known about empowerment, community mediation, and the link between mediation participation and empowerment as a result of this study, and some of the implications for further research, praxis, and policy making. I also discuss the possible or probable future of the community mediation movement and its potential for personal and social transformation. At this time in the development of the community movement there are competing models and different ideological projects that are vying for ascendancy. Some of these models and projects emphasize human growth and social transformation, while others emphasize the need for professionalization and standardization of mediation and may support the maintenance of the present political and legal status quo. One direction represents major transformation of existing structures, and the other implies perhaps minor reforms. One direction would enable both personal empowerment as well as political transformation, while the other, which focuses on cost-effective delivery of conflict management services, may incidentally develop some degree of personal empowerment.

Empowerment has provided an important symbolic resource for the community mediation movement, and in addition, it is equally important to other transformational movements and projects. In chapter 8 I discuss the further development of empowerment theory, its linkage to participatory democracy and communitarianism, and its potential as a paradigm for Transformational Politics.

Finally, I close with some remarks on the future of Transformational Politics not only as a scholarly endeavor but also as a social movement in its own right. We are at a crucial point in world history, perhaps a "democratic moment." We do have some power to shape the future. But the way is not clear and the obstacles are many. It is easy to be discouraged or overwhelmed by the complexity of the tasks ahead. While the difficulties are great, perhaps this is truly a transformational moment in history. Should we be optimistic or pessimistic about our future prospects?

2

The Community Mediation Movement: Models, Ideology, and Mediators

This chapter provides a general overview of the Alternative Dispute Resolution (ADR) movement and community mediation. It discusses the importance of mediation ideology and the core value of empowerment. It describes the citizen volunteer mediators, their roles, and the strategies they use to mediate disputes. This material provides a background for understanding the community mediation movement and its potential for the empowerment of individuals and communities.

THE ADR MOVEMENT AND MEDIATION

Growth and Development

Americans feel entitled to use the legal system for help with their legal problems and conflicts with friends, neighbors, lovers, or strangers. A generation who has grown up with "Perry Mason," Judge Wapner, and "L.A. Law" naturally see the court as an institution that will protect their legal rights and property. They turn to the formal legal system as the place to go for "getting justice and getting even" (Merry 1990).

In recent years, however, the courts have come under heavy criticism for their perceived shortcomings, such as: (1) excessive legal costs that limit access to justice for the poor, (2) the long delays in processing cases caused by an unwieldy court system, (3) the unfairness of many litigation outcomes that tend to favor the wealthy, and (4) the limitations of legal remedies that address situations, instead of the causal aspects of disputes (McGillis and Mullen 1977; Folberg and Taylor 1984; Pruitt and Kressel 1985).

Over the last twenty years the American judicial system has witnessed the rapid proliferation of informal alternative dispute resolution (ADR) programs driven in part by widespread dissatisfaction with the performance of the formal legal system. ADR has been suggested as a replacement for, or as a supplement to, the formal American court-based, lawyer-dominated, dispute-processing system. It provides options to routine court processing for handling many of the disputes that arise among citizens.

The current wave of alternative dispute resolution is only about twenty years old, but its historical precedents can be traced to colonial America, where forms of mediation were used by Quakers in Philadelphia, the Chinese in San Francisco, Scandinavians in Minnesota, Jewish immigrants in New York, and communal groups and businessmen (Auerbach 1983). There is also evidence that early Native American tribal cultures, including Navahos and Lakotas, used mediation to resolve disputes (Garrett 1994).

Endemic forms of informal dispute resolution are found throughout the world in other cultures, such as China (Li 1978; Cohen 1977), Japan (Miyazawa 1987), the Philippines (Pe and Tadiar 1979), Sri Lanka (Tiruchelvam 1984), and Melanesia (Johnny 1987). In Hawaii, the traditional form of Hawaiian dispute resolution, called "Ho'oponopono," is still practiced today (Ito 1985; Shook 1985).

The modern ADR movement in the United States is usually traced to three diverse influences: labor mediation models (Kolb 1983), African moots (Danzig 1973), and the people's courts system in the Soviet Union (Henry 1983). Growth over the last twenty years in the United States has been rapid, from a dozen dispute resolution programs in 1975 to over 485 programs operating today in forty-four states, the District of Columbia, and Puerto Rico (American Bar Association Dispute Resolution Directory 1986). A study of the ADR movement (Keilitz, Gallas, and Hansen 1988, 10) indicates that "the adoption of ADR is hovering around the base of the J-curve . . . the movement is poised for a second generation of programs that will refine and improve the ADR process."

The emergence of the ADR movement is marked by growth in membership and attendance at conferences of professional organizations, such as the Society of Professionals in Dispute Resolution (SPIDR) and the North American Conference on Peacemaking and Conflict Resolution (NCPCR). The development of dispute resolution programs at the University of Hawaii, George Mason University, and other universities, and increasing course offerings in ADR at law and business schools (ADR Report 1988), imply that it is an "idea whose time has come" (Sandole 1985). Other significant indicators are the increased research funding from Ford, Hewlett, and other foundations, and the proliferation of articles and mediation books published in the last five years.

Given this rapid growth, some observers have suggested that ADR may constitute a social movement (Adler 1987) or represent a paradigm shift (Sandole 1988) or a political system (Burton 1988). ADR is a general phrase that describes an array of techniques that can be used to resolve disputes without formal adjudication. The types of alternative dispute resolution commonly included are negotiation, conciliation, mediation, mediation/arbitration, and arbitration. A number of approaches have been used to compare and contrast these conflict resolution processes. For example, some scholars of dispute resolution suggest that these processes can be viewed on a continuum of increasing coercion, with conciliation the least coercive and arbitration the most coercive (Marks, Johnson, and Szanton 1984), arranged on a scale of decreasing external involvement, with two-person negotiation having the least external involvement and arbitration the most (Sander 1982, 27), or organized in a taxonomy based on their structural characteristics (Goldberg, Green, and Sander 1985).

Other scholars have argued that these efforts at classification represent misleading essentialism, and contend that, in reality, "dispute processes are flexible and adaptive, their boundaries are blurred, and their capacities are uncertain" (Sarat 1988, 709). Therefore, any attempts to define the essential attributes of mediation and the other forms of dispute resolution are seen as problematic, if not misguided.

Mediation is by far the most widely used of these dispute resolution processes. Mediation programs have rapidly expanded their services to include a variety of community, commercial, family, environmental, and public policy disputes (Folberg and Taylor 1984; Marks, Johnson, and Szanton 1984; McGillis 1986). There is often confusion about the meaning of the term "mediation" in part because it is used to encompass a variety of related but distinctive conflict resolution processes, including labor mediation, environmental mediation, international commercial mediation, international political mediation, and community mediation. Although the general definition of mediation given above would cover all of these conflict resolution processes, there are significant differences among them (see Sandole and Sandole-Staroste 1987). This study focuses specifically on community mediation.

Community mediation has spread rapidly in recent years and is now used in many American communities. But mediation can be done in somewhat different ways in different communities. In one model, mediation is closely tied to the formal court system and sometimes done for a fee by professional mediators, such as lawyers and therapists. In other cases, community mediation is based on a grass roots community model, or a human services agency model, and mediation is done by citizen volunteer mediators as a community service, usually without financial remuneration.

These different models of community mediation and the use of professionals or citizen volunteer mediators may have profoundly different implications for the present impact of mediation on the participants and the community, as well as for the future of community mediation itself. These implications will be considered later. Because this study is concerned specifically with the linkage of community mediation and citizen empowerment, as well as the relationship between citizen participation and democratic theory, the research participants chosen for this study are the citizen volunteer mediators who are motivated to serve their communities out of altruism and perhaps the desire for personal empowerment.

Despite the rapid spread of community mediation programs in recent years, relatively little is known about the impact of community mediation programs on the participants or the community, and research efforts are in an early stage (Pruitt and Kressel 1985; Wall and Lynn 1993). To ascertain the impact of these programs on the formal legal system we need more data on cost-effectiveness, the quality of justice rendered, access to justice, and client satisfaction compared to the alternatives offered by the formal justice system. On the other hand, in order to understand the broader social and political implications of these community dispute-resolution models, we need to learn more about how these programs might impact the disputants, the local community, and the citizen volunteer mediators who facilitate the mediation process.

A major purpose of this study is to learn more about how citizen volunteer mediators are affected by their mediation experiences. These community mediators are important candidates for inquiry both because of their key role in the mediation conflict management process and because of their increasing numbers. There are presently over 25,000 active mediators, with thousands more being trained each year (McGillis 1986).

Mediation's advocates often claim that community mediation has an empowering impact on both the participants and the community. Whenever empowerment is discussed in the mediation literature the focus is primarily on conducting the mediation process in ways that will empower the disputing parties. However, some long-time observers of community mediation, such as Sally Engle Merry (quoted in Beer 1986) and Judy Rothschild (1986), have suggested that if anyone is empowered by mediation, it is more likely to be the mediators.

There are several reasons why mediators are more likely than the disputants to be empowered by the mediation process. First, compared to the experience of most disputants, who are only exposed for a few hours to the mediation process, volunteer mediators are involved with the mediation process over a long period of time. Second, the mediators receive intensive mediation skill training designed to increase their self-confidence and personal competence and thus be empowering. Third, they may have been motivated to become mediators not only by the desire to help others and to serve their community, but also because of their belief that mediation would enhance their self-empowerment. In other words, personal empowerment is a conscious goal for many citizen mediators but not for disputants who are only seeking solutions to their disputes.

If the community mediators become empowered, they may in turn have an empowering impact on the larger community. If empowering skills, attitudes, and behaviors are transferred from the mediation setting to other community settings, mediators are most likely to be the primary transmitters. Thus, mediators may act as political change agents and consciously or unconsciously facilitate political transformation. While many community mediation programs have the empowerment of the disputing parties as their stated objective, the empowerment of the mediators may be the major unforeseen benefit. From a public policy perspective, this empowerment outcome may be as important as the settlement of disputes if the result is personal and political transformation.

These ideological claims that community mediation has potential for personal and political transformation have important implications for conflict management theory and practice, democratic theory, community building, political praxis, and public policy. But while these ideological claims have been widely accepted in the community mediation movement, so far there is little hard evidence to support them. The challenge for theorists, practitioners, and policy-makers is to move beyond the ideological assumptions of mediation's proponents and to empirically test claims that mediation participation is empowering. The types of mediation participation of concern to this study include the major activities of mediators, such as the mediation skills training, the mediation of disputes, and leadership roles in the organization.

Despite its many advocates who claim that mediation has substantial advantages over the formal litigation process, mediation is not without its critics. Serious questions are being raised about the legal, social, and political implications of the mediation movement and its future. Mediation's critics, such as Roman Tomasic (1982), argue that the claims for the superiority of mediation for solving conflict in comparison with the formal justice system are untested and unproven.

Many of mediation's critics are apprehensive about the possible negative implications for the poor and middle classes (Abel 1982). For example, some of them argue that mediation is actually a conservative force that operates to maintain social control instead of a mechanism for social transformation (Neubauer and Shapiro 1985; Rothschild 1986). As Sarat argues, these techniques may "serve social control purposes and inhibit the development of coherent political opposition by individuating grievances" (1988, 711). Other critics are concerned about the need for quality assurance in service delivery and the lack of standards. They call for more regulation of the practice of dispute resolution and greater institutionalization (Burton and Dukes 1990).

Present State of Research

The debate between mediation's advocates and its critics is likely to continue for some time given the paucity of research that has been done so far. In their survey of mediation research, Kressel and Pruitt (1985, 179) point out that "we are still in the relatively early stages of sustained research on mediation," and they argue that it is difficult to make any assertions since the "measures employed in these studies are inaccurate or unreliable" (187). They note that "the enthusiasm and inventiveness of mediators has thus far outdistanced the ability of researchers to comprehend the mediation process and to accurately assess its value" (196). The mediation literature is scattered among a diverse collection of law and social science journals. Two journals, the *Mediation Quarterly* and the *Negotiation Journal* have begun to provide more focus, and a few books (Folberg and Taylor 1984; Goldberg, Green, and Sander 1985; Moore 1986; Burton 1990; Burton and Dukes 1990; Duffy, Grosch, and Olczak 1991; Merry and Milner 1993) have started to organize the field of dispute resolution.

Most of the literature consists of case studies. An assessment of empirical studies on mediation notes the "paucity of studies" and "the rather crude designs which typify the research literature" (Kressel 1986, 4). The tendency has been to focus on measures that are easily quantifiable and satisfactory for basic evaluation research questions, such as the number of cases processed, number of agreements, cost per case, and client satisfaction. Other potentially significant social and political measures that seem less tangible and more difficult to grasp conceptually have been less studied (see Lowry 1993; Wall and Lynn 1993).

Merry argues that, in order to understand mediation and its potential role in American society better, we need "broader definitions of effectiveness and success which describe more fully what Neighborhood Justice Centers (NJCs) can provide in the American context" (1982, 173). Some of these success measures, which are not easily susceptible to quantification but are nevertheless crucial to understanding the social and political implications of mediation, are its potential impacts on community quality of life, enhancement of the individual's sense of mastery and control, viability as a vehicle for social change, and "the development of local leadership and dispute settlement skills which can be applied outside the centers" (1982, 189).

To the extent that this study contributes to theory building and the development of these crucial but less tangible success measures, it will advance the assessment of mediation's impact on individuals and communities, have practical value for program evaluation, and contribute to the further development of knowledge about alternative dispute resolution.

MEDIATION IDEOLOGY AND EMPOWERMENT

The Functions of Ideology

Many social movements develop a coherent ideology that explains how the world actually works and provides a vision of how the world should work.

Ideologies provide a world view, a guide for action, the glue that holds social groups and communities together, and an effective means for social control.

Mediation ideology serves a variety of important functions for the mediators, the community mediation centers, and the ADR movement as a whole. Ideology is a key factor in understanding what attracts, motivates, and empowers mediators. For the purposes of this study, I define ideology as *the assumptions, values, beliefs, concepts (both factual and normative), and myths that purport to explain and justify what mediation is, why it is important, and how it compares with, and is superior to, the formal legal system.*

Mediation ideology serves the community mediation movement in many important ways. First, ideology provides a vision and mythology for mediation that mobilizes the resources necessary for its survival and success. As Adler, Lovaas, and Milner (1988, 2–3) point out, "Ideologies are broad statements of public purpose that are rooted in socially compelling visions of reality. Such visions are at the core of social movements. They determine the way reality is conceptualized and how problems are defined."

Second, ideology legitimates and promotes community mediation to its diverse constituents, such as judges and lawyers, anti-law reformers, business leaders, and grass roots community organizers. Third, it provides a marketing rhetoric by arguing that mediation has substantial advantages over the formal litigation process, including lower costs, greater accessibility to dispute resolution services, and the possibility of creating mutually satisfactory, durable agreements that are voluntarily crafted by the disputants. Fourth, by legitimating the support of mediation's adherents, ideology dampens internal and external threats to the community mediation movement.

Ideology also serves important functions for the individual community mediation programs. First, it provides the neighborhood mediation center with a skilled and cost-effective labor force by rationalizing the use of citizen volunteers to deliver conflict resolution services because of the benefits that are claimed to be provided to the disputants, the general public, and the mediators themselves. Second, mediation ideology helps to substantiate the claims of widespread community participation and community ownership that support the community mediation center and justify the requests for increased funding from local foundations, government, and business.

Perhaps most importantly, mediation ideology attracts both the disputants as well as the volunteer mediators to the community mediation centers. American citizens generally perceive the formal legal system as the primary arena for handling many types of disputes. Most citizens are unfamiliar with the conflict resolution alternatives provided by community mediation. This lack of public knowledge about the availability and advantages of mediation represents a serious problem for community mediation centers, which need a substantial caseload of disputes to justify their continued existence and expansion.

In order to "sell" prospective disputants on the virtues of community mediation compared to the legal alternatives, and to persuade them that mediation will help them to solve their disputes in a relatively convenient and cost-effective manner, the mediation center intake staff members and mediators use ideological rhetoric about the virtues of mediation to state their case persuasively. It is essential to both the success of mediation as a dispute resolution process, and as a social movement, that the disputants "buy in" sufficiently to voluntarily submit their case to the community mediation center. The disputants must also willingly accept the guidance of the mediator, since the mediator lacks the formal legal authority held by the court system to ensure the disputants' cooperation in the dispute resolution process.

Many of the citizens who apply to become volunteer mediators are initially attracted by the ideological claims made about the benefits of community mediation for empowering individuals and the community. The volunteers will often continue to mediate for years without financial remuneration because they believe in the value of mediation and they accept on faith that the claims made for the superiority of mediation are valid and proven. These dedicated citizen volunteers must believe "in the mediation process" in order to mediate effectively and without remuneration.

Mediation ideology also serves the mediation center as a device to screen prospective mediator applicants. During interviews with the center staff, those applicants who do not appear to share enthusiastically in the values and beliefs of mediation ideology are weeded out. In order to make the strong commitment required to go through the intensive training, and commit to monthly mediation requirements, applicants must believe strongly in the value of mediation. Thus, mediation ideology inspires commitment, and binds the center staff and volunteers to the program.

In addition, ideology helps to create a feeling of community of purpose and organizational culture. As in all cultures, truths, realities, beliefs, and values are what members agree they are. New community members are enculturated through the mediator training experience, through metaphors, and through retelling of the organizational history and myths.

By influencing the social construction of reality for mediators, ideology becomes a major factor in guiding organizational behavior and stimulating the discourse about mediation. Organizational culture provides the social energy that moves people to action. Mediation organizations have patterns of behavior that reflect and operationalize their distinctive ideology—the commonly held set of doctrines, myths, and symbols. The organization's ideology has a profound impact on the effectiveness of the organization. Ideology influences the most important issues in the organization's life: how decisions are made, how human resources are employed, and how people respond to their environment.

Finally, ideology can be an important factor in empowering citizen mediators. First, it provides them with an understanding of the reality of social conflict and the formal court system and various dispute resolution alternatives. Second, especially in some of the grass roots mediation programs such as the San Francisco Community Boards, ideological beliefs and analysis may create awareness of the social inequities that are believed to be the root causes of social conflict, and structural problems and other difficulties associated with the formal legal system and the existing political system. Third, by providing a vision of a "better way" for solving disputes and bringing peace and justice to the neighborhood, mediation ideology can provide a sense of personal mission that is vital to meaningful self-empowerment. Believing that one is a valued participant in an important social movement can enhance self-esteem and provide social status in the community, especially if that community views the community mediation movement as beneficial and desirable.

Assumptions of Mediation Ideology

What are the basic assumptions of mediation ideology? Despite some of the major differences between mediation programs and models, Roman Tomasic and Malcom Feeley (1982) argue that there is a discernible ideology that is used as a legitimating device to promote the growth of mediation as an alternative for, or supplement to, the formal legal system. According to Tomasic and Feeley, the key assumptions of this ideology concern factors such as the nature of disputes and disputants, the qualities associated with the mediation process and the citizen mediators, and the comparisons made between community mediation and formal court processing.

First, this ideology contends that the mediation process is able to "deal with a wide range of problems," as well as to deal "with the roots of problems." Second, the community mediation process is considered to be "noncoercive," especially when compared to the adjudication process, and it is "voluntaristic as it allows disputants to solve their problems themselves." Third, it is claimed that, compared to adjudication, mediation is speedier, less costly, more equitable, and "more effective than adjudication in dealing with recidivism." Fourth, it is argued that mediation "improves the communicative capacities of disputants." Fifth, it is believed that mediation can "reduce court congestion and delay," and that it "is a means of reducing tension in the community." Sixth, mediation's advocates contend that mediation centers are "nonbureaucratic, flexible and responsive" and that they "provide easier access to the legal system."

It is argued that community mediators are "not professionalized," and unlike judges and lawyers citizen mediators "represent the community and share its values." The community mediators are not "strangers but are friends of the disputants." Consequently, according to the ideology of mediation, "disputants want to get away from the courts and into the mediation centers" (Tomasic and Feeley 1982, 238–242).

According to Tomasic and Feeley, these ideological assumptions constitute the hypotheses upon which community mediation centers have been based, and each assumption represents a key feature of the rhetoric of the neighborhood justice movement. Tomasic and Feeley point out that while not all of the assumptions are accepted by any one mediation center, they would all be endorsed somewhere in the movement. They further contend that these assumptions are generally not questioned, but are taken on faith by mediation's supporters and advocates. Tomasic and Feeley conclude that there is a "gulf between rhetoric and reality in these areas" and therefore much more research to test these ideological assumptions is needed (242).

Empowerment: A Core Value of Mediation Ideology

In a case study of the San Francisco Community Boards, Judy H. Rothschild (1986) extended Tomasic and Feeley's list of ideological assumptions with seventeen additional propositions about mediation ideology. Some of these propositions are directly relevant to my concerns about the linkage of empowerment to mediation. First, it is contended that mediation "is educational not only for disputants and mediators, but for the community at large as well." Second, it is believed that mediation can therefore "be a vehicle for empowering communities and encouraging positive social change within communities" (33–34). While these empowerment propositions would appear to be particularly relevant to community-based programs, Rothschild argues that they "appear in the practice and promotion of both community-based and court-affiliated mediation" (33).

The mediation literature provides an extensive discourse regarding empowerment. James Laue (1982) for example, argues that empowerment is a core value and the key to development of an ethical framework for mediation. Peter Adler (1987, 26) contends that the two foremost themes of alternative dispute resolution (ADR) are "voluntarism and empowerment." Joseph Scimecca believes strongly "that the notion of empowerment is a staple of any conflict theory worthy of the name as well as being one of the most important, if not *the* most important, idea within the field of conflict resolution" (1987, 30).

Empowerment is a complex multi-dimensional and multi-level concept that can be applied to individuals, to mediating organizations, to communities, and to the larger society. First, looking at the individual level, most of the emphasis in the mediation literature is given to the potential of the mediation process for empowering the disputants (Folberg and Taylor 1984; Davis and Salem 1984; Wall 1981; Wahrhaftig 1984; Wolff 1983).

For example, in his influential text on mediation, Christopher Moore (1986) describes how mediators can empower the weaker disputants when asymmetrical power relations exist: "Empowering moves may include assisting the weaker party in obtaining, organizing, and analyzing data and identifying and mobilizing his or her means of influence; assisting and educating the party in planning and effective negotiation strategy; aiding the party to develop financial resources so that the party can continue to participate in negotiations" (242).

In explaining how to deal with the problem of power imbalances in mediation, Albie Davis and Richard Salem contend that mediation is well suited to dealing with most situations of power imbalance because it is a naturally empowering process. They argue that "mediation assumes that the parties are competent to resolve their own disputes. Often people who have been socialized to feel powerless rise to the occasion during mediation. . . . Knowledge is power, and in many mediations the surfacing and sharing of information is an imperative step in reaching an equitable settlement. This aspect of mediation has a strong empowering impact" (1984, 19–20).

Davis and Salem are concerned with mediation's empowering benefits for the disputants and do not specifically discuss how the mediators might be affected by the process. However, as one reads through their description of what mediators do, it would seem that the mediator must also be substantially self-empowered in order to conduct such an empowering process for the disputant. Davis and Salem point out, for example, that the mediators are able to "model respectful behavior, . . . foster open exploration of options, . . . provide a safe place in which to display anger and rage, . . . are impartial and non-judgmental, . . . [and] encourage information sharing" (19–20). These exceptional attitudes and behaviors, which are considered to be characteristics of good mediators, would indicate the possession of strong empowerment competencies.

The mediation literature refers to other attributes of individual empowerment that are relevant to both the disputants and mediators, including self-esteem, skill development, personal growth, efficacy, and critical consciousness (Shonholtz 1984; Moore 1986; Folberg and Taylor 1984). How these empowerment concepts may be interrelated, whether there is a developmental sequence with skill development preceding self-esteem, for example, or if there is a hierarchy of attributes is not clear from the discussion in the literature. These questions are considered more fully in the development of an empowerment framework in chapter 4 and are addressed in the empirical analysis.

Second, research on the empowerment of organizations is also relevant to community mediation (see Vogt and Murrell 1990; Bachrach and Botwinick 1992). Looking at empowerment from the perspective of the organizational level, a community mediation center can be studied as a setting in which the empowerment of individual disputants and mediators occurs. Or alternatively a community mediation organization can be discussed as an entity that becomes empowered itself as a function of its empowering mission and ideology and because of the empowering activities that take place there. In this case, the mediation center becomes an empowered community with an organizational culture which nurtures, and in turn is supported by the mediators as a consequence of their personal empowerment.

Third, moving to the community level of analysis, what is the possible linkage between community mediation centers and the level or type of community empowerment? According to Raymond Shonholtz, first Director of the San Francisco Community Boards (SFCB), the empowerment of individuals and community empowerment is an interactive process. "The inculcation of skills and the development of a community-church support base for the dispute resolution service make the program an authentic community building and empowerment process" (1984, 17). Because community building and empowerment are viewed as vital aspects of the organizational mission, the Community Boards train many more volunteer mediators each year than are actually needed to handle the center's mediation caseload. The SFCB goal is to train large numbers of people in the community with mediation skills. Their expectation is that these mediation skills will be useful not only directly in the mediation center for dispute resolution but also in other community settings, such as the workplace or family. In this way the community mediation center will enhance democratic participation and the quality of life throughout the community.

A similar view about the empowering potential of mediation for individuals and the community is held by the Tribal Council, an Indian mediation program modeled after the San Francisco Community Boards. In its written materials the Tribal Council makes a clear distinction "between 'power' a negative concept that the council associates with the outside culture, and 'empowerment,' a desirable concept that they believe strengthens the tribal culture and the individual" (Milner, Lovaas, and Adler 1987, 13). According to their belief system, the tribal mediation center offers "a way of rebuilding the tribe and its internal and interpersonal linkages," thus resulting in community empowerment for the tribe (Adler, Lovaas, and Milner 1988, 21; see also Garrett 1994).

Finally, looking at empowerment from the societal level of analysis, community mediation is seen by some advocates as a vehicle for social change and a potentially powerful instrument for sociopolitical transformation. Scimecca, for example, argues that any mode of conflict resolution that advocates empowerment must be considered to be anti-status quo because, "By introducing empowerment, the conflict manager is offering an education in sociological analysis." As a result of this educational process, the underlying structural roots of the individual's problems are revealed, and consequently people can learn how to take "charge of their own destinies" by transforming the social structures that oppress them (1987, 32).

Similarly, Christa Slaton and Ted Becker point out that "there are those who see mediation skills as being important to pass on to local community members, or as a means for decentralizing official power. In other words, there are those who see community-based or community-oriented mediation as a mode of reversing and/or reducing the general social trends leading to massive psycho-logical alienation and powerlessness" (1981, 2).

Mediation Models and Ideological Projects

Some mediation scholars have attempted to delineate different kinds of models of community mediation and distinguish between their ideological agendas and their public policy implications. For example, there are agency models that are linked to the formal court system, grass roots community models, and mixed models combining attributes of both. These models differ on the meanings of empowerment as well as on the importance given to empowerment as an outcome of mediation. In a study comparing the ideologies of six different mediation programs, Adler, Lovaas, and Milner (1988) distin-guished two general views of empowerment. According to their analysis, the community mediation programs emphasize the need for social change and the importance of empowering individuals and the community. The court-affiliated agency models, on the other hand, describe the empowerment of disputants primarily in terms of providing public access to professional problem-solvers for those in conflict.

These two views of empowerment obviously have quite different implica-tions for social and political transformation. Can these two different views both be accommodated by the empowerment construct, or does the agency view imply a paternalistic perspective and professional-client relationship that is alien to the spirit of empowerment as understood by most practitioners and scholars?

Theodore Becker also distinguishes between the transformational potential of different types of mediation organization. He sees the possibility of sociopoli-tical transformation occurring only as a result of the operation and proliferation of the "pure" community mediation centers and the university-based mediation models that are specifically focused on "people empowerment" as part of their mission (1986, 110). On the other hand, Becker does not believe that the agency or quasi-agency mediation models that are usually an arm of the court system have potential for social change. In fact he believes that they primarily function to maintain social control and support the political and social status quo.

Christine Harrington and Sally Engle Merry (1988) studied three different models of local mediation programs in New England and identified three analytically distinguishable ideological projects. One of these mediation mod-els was closely affiliated with a court, the second mediation program was based in the community, and the third program was affiliated with a social service agency.

The first ideological project emphasizes the delivery of dispute resolution services. According to this project, the courts are considered to be too slow, too adversarial, and inappropriate for dealing with interpersonal problems. On the other hand it is believed that mediation offers greater efficiency, relief of court congestion, and a more appropriate forum for certain kinds of dispute. The service project is primarily a reform project and is associated with the mediation programs structured as adjuncts to courts.

The social transformational project, in contrast with the service project, envisions a restructuring of human society through community empowerment, decentralized judicial decision making, and use of community members instead of professional dispute resolvers. According to Harrington and Merry, "This project advocates community mediation completely independent of the judicial system, with its authority based on the local neighborhood rather than on the state" (1988, 715).

The third ideological project focuses on personal growth and development. Mediation is seen as a voluntary consensual process that permits the participating individuals to take control of their lives and to learn conflict resolution skills that can be used in future conflict situations. This project suggests that mediation can be more humane and more concerned with meeting human needs than the courts are. The personal growth project is likely to be associated with both community-based as well as social service agency models. This personal growth ideological project is also closely associated with the community mediation center that provides the case study for this research project.

Surprisingly, despite its importance as a "theme" and "core value" of mediation, there has been very little effort by scholars or advocates of mediation to clearly define empowerment or to develop a theory of empowerment relevant to conflict resolution. Therefore, there is a clear need for conceptual analysis to explore the dimensions of empowerment pertaining to mediation, to understand more clearly what it is, and to develop the theoretical framework necessary for interdisciplinary research and comparative analysis of mediation models.

At the same time, empirical analysis is needed to determine whether personal empowerment occurs as a result of participation in community mediation. Given the rapid growth of mediation in the United States and other countries, the uncertainty of its impact on participants and the community, and the lack of research, this is an area requiring both systematic theoretical analysis and rigorous empirical study. In short, as Tomasic and Feeley (1982) have urged, there is a need to begin to distinguish the rhetoric about empowerment from the reality of community mediation.

EMPOWERING MEDIATORS

While most of the community mediation researchers and advocates have focused their attention on the importance of the empowerment of the disputants, a few of them, perhaps most prominently Raymond Shonholtz, the founder of the San Francisco Community Boards, also acknowledge the importance and value of empowering mediators. Shonholtz argues that a major value of his program is that "individual volunteers experience personal and skill growth that heightens their self-esteem and sense of competence through civic involvement, which serves to combat the alienation that pervades urban communities" (1984, 17).

Thus, in the San Francisco mediation program and other community mediation centers modeled after it, such as the Tribal Council, the mediator is viewed as both an agent of empowerment working on behalf of others to resolve community conflicts and also as a prime candidate for self-empowerment as a result of intensive mediation skills training, civic participation in community mediation, and other empowering experiences.

What Mediators Do: Roles, Attributes, and Strategies

What exactly do these mediators do? And in what ways might their mediation experiences be empowering? The brief answer is that the mediators manage the dispute resolution process. In order to successfully manage conflict, mediators must consciously cultivate nonjudgmental attitudes; develop special communication, problem solving, and negotiation skills; and attempt to understand human feelings and behavior. In addition, they must acquire specific contextual knowledge relevant to the particular dispute, perform tasks like exploring options and reality testing, and use effective agreement-building strategies to achieve conflict resolution.

We can understand more clearly what mediators do by considering the mediation process in more detail. According to Christopher Moore's book, *The Mediation Process*, "*Mediation* is the intervention into a dispute or negotiation by an acceptable, impartial, and neutral third party who has no authoritative decision-making power to assist disputing parties in voluntarily reaching their own mutually acceptable settlement of issues in dispute" (1986, 14).

Unpacking Moore's definition reveals exactly what mediators do. The mediator is a neutral third party who intervenes in a dispute between two or more parties in order to facilitate settlement of the dispute. The mediator brings to the dispute situation new skills, specialized knowledge, and additional resources needed by the disputing parties. The parties voluntarily accept the mediator's intervention. If the mediator is not acceptable to both parties, they can either choose a different mediator who is satisfactory to both or choose to terminate the mediation process.

Most descriptions of community mediation emphasize that the mediator should be both impartial and neutral. "*Impartiality* refers to the attitude of the intervener and is an unbiased opinion or lack of preference in favor of one or more negotiators. All parties should be treated the same way procedurally and substantively. *Neutrality*, on the other hand, refers to the behavior or relationship between the intervener and the disputants" (Moore 1986, 15).

While mediators are expected to have a commitment to ensuring that a fair mediation process is conducted, they should not have a personal preference in the settlement agreed to by the parties, unless it appears to be unfair. If the mediator is not impartial and neutral, it is unlikely that the disputing parties will trust him or her sufficiently to willingly mediate. The mediator's job description may include a variety of roles and functions related to assisting the disputants in improving their communicating and problem solving. According to the American Arbitration Association, some of the mediator roles would include: *the opener of communications channels, the process facilitator, the problem explorer, the agent of reality, and the leader* (American Arbitration Association, cited in Moore 1986, 18).

To this list of mediator roles I would add others, such as:

The reframer. In addition to summarizing and clarifying the interests, issues, and positions relevant to the disputes so that they are understood by all parties, the mediator should also reframe into more neutral language any hostile comments or objectionable language that might lead to an impasse or to an escalation of the conflict. The objective of reframing is to present the essential information that was communicated in a hostile fashion in a way that can be more easily heard and understood by the other party.

The ventilator. While most mediators try to avoid acting as a psychological counselor, a major part of the mediator's job is to acknowledge the validity of the strong emotions that may be expressed in the mediation and to enable the parties to ventilate their feelings and communicate them to the other party. It is believed that failure to deal with strong emotions when they emerge may lead to an impasse in the dispute or result in an unsatisfactory settlement that will not last.

The guardian of the process. In addition to managing the mediation process the mediator must make sure the process is not subverted by a disputant who does not intend to negotiate in good faith. Some disputants may attempt to exploit the mediation forum for undesirable purposes, such as a delaying tactic for stalling legal action or an opportunity for attacking and intimidating the other party. According to mediation procedure, if all of the parties involved are not willing or able to negotiate in good faith the mediation process should be closed down.

The power balancer. In those cases where a great power imbalance exists between the disputing parties, some would contend that mediation is an inappropriate approach because the weaker party would be unable to negotiate effectively face to face with the dominant party. However, advocates of mediation would counter that it is not only often appropriate, but also it may actually be the preferred approach because when done well the mediation process can be empowering and especially effective in many cases of power imbalance. The mediator can use a variety of balancing strategies such as providing vital information, teaching negotiation skills, or referring to other resources to strengthen the weaker party and enhance the prospects for achieving a fair agreement (Davis and Salem 1984).

The agent of empowerment. This is a meta-role that combines many of the other roles, especially those of the educator, resource expander, problem explorer, ventilator, reframer, and power balancer. The mediator should constantly seek to enhance the disputant's levels of self-esteem, self-sufficiency, knowledge, skills, resources, and effective behavior, which enhances the personal power of the parties. This role assumes that there is a general commitment by the mediator to empower all parties as well as the intention to intervene in situations of power imbalance to empower the weaker party if necessary.

Carrying out these empowering mediator roles presumes the special personal attributes often associated with mediators in the literature. It is suggested that mediators should ideally be: empathetic, flexible, forceful, persuasive, nondefensive, articulate, imaginative, good listeners, honest, patient, persevering, optimistic, objective, intelligent, reliable, endowed with a good sense of humor, and highly respected in the community (Folberg and Taylor 1984; Stulberg 1987). These personal attributes would of course also be associated with individuals possessing high levels of personal empowerment.

Mediator Styles and Use of Power

There are at least two schools of thought about the mediator's role relevant to professional conduct and especially use of power. These two schools contrast the "mediator as facilitator" with the "activist mediator." The facilitation school argues that mediators are responsible for conducting the mediation *process*, but they should not be concerned with the *content* of the settlement agreement, which is the exclusive responsibility of the disputants. According to this view mediators should resist being too directive about possible specific bargaining options and avoid pressuring the parties to reach agreement. Conducting a fair and competent process is the key concern for the mediators. Whether or not the disputants ever reach an agreement should be a lesser concern to the mediators (Moore 1986).

The activist school of thought is somewhat more directive and contends that although the mediator should strive to be impartial and neutral, he or she should work closely with the parties on substantive matters in order to develop a fair and durable agreement. In this view the mediator plays a more active and more directive role in the scenario, with much more emphasis being placed on the importance of reaching a settlement. In this approach the mediators will often suggest and even argue for specific options being adopted, and they will sometimes even use techniques of "muscle mediation" to get the conflicting parties to settle. This strong approach has been vividly described by an attorney who both works as a professional mediator and serves as a volunteer mediator at a community mediation center.

Every mediator has his or her own style. Mine is the bulldog approach, not in the sense that I growl at or antagonize the contending parties, but in the sense that I sink my teeth into the case and determine that I won't let go until an agreement is signed, whether it takes all day and night or all week. I have a set procedure, first talking with both parties together and then shuttling between them with offers and suggestions, but my tactics vary with the personalities and circumstances. I'll wheedle, cajole, promise, threaten, praise, challenge, confront, blast, manipulate, anything within the bounds of ethics and propriety to get those signatures on a durable agreement. (Knebel and Clay 1987, 245)

In a major study of federal and state labor mediators, Deborah Kolb (1983), distinguished between two similar approaches, which she labeled the "orchestrator" and the "dealmaker" styles. Susan Silbey and Sally Engle Merry (1986), made similar distinctions in their study of three types of community mediation programs. They point out that the wide variation in mediation approaches "seems to range between a bargaining process conducted in the shadow of the court to a communication process which resembles therapy in its focus upon exploring and enunciating feelings" (7).

According to Silbey and Merry, the bargaining and the therapeutic mediator styles describe regular patterns of dealing with problems and of using mediator power. The "bargaining" style reflects a more structured process with more control and use of power *over*, by the mediator, more private caucuses with each disputant, and more emphasis placed on reaching a settlement. There is more concern for determining the disputant's "bottom line," and the settlement is achieved by the exchange of benefits. According to this approach, conflicts are generally caused by differences of interest, and the mediator must act as an "agent of reality" to clarify the drawbacks associated with nonsettlement when the parties resist. At the same time the bargaining mediators clearly and constantly stress the benefits associated with settlement.

In contrast, the "therapeutic" style of mediation emphasizes the key importance of communicating feelings and attitudes in conflict resolution. It stresses the central importance of healing the damaged relationship between the disputants and the need for encouraging mutuality and reciprocity in resolving conflicts. The focus of the mediators is on conducting the mediation process properly, rather than achieving any particular outcome. This approach assumes that most interpersonal conflicts are caused by miscommunications, misperceptions, or misunderstandings and are basically communication problems that can be resolved and perhaps prevented in the future if the disputants are willing and able to improve their communication skills.

Despite the fact that Kolb was studying labor mediation and Silbey and Merry were studying community mediation (two very different types of mediation), the patterns of mediator behavior they observed and described have a good deal of similarity. The "dealmaker" and the "bargainer" style of mediators are kindred spirits with their emphasis on determining the "bottom line" and controlling the negotiating process in order to get a settlement. On the other hand, the "therapist" and the "orchestrator" mediators both share a relatively nondirective style, giving the disputants more responsibility for any agreements reached.

These different styles of mediation represent ideal types. Many experienced, versatile, and pragmatic mediators use a mix of techniques or styles to some extent depending on the circumstances of the case, although one style will tend to be dominant. However, other mediators from the community mediation centers that have a strong empowerment ideology may refuse to use strong, directive techniques under any circumstances, because personal and social transformation has a higher value for them than does conflict resolution (see Shonholtz 1984).

These two contrasting styles of mediation suggest that community mediators may use power differently and consequently take different paths to self-empowerment. Silbey and Merry (1986) have observed that the mediators who use a bargaining style will present themselves to the disputants as representatives of some larger authority. Silbey and Merry explain, "The mediator wraps him or herself in the same mystical cloth as the jurist, the rabbi, or the priest; and, while not proclaiming openly that he is the embodiment of the law or of God, he nevertheless proclaims access to knowledge and wisdom derived from a special school of trained neutrality. He dispenses decisions, which from the perspective of the contending parties carry the same kind of authoritative weight as the law or God" (27). This approach may be empowering for the mediator but is probably less so for the disputants who work with this authority figure.

In her study of the Community Dispute Settlement (CDS) mediation program founded by Philadelphia Quakers, Jennifer Beer (1986) agrees with the view that mediator empowerment may be an outcome of mediation participation, but describes a different process and a different style. "Professor Sally Engle Merry frequently remarks that community mediation seems to empower mostly the mediators. This is unquestionably true for CDS volunteers. The task is one which pushes and pulls people to change, sometimes in unexpected ways. Those changes are not just the development of new skills but the reshaping of attitudes . . . person after person testifies to the difference it has made in their lives" (75).

Beer explains that the CDS program is shaped by two strong influences: first, the underlying Quaker philosophical principles, and second, the influence on the center of strong women's leadership. The Quaker traditions in which the program was founded emphasize the values of reconciliation, community responsibility, anti-authoritarianism, and individual freedom. While one-third of the CDS mediators are men, Beer claims that both the male and female mediators see their mediator role in the traditionally female terms of helper and peacemaker. The touchstone for members of the CDS program is the "vision of empowerment" for disputants, mediators, and the community. Beer observes that most of the mediators in the CDS program use the "therapist" approach to conflict resolution.

In short, mediators who use a bargaining style or the therapist approach may both be empowered, but in somewhat different ways. Perhaps, as Silbey and Merry suggest, bargaining mediators empower themselves by taking on the mantle of authority and using power actively and directively to achieve dispute resolution. The bargainers understand the dynamics of power *over* or power *for* in mediation and know how to develop and use their own personal power in the mediation context and perhaps in other personal and professional settings.

The mediators who use the less directive therapeutic style and are motivated by visions of empowerment and personal or social transformation may be affected differently and create a different outcome for the disputants. While they may feel less comfortable than the bargainers in actively using power *over* others, and reluctant to present themselves as conflict resolution experts, there may be more subtle kinds of self-empowerment taking place as a result of their mediation experience, such as changes in their conceptions of themselves and society, critical insights, and heightened awareness.

The use of power in mediation and the relationship of power to empowerment is a source of some confusion and controversy in the literature. As Moore's definition of mediation clearly states, a mediator "has no authoritative decision-making power" (1986, 14). This important distinction points out that in contrast to a judge or an arbiter, the community mediator has no legal power to make a binding decision for the disputants. This is sometimes mistakenly interpreted to mean that the mediator has no power over the disputants.

In addition, many volunteer mediators view power negatively and are uncomfortable with its exercise (see Beer 1986). But while community mediation is considered to be voluntary in that the parties can withdraw at any time, this rarely happens once mediation has begun, and the mediator does have a variety of powers that can be employed to further the process. In order to be truly effective, the mediator must be aware of power in mediation and know how to exercise it equitably on behalf of the disputants. The use of power is a natural and necessary consequence of the mediator's roles in the mediation process. The effective mediator uses power to control the process, to help the parties achieve fair and mutually acceptable outcomes, to empower the parties, and to address any power imbalances that may endanger equitable use of the process.

Moore (1986, 272) discusses twelve forms of power or influence that mediators can use, including management of the negotiation process, control of communication between parties, the arrangement of physical settings, timing of the negotiations, expertise influence, the use of institutional authority, the use of rewards and benefits to enhance cooperation, and the use of coercive influence by threatening to withdraw and shut down the mediation if there is a lack of cooperation or impasse.

Looking at the process from another perspective, Beer (1986, 84) distinguishes between the mediator's "real" authority and "perceived" authority. Real authority is derived from his or her control of the process, from the ability to persuade and coerce, from the mediator's experience and expertise in the subject in dispute, and from some control over the emotional levels of the mediation session. Perceived authority, on the other hand, is based on the mediator's roles, self-confidence, appearance of impartiality, and personal attributes such as age, race, and profession.

Silbey and Merry suggest that mediators "empower themselves by claiming authority for themselves, their task, or the mediation program based upon values external to the immediate situation, or they manipulate the immediate situation so that settlement" (1986, 7) is more likely. Four power strategies were employed by the mediators they studied. First, the way the mediators presented themselves as experts in conflict resolution and the community mediation program as superior to the formal court process. Second, the mediators controlled the mediation process by controlling the communication flow and rephrasing or redefining the dispute. Third, they maintained control of the substantive issues of the dispute by broadening the dispute, selecting, concretizing, and postponing issues. Finally, the mediators exercised power by activating commitments (using norms and values, such as community and harmony), which encourage settlement.

There is a tension in the way the mediation process is conducted, between the necessary use of power by the mediator to maintain control of the process, and the desirable outcome of empowering the disputants. Determining ethical boundaries for the use of mediator power are a matter of debate, but using power to support the process is far less controversial than is the use of power to achieve specific outcomes or to modify the power relationship of the parties.

In summary, the ethical management of power within the framework of mediation, and in keeping with the constraints of the mediator role, may be self-empowering for the mediator. Many scholars (Maslow 1962; McClelland 1975; Glasser 1984) consider power to be a basic human need. The use of power in the context of the mediator role may enhance the mediator's self-esteem, conflict resolution skills, and sense of personal efficacy. When a mediator acquires an understanding of the dynamics of power in the context of mediation and negotiation, and has learned how to use power more comfortably and effectively, these new skills and insights may transfer to other social and political settings. How this empowerment process develops and is utilized is discussed more fully in the following chapter.

3

Community Mediation and Citizen Mediators

The research setting for this study was the Neighborhood Justice Center of Honolulu (HNJC). This chapter describes its history, organizational development, mission, ideology, and program operation in sufficient detail to enable understanding of the organizational environment in which community mediation participation takes place. This chapter also discusses the HNJC volunteer mediators: their recruitment and selection and their major training, mediation, and leadership activities. While the possible relationship of mediation participation to empowerment is discussed briefly here, a more detailed explication of that relationship is presented after a theoretical framework for empowerment has been developed. The information about the operation of the mediation program presented here will also be used in later chapters to interpret the empirical findings and assess their generalizability to other community mediation and non-mediation settings.

COMMUNITY MEDIATION IN HAWAII

Despite its relatively small population and geographic isolation, Hawaii is a leading center for mediation research and practice in the United States, with strong support from the community, government, and the University of Hawaii. Community mediation activities in Hawaii began in the late 1970s with the cooperation of individuals in the community and university groups who were interested in exploring new forms of alternative dispute resolution.

In the fall of 1978, two political scientists from the University of Hawaii established the Neighborhood Justice Center Project (Slaton and Becker 1981).

They mailed information questionnaires about mediation to over thirty Neighborhood Boards and spoke at public meetings to generate community interest in establishing a mediation center. At about the same time another group, the Makiki Neighborhood Board, formed a Neighborhood Justice Center Committee (Barnes and Adler 1983). Initially the two groups agreed to develop a joint planning committee for a Makiki Neighborhood Justice Center—combining the resources of the University and the community-based group.

After a short time, however, serious disagreements developed about policy and procedures, and the joint-planning group split into two. In August 1979 the neighborhood board group incorporated as a private nonprofit organization called the Makiki Neighborhood Justice Center designed to serve the Makiki area of Honolulu. They sought funding from the Law Enforcement Assistance Administration (LEAA). In February 1980, the name was changed to the Honolulu Neighborhood Justice Center (HNJC) to reflect the center's expanded interest in serving all residents of Honolulu.

The University of Hawaii group, composed of university students, faculty, and community members, decided to set up a university-based mediation center that would mediate disputes throughout Honolulu. In November 1979, the university-based Community Mediation Service (CMS) began providing mediation services. Based on a community mediation model similar to the San Francisco Community Boards, it emphasized the importance of empowerment for all participants. The CMS used a two- or three-person mediation panel, and its Board of Directors was composed of all staff members and mediators. Students were trained to be mediators through an on-campus internship program, and mediation hearings were held in various locations in the community.

After months of successful operation, the city and county of Honolulu agreed to fund CMS to set up a Honolulu Neighborhood Mediation Network (HNMN) with four independent regional mediation outreach centers to begin operation in the fall of 1980. However, the November 1980 election brought in a new mayor and city administration with a different agenda, and the network was not funded. Some of the HNMN staff and mediators then joined the Honolulu Neighborhood Justice Center.

THE NEIGHBORHOOD JUSTICE CENTER OF HONOLULU

Program Operation

Since the early 1980s, the HNJC has continued to grow and add new staff and programs, and with a paid staff of over ten full-time employees, it is now one of the largest community mediation programs in the nation. Over 200 volunteer mediators and case intake volunteers contribute more than 6,000 hours of service to the mediation center each year. The HNJC budget exceeds

$600,000 annually, and the diversified funding it receives from private and corporate memberships, service fees, private donations, trusts and foundations, state judiciary grants, and the Aloha United Way, reflects its widespread government and community support.

According to their case statistics, the HNJC provides mediation service that is fast, with an average of fourteen days from intake to disposition; successful, with an overall agreement rate of 70% in 1,625 cases mediated or conciliated; accessible, with over 60% of the cases being mediated in the evenings or on weekends; and relatively cost effective, compared to similar cases processed through the formal court system, averaging $151 per mediated case (*HNJC Annual Report* 1987).

The HNJC mediation caseload has increased steadily each year although the mix of cases has changed over time, with neighborhood dispute cases declining in recent years compared to family conflict cases. In 1987–1988, the center received 2,037 requests for assistance, 12% more than the previous year. Out of that number 1,224 (60%) were mediated or conciliated. The overall settlement rate approached 75%. The breakdown of the 2,037 case total by case type was: family disputes 764 (38%), juvenile restitution cases 565 (28%), landlord/tenant disputes 207 (10%), consumer/merchant disputes 167 (8%), neighborhood conflicts 129 (6%), and other disputes 215 (11%).

The data collected on disputants in 1988 indicated that more males (56%) than females (44%) used the HNJC services. The disputants tended to be relatively young, with 9% under twenty, 26% in their twenties, 32% in their thirties, 18% in their forties, and the remainder of the disputants over fifty years of age. Caucasians are highly over-represented with 48% of the disputants, compared to 23% in the general population. The participation of other ethnic groups is much lower, with Japanese comprising 15%, Filipinos 13%, Chinese 7%, and African-Americans 4%. Eleven percent of the disputants earn less than $5,000, 16% earn between $5,000 and $10,000, 33% earn between $10,000 and $20,000, 26% earn between $20,000 and $30,000, and 14% earn more than $30,000 annually (Goldstein and Chandler 1988, 2).

Program Mission and Ideology

According to the HNJC's statement of philosophy, "In a broad sense the Justice Center is an expression of a commitment by many members of this community to seek a more just society and to build our collective capacity to resolve conflict without violence, suppression, or unnecessary litigation. This is no small task, but it is one that we share with a growing number of individuals, agencies, and institutions both here and elsewhere" (*HNJC Annual Report* 1987, 5).

The HNJC staff and advocates believe that it is unique in that it has managed to combine the best elements of both community and agency models. They contend that they have retained the community values of voluntarism and personal empowerment, while at the same time they have developed the professional dispute resolution services, government linkages, and the high caseloads associated with the agency models. For example, in a recent *HNJC Annual Report* (1987, 3), the President of the HNJC Board of Directors points out with pride that, "We have also continued to expand the use of our volunteers to assist in both the training and intake processes of the center. This marks a new approach to the delivery of social services that challenges the agency model and offers the possibility of personal empowerment."

Thus the HNJC ideology shares many of the assumptions about mediation that were set forth by Tomasic and Feeley (1982), believing as they do that mediation should be a voluntary and noncoercive process, that it improves communication, that it is able to deal with a wide range of disputes, that it is more accessible, speedier, less costly, fairer, more humane, and more empowering than formal adjudication. The development of the HNJC program reflects an ongoing concern with individual empowerment as well as with community empowerment. The advantages cited for the development of mediation in Hawaii include a variety of benefits relevant to personal and societal transformation, such as

the growth of a sizable group of citizens who not only can apply mediation skills in their everyday lives, but may further act as catalysts within their own communities. . . .
The development of a pool of over 200 Hawaii citizens trained as mediators is contributing a vast social benefit to our society. . . . Out of the mediation process itself flows the notion of empowerment. . . . Neighbors become responsible for what goes on in their own neighborhood and people in conflict situations become responsible for the outcomes of their own disputes. . . . People trained in mediation find themselves using the same skills in their daily interpersonal life, at home, in the workplace, and with friends and acquaintances. (Barnes and Adler 1983, 38–39)

The ongoing concern with personal and community empowerment is reflected in the HNJC mediator training manual, which mentions empowerment frequently, as well as in reports, brochures, and the HNJC newsletter. In a recent newsletter, for example, the President's Message states quite clearly the President's belief: "Mediation empowers both people in conflict and the volunteers trained to provide the process for resolving those conflicts" (*The Center Letter*, Spring 1988, 2). Thus this concern with the empowerment of the disputants served by the center, the empowerment of the local community, and the empowerment of volunteer mediators is an important ideological leitmotif and a symbolic resource for the HNJC program.

HNJC MEDIATORS

Motives and Expectations

The citizen volunteer mediators contribute in many ways to the successful operation of the HNJC mediation program, and they receive a variety of nonmonetary benefits in return. They provide for a high degree of community participation in the mediation program and enable the HNJC program to keep down the costs of dispute resolution services. Their participation may enhance the prospects for individual and community empowerment.

Voluntarism is a core value of the HNJC ideology. According to the first Executive Director of the program, "The Hawaii model . . . keeps mediation a voluntary activity done by volunteers. . . . Volunteers are offered professional training and education in dispute resolution. In exchange, they are asked to help settle real conflicts in their own area . . . free-of-charge. Skills are disseminated, cases are settled, and the rise of a mediation bureaucracy is short-circuited" (Barnes and Adler 1983, 44).

When the volunteer mediator applicants are asked to explain their reasons for wanting to become mediators at the HNJC, their responses clearly reveal their motivations, expectations, and attitudes toward conflict, mediation, and empowerment. The personal statements given below, from a recent trainee group, indicate their strong interest in their own self-empowerment, in the empowerment of the disputants they hope to work with, and in the empowerment of the community.

1. I derive great personal satisfaction from helping people develop their own solutions to their disagreements. . . . From a selfish career standpoint, I can see potential for great benefit in mediation training. But I am also very much interested in being of service to the wider community in the area of conflict resolution.

2. I want to explore more the nature and process of community mediation. I hope to learn more about how the Hawaiian multi-cultural community operates. Also, I feel that the deepening of these skills can only enhance my personal life and my relationships with others.

3. I feel I can be of benefit to my community while learning a valuable skill which should have great impact in all areas of my professional and private life. I would like to be instrumental in any effort which will allow individuals to settle differences without the emotional and financial drain of entering the court system.

4. First, I respect the goals of the Neighborhood Justice Center and believe that they add greatly to the quality of life in our community. If I am selected as a mediator, I would be a part of this worthwhile effort. It offers me an opportunity to help the community in ways that particularly interest me, both as a neighbor and as a member of society.

5. I see each individual as the foundational building block for families, neighborhoods, societies, cities, and nations. Thus, I believe in the concept of shared humanism, a harmonious blending of individual worth, dignity and rights. I would like to help those people to understand each other's needs and to create their own individually tailored solutions to their problems. I would like to see more mutual understanding, trust, order, and self-direc-

tion; and less individual fear, doubt, confusion and stand-offs. I want to be
an advocate of shared humanism in a more tangible empowering way.

These statements from prospective citizen mediators reveal their altruistic
motives of wanting to help individuals in conflict and to contribute to their
community. They also reveal their desire to develop the personal empowerment
skills and attitudes they believe will be useful in dealing with problems in their
personal relationships and would enhance their professional skills. Judging
from the statements above, many of the prospective mediators are already
familiar with the language of empowerment and persuaded of its value. It is
interesting to compare these statements given *prior* to training with the comments appearing later in this chapter, made *after* training, where an awareness
of the possible linkage between the mediation process and personal and
community empowerment is even more directly and clearly articulated by the
new mediators.

Mediator Recruitment and Selection

The procedures used by the HNJC staff for mediator recruitment and selection determine who will become an HNJC mediator and be given the opportunity to learn mediation skills. These recruitment and selection procedures
partially explain why and how the citizen volunteer mediators differ in many
important ways from the disputants who bring their disputes to the center, and
from the general adult population in Hawaii. Demographic information on
mediators will be used in a later chapter to interpret the empirical findings and
to assess the generalizability of this study.

The procedures for mediator recruitment may vary widely from one community mediation program to another. They are a function of each individual
program's needs and ideology. The criteria used for selection are based on
assumptions about what makes a good mediator, and they determine the type
of person who will be chosen to mediate. In some community mediation
programs, like the San Francisco Community Boards (SFCB), the primary
criteria for selection of mediators are that the prospective mediator should be a
neighbor and reside in the area where the dispute originates. The main emphasis
in the SFCB program is on "neighbor helping neighbor" and on community
mediation as a vehicle for community building. There are few other selection
criteria used, and nearly all of those who apply are accepted for training (Du
Bow 1987; Rothschild 1986). Indeed, because the SFCB program is primarily
concerned with community empowerment by training many citizens as mediators, trainings are conducted frequently and many more mediators are trained
than are actually needed to handle the yearly caseload of disputes to be
mediated.

In contrast, the HNJC mediator selection process is more formalized and has many steps and criteria that have been carefully refined over time. There are several practical, ideological, and theoretical reasons for following a careful selection process. First, the process is designed to select persons who are capable of mediating all types of disputes, either working alone or teamed with a co-mediator. Providing professional service to the disputants and maintaining quality assurance are primary concerns of the HNJC program staff. Second, it is very important to select those individuals who have a high likelihood of successfully completing the intensive and lengthy mediation training program. Training workshops are expensive to conduct and time consuming for the paid staff and volunteer trainers. Class size must be limited to ensure quality instruction, therefore it is important to minimize dropouts and those who for various reasons must be screened out by the staff after training has begun. Mediator retention is another vital concern for the HNJC staff because of the high cost of replacing mediators, and so the candidate's level of commitment to community mediation and the HNJC are carefully assessed along with their abilities and attitudes.

Recruitment of citizen volunteers is done both through the media and by word of mouth. In order to enhance maximum diversity in the mediator pool, special efforts are made to recruit from certain ethnic and age groups that reflect Hawaii's multicultural complexity. The HNJC staff believes that whenever possible it is desirable to be able to provide mediators who have ethnic or cultural backgrounds similar to the disputants. It is believed that this matching of mediators with disputants may facilitate cultural understanding relevant to the dispute and help to establish the mutual trust and rapport that can increase the probability of a successful resolution of the dispute.

In addition to meeting the specific selection criteria described above, applicants must be willing and able to commit to a number of other practical requirements, such as taking fifty hours of intensive basic and family mediation training as well as ten to twenty additional hours of advanced training during the first year. They must also be willing and able to mediate a minimum of twelve cases or fifteen mediation sessions the first year, pay a training fee for course materials, and pay a small membership fee for joining the HNJC organization.

While not an explicitly articulated criterion for selection, desirable applicants should also appear to share the values and ideology of the community mediation movement. In fact, the mediator screening process functions as the first step in inculcating the ideology of mediation. In the process of reading over the HNJC materials, viewing videos on the mediation process, having conversations with program staff, and undergoing the entry interview, the applicants become familiar with the values, ideology, and language of community mediation. Those individuals who do not appear to resonate to these mediation values may decide to drop out at this point in the process or they may be screened out by the staff interviewer. It is typical of many organizations, particularly social movement organizations that have a specific vision or culture, to seek out like-minded individuals as new members and to eliminate those members who do not fully support the organizational values, goals, and objectives.

Applicants who match the selection criteria are invited to participate in the basic mediation training. Their evaluation by the staff and volunteer trainers continues throughout the training sessions, and the trainees can be screened out at any point in the process if difficulties are encountered. After completion of their training there is a one year probationary period, which requires ongoing training with experienced mediators before a trainee receives a graduation certificate.

This careful screening process presents significant barriers to entry into the mediation community. Many more apply than are accepted. HNJC's own statistics demonstrate how selective their screening process is. For recent training sessions, "Over 200 applications were submitted; 80 applicants were interviewed and twenty-nine selected" (*The Center Letter*, Fall/Winter 1988). Contrast this selective winnowing process with that used in other mediation programs like the San Francisco Community Boards that will accept into the training program nearly all who apply to be mediators (Du Bow 1986). It should be noted that the HNJC mediation selection process is designed to select those exceptional people who already possess many of the attributes and skills usually associated with high levels of personal empowerment.

After their selection, mediation participation consists of three major activities: (1) intensive mediation training, (2) mediating a variety of dispute cases, (3) and for some of them, participation in HNJC organizational governance tasks. These three types of mediation participation are described below in sufficient detail to provide the reader with an understanding of their nature and their potential for personal empowerment of the participants. The relevance of these activities to mediator empowerment is briefly mentioned here, but the explicit linkage is made in the next chapter after the development of a theoretical framework for empowerment.

Training

The length, intensity, and type of training given to citizen volunteer mediators varies somewhat among different mediation programs, although the substantive content tends to be similar across most community mediation programs. The length of the training for most mediation programs is usually between twenty and forty classroom hours. The content of training depends to some degree on a number of factors, such as the program's mission, the kind of mediation model used, the type of disputes handled by the program, and the kind of mediators selected for training. For example, the San Francisco Community Board program's primary mission is stated to be social transformation and the rebuilding and strengthening of the local community. The mediation model used in San Francisco consists of a five-person panel that mixes mediators with different levels of experience and expertise, and different ethnicity. The disputes they deal with are limited to relatively simple neighborhood issues, and all or most mediator applicants are accepted for training (Du Bow 1986). For these reasons, their training content, length, and intensity of training differ in important ways from the training workshops developed by HNJC.

The primary mission of HNJC is to provide expeditious and impartial dispute resolution service. Their mediation model uses one mediator for most of the simple types of dispute cases, such as neighbor-neighbor conflicts, and two mediators (female and male teams) for divorce mediation, which is often complex and lengthy and may require multiple mediation sessions. The types of disputes that are mediated by HNJC include neighborhood conflicts, commercial disputes, juvenile restitution cases referred from the courts, and complex divorce mediations. Therefore, the training can and must be intensive and focus on developing sophisticated communication and negotiating skills and specialized knowledge of matters such as the psychological dynamics of divorce for adults and children.

The training of citizens as mediators is considered to be a major key to success for many community mediation programs because the bulk of their dispute resolution services are delivered by volunteers instead of by a paid professional staff. Using these citizen volunteers keeps program costs much lower than they would be if all of the mediators had to be paid for their services. Using citizen volunteers also generates vital public relations and community support for the program because the volunteers usually become strong advocates for the benefits of mediation. The HNJC program is well known across the country for the high quality of their training, and it probably devotes more resources to training than is typical for community mediation programs. The training has been described by the HNJC Director of Training as a process of "professionalizing volunteers."

The structure and content of the training program has remained relatively stable over the past four years, but continual refinements are made to reflect advances in the field and the expansion of the HNJC program into new areas of mediation such as family and condominium disputes. Veteran mediators are given the opportunity to be updated continually with ongoing seminars and by their interaction with new trainees who have learned the latest techniques and tactics.

The complete HNJC training program consists of three components. The first component covers the theory of conflict, as well as negotiation, and basic communication skills, and it lasts for twenty-five hours. The second component focuses on family mediation training, and it equips the mediator to deal with the dynamics of relationships between divorcing couples, and the complex issues around child care and property division they are likely to face in dissolving the relationship. This component also takes twenty-five hours. In the third module, trainees are taught advanced techniques in mediation, such as how to deal with domestic violence, understanding cross-cultural issues, and working with parents to develop positive parenting plans. This session requires the final twenty hours. These training components are designed to develop the desired mediator attitudes, skills, and knowledge. They also serve a crucial socialization function, which inculcates the ideology of community mediation.

All of the trainees are given a reference manual before the first training session begins. This manual explains in great detail the existing HNJC policies and the various office procedures carried out by the paid staff, such as the client intake, case management, and mediator scheduling. In addition, the manual provides basic material on conflict theory and analysis, useful negotiation tactics, the basic mediation principles and process, the Hawaii model of family mediation, and other special applications of the mediation model. Throughout the course of the training the trainees are told in many ways that they are special people, with an opportunity to be involved in an exciting and challenging new social experiment that will benefit both themselves and their community in significant ways.

The first evening is spent getting acquainted with each other and with the HNJC program. Small group exercises are conducted early on to help the new trainees get in touch with any personal biases that may adversely influence their neutrality as mediators. In the first meeting they are also exposed to the language of mediation and empowerment.

The subsequent meetings are spent in learning and practicing the steps of the mediation model and process, and mastering specialized communications and conflict management skills, such as attentive and reflective listening, asking focused and open-ended questions, facilitation, problem solving, negotiation techniques, and agreement writing. In addition to formal lectures, the training sessions include numerous opportunities for skill practice and extensive role plays of several basic mediation scenarios.

The training experience is consciously structured, with the goal of teaching information and skills in ways that are maximally empowering to the participants. The emphasis is on using small group activities, peer teaching, dialogue, and other pedagogic techniques to teach and to develop a sense of social bonding and community affiliation. The staff and volunteer facilitators attempt to support the trainees in structuring their own learning experiences, and to pose problems and questions in ways that promote critical consciousness of the self and consciousness of the mediator's responsibility to empower disputants, especially in situations where a power imbalance exists. Teacher-student distinctions are de-emphasized, and the trainees are encouraged to become increasingly active in the learning process.

The second training module is presented two weeks later on advanced mediation skills and tactics for dealing with divorce issues and problems.

Divorce cases are especially difficult to deal with for many of the prospective mediators for several reasons. First, there are often stronger emotions expressed (i.e., anger, fear, anguish, and self-pity) than in other types of disputes. The mediator trainees, especially those who have personally been through a difficult divorce experience, sometimes find it difficult to cope with their own emotions as their painful memories of that experience return to the surface. For many trainees, however, the training experience appears to be therapeutic, and they often express the strong desire to help others avoid some of the pain they had experienced in fighting out a bitter divorce battle that was exacerbated by the adversarial formal legal system.

Trainees are also taught how to deal with situations of domestic violence. This is emerging as a growing problem in American society today, and it is a new and experimental area for mediation programs. Given the complexity and sensitivity of these mediations, trainees in the divorce mediation component must learn how to adapt the basic mediation model for divorce cases and how to master and apply advanced conflict management skills to deal with impasse situations.

Throughout the training, the participants are encouraged to view themselves as community peace-makers and problem-solvers who can help others in conflict to reach fair, durable, and mutually satisfactory resolutions. They are taught that empowerment is a core value of mediation and that mediation is superior to handling disputes through the formal legal system. If done correctly, mediation should result in the empowerment of the disputants rather than the disempowerment that often occurs in the formal court system. It is believed that mediation can result in the crafting of voluntary durable agreements and the healing of ruptured relationships.

As mentioned earlier, prior to their training the trainees often assert that they are motivated by seeking personal growth opportunities, and they believe that mastering mediation skills and new positive attitudes will make them more efficacious in other areas of their lives. After completing the training, many graduates specifically cite these positive personal changes as among the major benefits they believe they have received from the training experience. A sample of comments from recent graduates reflects both the depth of these feelings as well as an acknowledgment of the linkage that is believed to exist between the community mediation process and the empowerment of self and others.

1. HNJC mediation training is a powerfully empowering experience in the exciting area of mediation. As volunteers, we were exposed to dedicated professionals who held our hand through learning the tools of the process for dispute resolution. The intensity of this training, the hands-on involvement, the degree of real internal questioning and growth personally surpassed my expectations.

2. I felt very lucky that I had the opportunity to be part of this organization. It had certainly changed my previous view on problem-solving and negotiation. Had I learned this process earlier, a lot of my hang-ups would have been resolved. It is certainly one of the most enriching experiences I have encountered.

3. The training sessions I have just marathoned left me with the same kind of exhaustion and general euphoria of having run all those miles. To anyone wanting to get in touch with themselves, I recommend mediation. What an exceptional empowering experience!

4. The HNJC training experience was very rewarding because the staff taught the skills of empowering others by empowering us. I learned how affirming it is to be heard by someone reflecting back my thoughts and feelings, paraphrasing them, and then moving me on to new knowledge and skills.

5. The HNJC training institute has provided me with an invaluable set of skills that is not only applicable to mediating disputes but also to my day-to-day life activities. Mahalo, mahalo! I hope I can be of service and live up to the HNJC's expectations.

6. Volunteer mediation: a gift by the people of your community of caring, time and endless energy to help those who want to solve their woes. Consider the gift of helping others to hold onto peace by themselves. Join the mediation movement.

7. HNJC training is a well-designed, carefully administered act of love. Through the love, new skills are learned, old ones rekindled and bright new horizons unfold. The pain, anxiety and fears quickly give way to a new way of viewing ourselves and the world.

The synergistic themes of personal and community empowerment are reflected in many of these enthusiastic statements. These euphoric graduates express the belief that they have been transformed by the experience and that mediation will benefit them in many ways, with personal insights, growth, and valuable skills. They also believe that it will provide them with the opportunity to help others who are mired in conflict, and to serve their community and contribute to society. These statements reflect their inculcation with the values of the community mediation movement and their belief in the superiority of informal alternative dispute resolution over the formal legal system.

After completing their training, the new mediators first observe a variety of mediation cases, then they work with experienced mentors during a three- to five-case apprenticeship. The early mediations, and in all future mediations with a co-mediator, the pre-briefing period, the mediator caucus, and de-briefing periods all provide additional opportunities for new learning and refining of their skills.

Mediation Practice

The neophyte mediators are given the opportunity to further develop their skills by mediating a variety of neighborhood, juvenile restitution, commercial, and divorce mediation cases. As mediators they may assume a number of the roles discussed earlier to assist the disputing parties in resolving their conflict, such as the role of legitimizer, communicator, facilitator, educator, resource-expander, problem-solver, negotiator, or the agent of reality. These special roles provide a source of influence and status for the mediators despite their lack of formal authoritative decision-making power. Experienced mediators should learn how to use their power in a variety of ways to empower the disputants and manage conflict.

The mediation sessions provide ample opportunities to use the communication, problem-solving skills, and the specialized knowledge acquired in training. Mediators become increasingly adept in the exercise of power and control over the process, and they gain expertise and a sense of accomplishment. The mediation of disputes may prove to be empowering for the mediators in many ways that will become clearer as the process used by HNJC is described more fully.

Different community mediation models and programs vary in their potential for mediator empowerment as a function of factors such as the number of mediators used to mediate each case, the roles played by the mediator, the type of disputes handled, the frequency of opportunity for mediation, the ideology of the program, and the resources provided for ongoing support and education of the mediators.

The basic HNJC mediation model, which is illustrated in Figure 3.1, has two major phases. First is the "Forum" phase, which includes the first joint session and the first separate sessions. The Forum's objectives include discovering information relevant to solving the dispute—such as the issues, interests, and positions of all parties—and acknowledging strong feelings and ventilating emotions, developing rapport with all of the parties, enhancing communication, and assessing the willingness and ability of the disputants to bargain in good faith.

Accomplishment of these Forum goals and objectives lays the groundwork for the "Negotiation" phase, which begins with the second separate session. At this point the mediator's function shifts to managing the bargaining process. The purpose of this phase is to find mutually satisfactory solutions that might lead to a fair and durable agreement. The objectives in this phase include helping the disputants to brainstorm and explore options, working to determine the "bottom line" for each party, and then preparing them for face-to-face negotiations that might result in a written settlement agreement.

As indicated in Figure 3.1, mediation sessions begin with the preparation, or pre-brief stage. The mediators usually arrive twenty to thirty minutes early at the HNJC Center in order to review the case file, talk with the program staff,

Figure 3.1
HNJC Mediation Model

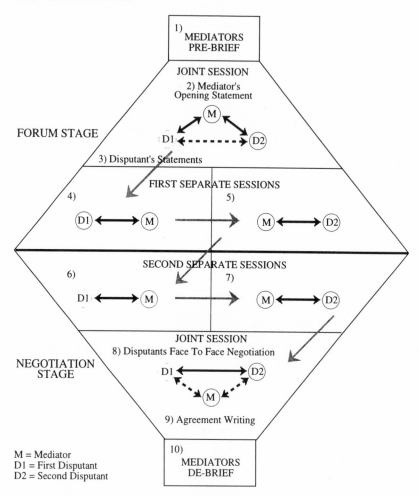

and prepare to meet with the disputants. If there are two mediators assigned to the case, as there are for divorce mediation, they will confer and decide what to do about their mediation strategy and seating arrangements, and how they will divide up the tasks and work cooperatively. The ideal of team mediation is to achieve a balanced interaction where neither mediator dominates the other or the mediation process. They may also discuss their personal goals for skill development, any perceived weaknesses, and specific areas where they would like to receive constructive feedback from the other mediator.

The basic HNJC model is highly structured, with specific objectives to be accomplished at each stage. Mediation skills and tactics are used to achieve the objectives, and new mediators are taught to be constantly aware of where they are in the model, and to think about what their objectives are at that point. New mediators are strongly encouraged to stick closely to the model until they thoroughly master it. They are taught to "trust the process" and to use the LAM (Listen, Ask, Move) skills as the tools that will help them achieve conflict resolution and a written agreement, if the disputants are willing and able to mediate in good faith.

After the disputants complete the HNJC registration form, they are greeted cordially by the mediator(s) and seated in the mediation room. A mediator begins the process with introductions of all participants and an opening statement, which includes an explanation of the mediation process and the mediator's role. This opening statement sets the tone for the session, which should be friendly and informal yet business-like. It assures the parties of the mediator's neutrality and impartiality and defines the parameters of confidentiality. A good opening statement is considered to be vital to setting the stage for what follows, and the mediator will often refer back to agreements the disputants have made at this point if there are any behavioral problems encountered at later stages of the process.

Next, the disputants take turns making opening statements that set forth their view of the conflict and how they feel about it. At this point in the process the disputants often state how they believe the conflict should be resolved. The mediator's objectives during this phase are to establish rapport with both disputants and to get a rich picture of the dispute, including the background of the people involved and the major issues and interests. The mediator's job is to help each side hear what the other has to say, and the mediators attempt to prevent premature bargaining, which might lead to poor solutions or to no settlement of the case. At this point in the process most of the disputants tend to talk directly to the mediator (indicated by solid lines in Figure 3.1), and to ignore the other disputant, so that the mediator becomes the primary communication conduit. If there are any serious interruptions, or insults, the mediator may intervene in the process to control the communication and keep the mediation process on track. The mediator uses specialized listening skills to capture the salient facts and to clarify and summarize issues, interests, and the position of each disputant.

Mediators are taught that it is important to acknowledge each party's feelings and to allow those feelings to be ventilated and communicated to the other party. However, any hostile statements are continually reframed or restated in more neutral language by the mediators to reduce the anger level and facilitate communication. Early in the mediation process communication techniques, such as asking open-ended questions and using affirming body language (leaning forward attentively and encouraging nods), are used to encourage the disputants to tell their story in their own words. Other specialized communication techniques are consciously used to guide the process and to keep it moving along from issue to issue and from stage to stage.

After each party has had an opportunity to tell their story, the next step in the process is the first separate session with each disputant (see Figure 3.1). At this point one of the disputants leaves the room for a short time while the mediator meets privately with the other. The main purpose of the separate session is to gather more useful information that might not have been revealed in the presence of the other disputant, and to build the trust with each party that may facilitate a resolution. The outcomes of this step depend on the mediator's skill and ability to generate sufficient trust to encourage each of the disputants to be open to possibilities of new options. Each step of the process is cumulative, and so it is believed that it is important to achieve the objectives for each stage before moving on to the next step. When the private session with the first party is finished, he or she leaves the room and then the second party returns for a private meeting with the mediator.

After concluding the first separate session with the second party, the mediator may decide to take a short break to consider what has been discovered about the major issues, interests, and positions of both parties, and to plan the next steps. If there are two mediators they may "caucus" at this point to consider several key questions, including: Are both disputants willing and able to mediate in good faith? Are most of the major issues and relevant interests, needs, and feelings on the table and fully understood? What additional information might be needed before moving on to the next stage of the process? What negotiation strategy or tactics would be most viable in this situation?

The co-mediators may also discuss their own mediation behavior and their feelings about the case or the disputants (especially if their feelings are negative, and therefore likely to affect their neutrality), any problem areas in style or techniques that need work, and their team interaction. These caucuses provide valuable feedback to both new and veteran mediators and serve to continue the training process.

If the mediators agree that the objectives for the Forum stage have been accomplished, they may prepare to shift gears for the next phase in the process, the "Negotiation" stage. If not, they may decide that additional private sessions may be necessary before moving on. In the Negotiation stage, the mediator's role shifts from being the facilitator of communication to being the manager of negotiation. The focus of the process in the negotiation stage is on exploring mutually satisfactory solutions to the dispute. The second separate session phase begins with another private meeting of the mediators and the first party. Confidentiality is vital in these sessions because the disputants must trust the mediator sufficiently to be open and flexible and to reveal their "bottom line" for a settlement of the dispute. In order to maximally empower the disputant, the mediator tries to be as nondirective as possible in generating options, and resists giving advice. The mediator uses brain-storming and problem-solving techniques and prepares the parties to deal directly with each other when they meet face-to-face in the upcoming "joint" session.

After meeting with both parties to explore acceptable options, the mediators may call another time out. In this caucus the mediator's objectives are to identify areas of close agreement on issues and any areas of strong disagreement, and then to determine the most effective order for dealing with the issues and the most effective bargaining strategies. If conditions seem favorable for a settlement, the disputants will be brought back together in a joint session; if not, more private sessions may be necessary.

When the mediation participants reconvene to negotiate a settlement, the mediator's objectives are to help the parties communicate directly with each other and to negotiate their own agreement. Ideally at this point, the mediators take a less active role (indicated by the dotted line in Figure 3.1) and encourage the disputants to bargain for themselves. This is considered to be especially important if the parties have an ongoing relationship as neighbors or parents, for example, that is likely to continue after they leave mediation. But an equitable face-to-face negotiation is sometimes difficult to achieve if there is a power imbalance between the disputants and the mediator has been unable to sufficiently empower the weaker person.

If all goes well, the bargaining process melds smoothly into the final agreement-writing phase. The written agreement is signed by each party as well as the mediator. Each party receives a copy, and one copy is retained for HNJC records. Mediators are taught that if the mediation process is followed scrupulously a good agreement will probably result that both parties will want to carry out, even without the need for external enforcement. It is believed that this kind of mediation process is empowering for the disputants, and that they may learn communication and problem-solving skills that will serve them well in any future conflict situations they may encounter.

In closing the session, the mediators congratulate the parties for their willingness to try a peaceful means of resolving disputes, and invite them to contact the center if they have further difficulties with this dispute or with future disputes. The parties usually thank the mediators for their hard work, and often express their gratitude and admiration for the mediators' skills and dedication. Sometimes the disputants will ask how they might become community mediators. These are indeed gratifying moments for most of the mediators.

After the parties leave, an additional twenty to thirty minutes is spent finishing HNJC report forms, and in mediator debriefing. Many mediators keep a journal of all sessions as a learning tool, and the HNJC Center provides a debriefing form that can be used to analyze the mediation session. If there are two mediators, they will often analyze the session in some depth, discuss alternative strategies, and ask for feedback on their skills and the team interaction. This is a part of the informal, ongoing training. For many mediators, co-mediation is a valuable and valued part of their mediation experience, and it meets some of their affiliation needs.

Most of the active mediators have a great deal of faith in the efficacy of the HNJC mediation model and take obvious pride in their roles as mediators. Being a mediator is satisfying and fulfilling for them, and they may have little desire to get involved in other kinds of organizational activities. A few of them, however, motivated by the desire to learn more about mediation, to contribute more to the HNJC and the community, or for other motives, may choose to become involved in a variety of organizational leadership roles.

Mediator Leadership Roles

The third type of mediation participation examined in this study involves leadership activities. The leaders are generally experienced mediators who have chosen to or have been encouraged to be active on the HNJC Board of Directors, on various program committees, or with the mediator training faculty. The board members of nonprofit organizations like the HNJC are responsible for making policy decisions and for overseeing the operation of the agency. They have the authority to hire and fire the Executive Director, and often assist the organization with public relations campaigns, fund-raising and resource development, and other vital organizational functions.

The members of the specific program committees help to develop the organization's long-range strategic plans, the mediation training curriculum, the volunteer-development procedures and materials, and policies and procedures that are essential to the maintenance, growth, and development of the organization. In return for their time and efforts these community leaders enjoy recognition and status in their community and with the community mediation center. They have the opportunity to develop additional leadership skills and valuable expertise in organizational governance and specialized areas, such as fund-raising, program budgeting, and strategic planning.

Leaders who participate on the mediator training faculty assist in organizing and implementing the training sessions several times each year and travel to Hawaii's "neighbor islands" to train mediators there. The senior trainers help to develop the curriculum and present the training modules. Others assist with the organization and logistics of the workshop and act as small group leaders and mentors to the new trainees. In return for their efforts and dedication these leaders receive recognition from the program staff and other volunteers, and they learn advanced training and mediation skills.

In many ways leadership provides opportunities for the empowerment of self and others. Studies of citizen participation indicate that one way to develop both a sense of control, and actual or perceived power, is to become involved in the decisions that affect the quality of community life. In this regard, studies of citizen leaders suggest that participation in leadership is particularly empowering. Community leaders typically believe in their political efficacy and have a strong sense of self-efficacy (Milbrath 1977). Kieffer's study of grass roots organizations (1984) found that local leaders had a positive sense of self-competence and self-concept. Zurcher (1970) found that leaders in grass roots organizations became less alienated as a result of their participation in leadership roles. Given the findings of these other studies of community leadership, it might be expected that the mediator leaders will be more empowered than the other mediators who do not play leadership roles in the organization.

The relationship between the three different types of mediation participation and empowerment that might result will be discussed more fully in the next chapter. But first it is necessary to examine more closely the concept of empowerment. Some of the confusion surrounding this concept may be dispelled by further conceptual development to explore its relationship to other concepts, such as power, locus of control, efficacy, and self-esteem. Chapter 4 reviews the literature on empowerment and extends the theory-building process.

4

Empowerment: Transforming Power and Powerlessness

In this chapter I pose three questions: (1) What is empowerment? (2) How do individuals become empowered or disempowered? and (3) What is the linkage between the mediation process and the empowerment process? In order to clarify the meaning of empowerment and facilitate theory building, I delineate empowerment's major components and develop a theoretical framework. This conceptual analysis provides a context for understanding the mediation perspective on empowerment. A model derived from the theoretical framework suggests how mediation empowers mediators and provides a foundation for the research design described in the following chapter.

CONCEPTUAL ANALYSIS AND THEORY BUILDING

The Empowerment Concept

Empowerment is a relatively new concept compared to the related concept of power, which has been traced back to the Greek philosopher Plato (Winter 1973). Over the last twenty years the term "empowerment" has appeared with greater frequency in many different fields and disciplines. It is now considered to be a core concept in education (Kindervatter 1979), political and economic development (Freire 1970; Kent 1990; Friedmann 1992), democratic theory (Boyte 1986), African-American politics (Hanks 1987; Bobo and Gilliam 1990), feminist politics (Schuler 1986; Bookman 1988; Deutchman 1991), mental health (Rose 1985), public health (Israel et al. 1989), community psychology (Rappaport 1985; Zimmerman 1990), human services (Solomon

1976), business (Block 1987; Hitt 1988), and the "new age" human potential movement (Robbins 1986; Zukav 1989).

The term "empowerment" is commonly used in the popular media, and most Americans have at least some idea of what they think it means. Julian Rappaport, a leading proponent of empowerment in the field of community psychology, claims, "Empowerment is a pervasive positive value in American culture" (1987, 121). The value of empowerment appears to be so widely accepted that it is embraced by people with quite different values and ideologies (Kelso and Swanson 1994), by theorists of the political right (Berger and Neuhaus 1977), as well as the political left (Freire 1970; Gaventa 1980; Gore 1993).

The term "empowerment" is complex and it has many components. It is used as if it were synonymous with a variety of other related concepts, such as self-esteem, self-reliance, self-actualization, self-transformation, personal competence, power, coping skills, citizen participation, community building, and social or political transformation.

Empowerment can be viewed from many different perspectives. For example, it is discussed as a plan of action (Hess 1984), as symbolic ideology (Katz 1984), as a way of being (Wolff 1987), or as a model for policy (Rappaport 1987). The recent political development literature suggests that development should be viewed as a process of individual, community, and societal empowerment. For example, according to George Kent's definition, "Empowerment is development: *to be empowered is to increase your capacity to define, analyze, and act on your own problems*" (1988, 5).

Charles Kieffer, a community activist as well as an empowerment theorist, points to both the transformational potential and the conceptual confusion associated with the concept of empowerment. "Empowerment is coming of age in the 1980s. An idea rooted in the 'social action' ideology of the 1960s, and the 'self-help' perspectives of the 1970s, empowerment appears with increasing frequency in discussions of strategies for prevention and community intervention. . . . [W]e seem to resonate intuitively to its psycho-social, political, and ethical connotations. But we have yet to define this term with sufficient clarity to establish its utility either for theory or practice" (1984, 10). Thus, despite the widespread and growing appeal of the idea and ideal of empowerment, little progress has been made in its conceptual development.

There are several reasons for this lack of conceptual clarity. First, conceptual confusion is a problem that is endemic to the social sciences. As Robert Merton, the eminent sociologist, pointed out over thirty years ago, "A good part of the work called 'theorizing' is taken up with the clarification of concepts—and rightly so. It is in this matter of clearly defined concepts that social science research is not infrequently defective" (1958, 114).

Second, in addition to the generic problems of social science research, conceptual difficulties also stem from the unusual complexity of the empowerment concept. The social science literature suggests that empowerment may be a multi-dimensional concept with many forms, and a multi-level concept with relevance for individuals, groups, organizations, communities, and larger systems. Rappaport attests to many of the difficulties involved in clarifying this concept:

It is a very complex idea to define because it has components that are both psychological and political. The word is used by psychologists and social workers, and by sociologists and political scientists, as well as by theologians. It suggests a sense of control over one's life in personality, cognition, and motivation. It expresses itself at the level of feelings, at the level of ideas about self-worth, at the level of being able to make a difference in the world around us, and even at the level of something more akin to the spiritual. (1985, 17)

As Rappaport alludes, empowerment is both familiar and elusive at the same time. It is widely used by people who seem to have some idea about what it means. Empowerment is a complex interdisciplinary concept with aspects of interest to psychologists, sociologists, and political scientists. Empowerment is considered to be a positive value by individuals and groups with very different and sometimes opposing ideologies.

These difficulties are exacerbated because its conceptual power and ideological appeal have made it attractive to many disciplines with diverse theoretical perspectives that emphasize different aspects of the concept. Fred Riggs (1988), a leading theoretician long concerned with conceptual development, argues that this tendency in the social sciences to assign multiple meanings to the same term creates interdisciplinary communication problems that result in a modern day "Tower of Babel."

Despite, or because of, these interdisciplinary difficulties, an attempt at concept clarification is warranted if we are to make advances in theory development. The Nobel laureate Sir G. Thomson has argued that all science "depends on its concepts. These are ideas which receive names. They determine the questions one asks, and the answers one gets. They are more fundamental than the theories which are stated in terms of them" (1961, 4). More recently, in addressing the "basic dilemmas in the social sciences," Herbert Blalock, an eminent sociologist and methodologist, urged "a strenuous effort . . . to strive for a much better consensus on concepts and definitions" (1984, 10).

This chapter represents an effort to achieve greater clarity about the concept of empowerment beginning with a reconnaissance of the social science literature. My intent is to provide a context for understanding empowerment in relation to community mediation and to justify the selection of empirical indices to operationalize the empowerment concept.

CONCEPTUAL ANALYSIS GUIDELINES

My conceptual analysis of empowerment follows Giovanni Sartori's (1984, 4) methodological guidelines. He suggests, "In reconstructing a concept, first collect a representative set of definitions; second, extract their characteristics; and third, construct matrixes that organize such characteristics meaningfully."

The conceptual analysis of empowerment has a number of stages. First, I began with an analysis of lexical definitions from a variety of general and specialized dictionaries. Second, I selected representative definitions from the leading scholars in the social sciences, public health, education, and mediation, and I delineated the key characteristics of empowerment culled from these definitions. Third, following Sartori's guidelines, I developed a matrix of meanings to organize the characteristics and clarify the major themes set forth by scholars and reflective practitioners. This process provided a context for understanding the comparative perspectives on empowerment found in the mediation literature and the views of HNJC mediators on empowerment.

Fourth, the reconceptualization stage develops a general definition for individual empowerment that links the various components of empowerment. In the final stage of this analysis I elaborate the definition into a general theoretical framework, which provides the foundation for the development of the mediator-empowerment model and the subsequent empirical analysis of the relationship between mediation participation and individual empowerment.

Lexical Analysis

I began the conceptual analysis with a survey of general and specialized dictionaries in order to determine current usage of the term. Webster's *New world dictionary* (1966, 476), defines empower as: "v.t. 1. to give power or authority to; authorize: as, the president is *empowered* to veto legislation. 2. to give ability to; enable; permit: as, science *empowers* men to control natural forces more effectively."

The *Random House dictionary of the American language* (1966, 468) uses a similar definition, and the *Compact edition of the Oxford English dictionary* (1971, 131) defines *empower* as: "1. To invest legally or formally with power or authority; to authorize, license. 2. To impart or bestow power to an end or for a purpose; to enable, permit. 3. To gain or assume power *over*." It further defines empowerment as: "the action of empowering; the state of being empowered."

All of these dictionary definitions assume a situation of authority or dominance *over* things or people. Empowerment is defined in these volumes as the process of the dominant power or legal authority permitting or *giving* power or abilities to another individual or a group having less power, or as gaining power *over* another person.

This notion of empowerment as giving power or abilities to others differs significantly from the current social science views, which strongly emphasize the role of *supporting or facilitating* others in becoming empowered. These dictionary definitions are also narrower in scope than the social science views, which link to other concepts that constitute a semantic field for empowerment. The lexical definitions stipulate that empowerment is an extension of the more familiar concept of power. In contrast, social science definitions suggest a wider range of denotations and connotations undoubtedly resulting from the increased usage and corresponding complex evolution of the concept in many disciplines in recent years.

We might expect to find that these more diverse meanings of empowerment would be reflected in the specialized social science dictionaries and encyclopedias, but a search of the major works for further guidance proves surprisingly disappointing. For example, a survey of *the International encyclopedia of the social sciences* (1968), *the Dictionary of philosophy* (1976), *a Dictionary of the social sciences* (1964), *the Encyclopedia of philosophy* (1967), *the International relations dictionary* (1969), *the American political dictionary*, 3rd edition, (1972), *the Harper dictionary of modern thought* (1977), *the Encyclopedia of education* (1971), *the Dictionary of key words in psychology* (1986), and *the Concise encyclopedia of psychology* (1987) failed to reveal a single definition for the term "empowerment." The omission of empowerment from the more recent social science publications is especially puzzling considering the widespread use of the concept in these fields.

The Social Science Literature: Reconstruction

A survey of the literature on empowerment was more productive. What do the major theorists, action researchers, and reflective practitioners from the social sciences, education, and public health mean by empowerment? In order to answer this question, I surveyed the major contributors to empowerment theory from these fields and compared their views to those of mediation theorists and to the views of active mediator practitioners.

Empowerment Definitions. A sampling of empowerment definitions selected from diverse disciplines reveals a variety of issues, orientations, and concerns, as well as a good deal of commonality.

1. "From the standpoint of psychology, Rappaport suggests that empowerment means to have (or gain) some positive sense of control over oneself and one's life opportunities. From a more sociological perspective, it probably also involves the feeling that one is part of a larger collectivity, a group in which one encounters 'people like myself.' Meaningful participation in such a collectivity involves formal or informal roles in a family, a friendship group, a race or gender group, a work group, an organization, or a total community." (Chesler and Chesney 1988, 231)

2. "Empowerment is viewed as a process: the mechanism by which people, organizations, and communities gain mastery over their lives. However, the content of the process is of infinite variety and as the process plays itself

out among different people and settings the end products will be variable and even inconsistent with one another." (Rappaport 1984, 5)

3. "Empowerment can be viewed as attainment of an abiding set of commitments and capabilities which can be referred to as 'participatory competence.' This state of being and ability incorporate three major intersecting aspects or dimensions: (a) development of more positive self-concept, or sense of self-competence, (b) construction of more critical or analytical understanding of the surrounding social and political environment, and (c) cultivation of individual and collective resources for social and political action." (Kieffer 1984, 31)

4. "The empowerment process appears to involve the ability to think critically and dialectically, about the world and one's position in it. This requires skills gained from dialogue with others, as well as knowledge gained about macro system structures, specifically, about the social, political, and economic systems. . . . Ideally empowerment involves reflective action directed towards responsible social change." (Torre 1986, 39)

5. "[Empowerment] links individual strengths, and competencies, natural helping systems, and proactive behaviors to social policy and social change. . . . [e]mpowerment can be understood at different levels of analysis. For example, organizations can be empowering because they influence policy decisions or because they provide settings for individuals to feel in control of their own lives. A community can be empowered because the citizens engage in activities that maintain or improve the quality of life and respond to community needs." (Zimmerman, quoted in Rappaport 1985, 18)

6. "Empowerment is dependent upon two concepts: *capacity* and *equity*. . . . Capacity has three components. It is an individual or group's ability to: (a) utilize power to solve problems, (b) gain access to institutions or organizations that are serving them, and (c) nurture. . . . Power involves skills and financial resources. . . . The defining elements of the nurturance dimension of capacity are human and community resources. . . . The principle of equity is defined by citizens in two ways: whether their investment (objective or subjective) is equal to their return; and whether their neighborhood organization is getting its fair share of resources." (Biegel 1984, 119)

7. "Empowerment is defined in terms of the extent of decision-making power that people actually wield in an organization. . . . The ideal of people acting to control their own lives is at the heart of democratic theory." (Gruber and Trickett 1987, 353)

This montage of definitions provides a brief but representative overview of the literature on empowerment. Using these interdisciplinary definitions and other material cited below, the next step in the conceptual analysis process was to delineate the empowerment concept into eight primary components, including self-esteem, self-efficacy, knowledge and skills, political awareness, social participation, political participation, political rights and responsibilities, and resources. The resulting matrix suggested by Sartori brings increased order to an analysis of the literature and provides the foundation for a theoretical framework. While the conceptual categories of the components discussed below are analytically distinct, the boundaries between them are often blurred in practice as well as in the literature.

The Eight Empowerment Components

The basic components of empowerment are briefly described below, and many of them will be elaborated on in a later chapter when they are operationalized and the psychological scales used to measure them are described. The first two components of empowerment that are mentioned in most of the definitions are self-esteem and self-efficacy. These key concepts refer to a set of attitudes and beliefs about the self and about the self in relation to the environment. The terms "beliefs" and "attitudes" are often used interchangeably, but Thurstone, a leading theorist in the study of attitudes, defines attitude as including (1) affect for or against, (2) evaluation of, (3) like or dislike of, or (4) positiveness or negativeness toward a psychological object (in Mueller 1986). In other words, attitudes refer to judgments about or preferences for or against an object. The psychological object of concern can include individuals, groups, actions, and institutions.

Beliefs are people's subjective knowledge about themselves and the world, and they are considered to be the primary determinants of attitudes. Values are a type of belief. Milton Rokeach suggests that a value is an "enduring belief that a specific mode of conduct or end state of existence is personally or socially preferable to an opposite or converse mode of conduct or end state of existence" (1973, 5). It is generally agreed that values are more abstract, higher-order constructs than attitudes. A formulation of the relationship between these constructs would suggest that a positive attitude toward an object would result from the belief that the object is positively linked to the attainment of important values (Fishbein 1967; Bem 1970; Scheibe 1970; Ajzen 1988).

1. Self-esteem. Self-esteem is the evaluative function of the self-concept. High self-esteem indicates a positive attitude toward oneself and one's behavior. It seems to be an enduring personal disposition, but self-evaluation may shift depending on one's ego strength, the love of significant others, and various environmental factors. Similar terms would include: self-worth, self-acceptance, and self-respect. Abraham Maslow (1962), the father of humanistic psychology and developer of the well-known "needs hierarchy," believed that self-esteem is a basic need and that it is strongly related to the process of becoming a "self-actualized" person. Self-esteem is basic to an individual's mental health and has been linked to democratic political participation (Sniderman 1975).

2. Self-efficacy. A sense of self-efficacy refers to the experience of one's self as a cause agent. High self-efficacy is a positive attitude toward one's control over the environment. Those with adequate self-efficacy can cope with the demands of the situations they encounter. Obstacles to making progress will only motivate them to increase their efforts. Albert Bandura, the major theorist in the development of the self-efficacy and personal competence concepts, contends, "Among the different aspects of self-knowledge, perhaps none is more influential in people's everyday lives than conceptions of their personal efficacy" because efficacious functioning "requires both skills and self-beliefs of efficacy to use them" (1986, 391). Bandura (392) defines perceived self-efficacy as, "people's judgments of their capabilities to organize and execute courses of action required to attain designated types of performances. It is concerned not with the skills one has but with judgments of what one can do with whatever skills one possesses."

An individual's level of self-efficacy may be a general disposition or it may vary across different activities, different levels of activity, and different circumstances. For example, an individual might feel competent to perform well in most academic situations, but feel totally inadequate in athletic competitions.

How is the concept of self-efficacy related to the concept of self-esteem? These concepts are often confused and used interchangeably but they are different phenomena. Self-esteem is the evaluation of one's self-worth, whereas self-efficacy is a judgment about one's personal capabilities. There are, for example, many athletes who feel efficacious and excel at sports but still have low self-esteem. Conversely, one could play golf or other sports poorly without any loss of self-esteem, especially if golf is considered to be only a trivial game or a source of leisure time relaxation. Bandura contends that both self-esteem and self-efficacy "contribute in their own way to the quality of human life" (1986, 410). In addition, both self-esteem and self-efficacy contribute positively and significantly to the formation of "psychological" empowerment.

3. Knowledge and skills. This component of personal empowerment refers to personal capabilities. I would include several kinds of knowledge here. First, the most important type of general knowledge relevant to personal empowerment is basic literacy (see Freire 1970). Also important are the kinds of practical knowledge that enable the individual to survive in a recalcitrant environment and facilitate the development of personal competence, such as knowledge about conflict dynamics and the mediation process. Third, self-knowledge such as one's goals, values, limitations, and strengths are fundamental to increasing and maintaining self-empowerment. Other kinds of specialized knowledge specifically relevant to political empowerment are included in the political awareness component described below.

Skills can be defined as a coordinated series of actions that help to attain goals or accomplish tasks. The skills considered to be essential to personal empowerment may vary somewhat according to one's view of empowerment, the cultural context, and other factors. The primary empowerment skills list usually includes things like stress management and coping skills (Marsella and Dash-Scheurer 1988), communication, negotiation, problem solving, and conflict resolution skills.

Social or political activists would emphasize the need for additional skills, such as community organizing, grass roots transforming leadership, and other political skills. These various types of empowering skills can be acquired by participating in social and political organizations at the grass roots or higher levels of governance or through workshops such as mediation training. In turn, the development of these basic empowering skills of democratic citizenship provide a major rationale for arguments on behalf of a significant political transformation favoring participatory or "strong" models of democracy to replace or supplement the current representative or "elite" model of democracy (see Shonholtz 1993a; Barber 1984; Warren 1992). In short, the knowledge and skills component, combined with the empowering attitudes of self-esteem and self-efficacy, provide the basis for development of social competencies or "social" empowerment.

4. Political awareness. One aspect of political awareness is critical consciousness, a special type of empowering knowledge that enables people to develop their own concepts of social justice and provides conceptual tools to realize those goals. The notion of critical consciousness is strongly associated with the influential Latin American liberation theorist, Paulo Freire (1970) and his ideas about "liberation education." Freire developed the transformational concept of *conscientization* in order to help oppressed people to think critically about their social and political conditions, to recognize themselves as human beings oppressed by political authorities and structures, and to develop political actions that would transform and alleviate their oppression. In opposition to traditional models of education that he views as tools of oppression, Freire's models for empowering education are based on a continuous dialogue between the teacher and learner in which there is always mutual respect and mutual learning for all participants.

Underlying my conception of political awareness are four related questions: What is, or where are we now? Where are we headed? Where should we be headed? And how do we get there from here? These are complex questions with no easy answer. The first type of political analysis requires the necessary theories, ideology, information, empirical analysis skills, political experience, and political intuition to determine *what is*. Understanding the political game is essential for all citizens especially in democratic societies. This includes mainstream politicians who wish to be effective and successful, conflict resolvers who believe that it is vital to get at the root (structural) causes of deep-rooted conflict, and reformers and transformationalists who seek to critique in order to improve or fundamentally transform the existing political system.

Understanding the political game requires identifying the power elite and key players and answering several key questions. How does the political-economic system operate? Who has the power and how is it used? Who benefits from the present system and who is exploited? What social or political strategies would enable one to be efficacious within the existing status quo system or if need be to transform the present system? This type of critical political analysis is crucial to understanding the nature of the existing system, the key factors related to disempowerment and social injustice, and the empowerment potential of any setting or system (see Freire 1970; Gaventa 1980).

The second type of political analysis, which flows from the first, asks *where are we headed or what will be?* Given our understanding of existing political systems and the apparent trends and transformations, changes and continuities, what does the future look like? Anticipating the future is perhaps even more difficult than understanding the present, but it is essential for future planning and developing effective policies. Anticipating what will be may be especially important if one believes that the consequences of present policies and trends will be disastrous in the long run, and there is a need for major preventive efforts to avoid the possible environmental and political disasters looming in the third millennium.

The importance of this question has spawned a large and growing futurist industry in universities and think tanks that use scenarios, forecasts, extrapolation, Delphi techniques, computer models, and other techniques in an effort to anticipate the future. Despite these efforts, the futurists debate continues between optimists and pessimists; among those who believe that major social, economic, and political transformations are occurring throughout the world; and among other scholars who stress the underlying structural continuity of these same systems.

The third aspect of political awareness, which follows directly from a critical analysis of the existing sociopolitical structures, is prescriptive analysis, or the ability to decide *what should be*. This normative vision of a better future should be based on a clearly articulated theory or ideology with basic values such as human survival (i.e., meeting basic needs), and values relating to *quality of life* (i.e., social justice, equity, or transcendence). In this regard, many theorists and political activists would suggest that a theory of empowerment would provide a desirable guide or vision for a preferred future. Of course, as we have discussed there are different perspectives on empowerment.

Some perspectives on empowerment view the possibilities of, and strategies for, empowerment in ways that seem to assume support for the existing economic, social, and political status quo. An example is the traditional view of mental health services, which assumes that the existing social structures are relatively fair and that problems of personal disempowerment should be dealt with primarily by mental health counseling and other interventions to help the individual to get access to existing resources and to learn the coping skills that will enable the individual to adjust to stress and to living more harmoniously in society. Thus, these experts and writers emphasize the need for the development of personal competencies as the primary path to empowerment, with perhaps some piecemeal reforms to eliminate bottlenecks in service delivery and generally improve system effectiveness.

Other more critical writers offer a significantly different analysis of the existing political system, and consequently they set forth different prescriptions for increasing the levels of individual and community empowerment. They contend that the present political and economic structures are oppressive and breed injustice and disempowerment for the majority of the citizens. Consequently, these critics emphasize the need for analysis of root causes of injustice and social violence, and major social and political transformation to restructure existing power relationships in society, in addition to, or perhaps instead of, personal transformation.

The fourth aspect of political awareness is the ability to develop viable transition strategies, or to determine *how to get there from here*. If one believes that the existing political-economic system is relatively fair or that it requires only a few minor changes, and that furthermore, the future indicators for a continuation of the status quo are salutary, then all that may be required are routine system maintenance activities or minor piecemeal reforms.

If on the other hand one believes that the present structures are oppressive, dysfunctional, and disempowering, or that these present structures are basically satisfactory but that they may be seriously deteriorating, then the task of achieving major structural transformation is somewhat more daunting. Under these circumstances, the ability "to get there from here" involves a combination of capabilities, such as the critical analysis of root causes of alienation and the barriers to transformation, as well as planning and transforming leadership skills to strategize and implement the individual and collective actions essential to the transformation of individuals and structures.

Political awareness as I have described it here is the core component of developing political competencies or of "political empowerment." In combination with the self-esteem and self-efficacy attitudes and the knowledge and skills components, political awareness enables a citizen to function quite effectively in the different types of political activities described below.

The first four empowerment components discussed above—self-esteem, self-efficacy, knowledge and skills, and political awareness—relate to different aspects of citizen empowerment. The next two empowerment components, social and political participation, refer to two types of social and political collective behavior that have the potential to transform individuals and societies. The empowerment literature usually does not differentiate between social and political participation. But because of the discussion above on system maintenance versus structural transformational perspectives, and the implications for theory building and public policy that will be discussed later, I will distinguish between these two types of collective behavior based on the intentions of the participants, the expected outcomes, and the potential of each type of participation for personal and political transformation.

5. *Social participation.* As I am defining it here, social participation includes participation in a broad spectrum of community groups, organizations, and activities, such as stamp clubs, investment clubs, garden clubs, community beautification projects, the Kiwanis, Lions, Masons, community self-help mutual support groups like Alcoholics Anonymous, traditional human service counseling, or therapy programs. Many citizens participate in what Peter Berger and Richard Neuhaus (1977) call "mediating" agencies such as church groups and various community volunteer activities like Big Brothers, Big Sisters, and the Heart, Cancer, and Arthritis Foundations, as well as the research setting for this study, the Honolulu Neighborhood Justice Center.

This type of social participation can be very valuable in meeting various individual needs for affiliation, meaningful service, and achievement. Social participation may provide a support system that helps people cope with stress. It offers the opportunity to help others as well as one's self, the possible development of new knowledge and skills, enhanced feelings of personal control, and increased self-esteem and self-efficacy.

At this point, research on the linkage of social participation and citizen empowerment is at an early stage, but most of the empirical studies have demonstrated a positive correlation between community participation and citizen empowerment. The specific nature of the linkage has not been established, but several variables appear to impact empowerment: the individual's motives for participation (e.g., self-help or helping others), the degree or frequency of participation (e.g., once a year, once a month, daily), the level or type of participation (e.g., part-time volunteer, core member, leader), and the kinds of tasks performed or skills learned (e.g., filing, envelope stuffing, fund-raising, organizational governance, or community mediating).

Other important variables relevant to citizen empowerment include the characteristics of the organization or setting, such as the organizational vision, ideology, mission, or purpose; the organizational culture or style; organizational leadership style (i.e., autocratic, transactional, transforming), as well as other characteristics. Little empirical research has been done on any of these individual or organizational variables, but compared to other types of community participation, community mediation with its emphasis on self-help and mutual help, ideology of empowerment, and opportunity for human growth and skills development would appear especially likely to have high empowerment potential.

At this point it should be noted that most of the community organizations discussed here, including the community social service agencies and mediation centers, assume that the existing political and economic system is basically fair and that people can exercise their rights and gain access to needed services and resources once they have the knowledge to understand how the system works.

Indeed, in some cases there is a tendency in the "helping professions" and with members of the public to "blame the victim" for their problems and perceived deficiencies when the underlying causes for social problems are structural in nature. Therefore, the preferred solutions for personal powerlessness or disempowerment are either to use techniques, therapies, or strategies for providing professional services and resources to dependent clients, or to *transform the individual* by developing the necessary knowledge and skills for personal competence and positive attitudes for dealing with problems.

Because many of the traditional social service agencies support the economic and political status quo, they are often perceived as a tool for maintaining social control and enhancing dependency by political activists, including many transformationalists critical of the existing system. As mentioned earlier, this critique is also leveled at many of the community mediation programs, especially those that function as an adjunct of the court system or are closely linked by funding or client referral to the courts and other governmental agencies.

While this critique may be valid, it should be noted that individuals may still become personally empowered by participation in community organizations despite the status quo political orientation of the organization. Furthermore, if individuals become empowered they are likely to be happier, and healthier, and to contribute to enhancing the quality of life in their communities. Perhaps if they become sufficiently transformed, they may be willing and able to assume an active role in transforming their communities and society. I will return to the relationship between personal transformation and political transformation below.

6. Political participation. I have divided political participation into four types or categories, which I will call "politics as usual," "Transformational Politics," "radical revolutionary politics," and "reform politics." These types of political participation will differ somewhat with regard to ideology, the kind of political analysis conducted, prescriptions suggested for political action and public policy, and potential for personal and political transformation.

"Politics as usual" refers to normal mainstream political participation in our representative democracy and includes voting, fund-raising, working with political campaigns, writing letters to the editor, advocating, lobbying, and running for political office. This is the kind of political behavior lauded in high school civics books. It supports the existing political system and may be personally empowering for some participants, but it is not intended to bring about political transformations. It is important to understand how the political game is played, who the power players are, and how to work within the system to be effective and personally successful. In this way it is possible that empowered individuals might prosper, even in a political system that is inequitable for the disempowered.

"Transformational Politics," on the other hand, usually begins with a political critique that attempts to reveal the root causes of alienation, injustice, social violence, and other systemic problems. It seeks to demonstrate structural and institutional shortcomings; and to prescribe transformational policies and programs to correct problems with the present system. In this view the existing social-political system is seen as inequitable, corrupt, inept, and oppressive for many citizens (see Parenti 1995). Band-aid solutions and piecemeal reforms are considered to be insufficient to solve the major social problems that stem primarily from structural defects.

In this view, individual transformation alone is not considered sufficient to solve the problems of powerlessness or disempowerment. The political economic system must also undergo major transformation in order to enable powerless and oppressed peoples to gain access to essential rights and resources. Transformationalists generally favor the spread of global democracy abroad and want to move from our present representative form of democracy to a much more participatory form of democracy similar to early American town meetings, where citizens were much more highly involved in day to day political decision making. Benjamin Barber (1984), a leading democratic theorist, calls this model "strong" democracy in contrast to the "thin" democracy model with low citizen participation that now exists in America. Some transformational theorists suggest that the revolution in telecommunications has provided the technology that makes a "strong" democracy and high levels of citizen participation possible. It is argued that high levels of citizen participation will lead to both citizen empowerment and political system transformation (Slaton 1992). Transformationalists debate whether individual transformation must precede structural transformation or vice versa, or whether both types or levels of transformation must be simultaneous. Transformationalists generally believe that major political change is essential but that it should be accomplished through noncoercive evolutionary means.

In contrast, the "radical revolutionaries" believe that the ruling power elite will never willingly surrender power and therefore that political violence and revolution may be necessary to accomplish major political changes. While some revolutionaries may intend to establish participatory democracies, others may plan to install another authoritarian system with themselves as a new political elite. Thus revolutionary political participation might result in personal empowerment for the participants, but the political outcomes could be either more democratic as in the American Revolution or more repressive as in the Russian Revolution.

By "reform politics" I mean something part way between "politics as usual" and "transformational politics." Reformers generally acknowledge that the present system is far from perfect. Congress may be viewed as a "dismal swamp," bureaucracies as unwieldy, inefficient, and often unresponsive to both citizens and politicians, and political corruption as an endemic problem at all political levels. However, reformers may argue that no political system is perfect, and the American political system is one of the best in the world. Most political reformers believe that it is possible to work within the system to substantially reform government and to elect leaders with vision to "reinvent" government.

Transformational theorists try to differentiate true political transformation, which is "noncoercive and evolutionary" from piecemeal reform. In some instances this distinction might be fairly clear cut; but in other situations the means and ends proposed by political reformers and transformationalists may be difficult to distinguish. For example, would the Clinton administration's proposals for "reinventing government," for creating "empowerment zones," or for "sustainable development" be considered to be part of a reform agenda or a transformationalist agenda? Is the newly emerging "communitarian" project (see Etzioni 1993b) that emphasizes empowerment and suggests restoring a balance between a citizen's rights and a citizen's responsibilities, considered to be a reform program or is it transformational? It is also possible that a policy intended as a reform in the short run may turn out to have a transformational impact in the long run or vice versa. Citizen participation in "reform" politics would probably result in some personal empowerment, and could bring about systemic changes that might be judged to be either reformist or transformational depending on the evaluative criteria used in the assessment and the time frame for evaluation.

Despite the analytic distinctions I have drawn here between social participation and different types of political participation, it should be pointed out that there are many areas of overlap between these types of citizen participation. First, individuals may participate in both social and political types of activity at the same time: being involved as a volunteer in a community program like community mediation, while also campaigning as a candidate for a transformational political party like the Greens. Second, an individual may become sufficiently empowered as a result of social participation to become more involved in political activities and causes that advocate political reform or transformation. Third, grass roots social organizations may initially attempt to work within the system to gain health or social benefits for their members from existing social services. But after a time they may become frustrated by experiences with impersonal, disempowering bureaucratic barriers and then they may become increasingly politicized as their levels of political awareness and power increase. Fourth, it is possible that different types of social and political participation, or different degrees of participation, may develop different kinds of empowerment. The type of participation that is most empowering for an individual may also depend on a number of personal and political factors, including the individual's characteristics and circumstances; the political system and its use of power and responsiveness to citizen demands; and the resources, commitment, and vision of the participants.

The last two empowerment components—political rights and responsibilities, and material and nonmaterial resources—are viewed as participation outcomes. These two components represent the basic needs of all citizens, their primary motives for social and political participation and collaboration, and the goals and objectives that are sought by people who are disempowered. In other words, those who lack access to rights and resources are considered to be disempowered.

7. Political rights and responsibilities. I am considering rights and responsibilities together here as one component of empowerment. Political rights refers to the traditional values of democratic societies, including the freedom of thought, conscience, religion, and political movement; the rights to free speech and free assembly; the right to organize politically, to run for office, to vote, to have a fair trial, and to be treated equally before the law; and the freedom from retroactive laws. Political responsibilities include voting, political participation beyond voting, payment of taxes, defense of the country, obeying the law, accepting majority decisions, and respecting the rights of others.

Until very recently most empowerment theorists focused on the centrality of rights and entitlements to increasing personal empowerment. A citizen's responsibilities were rarely mentioned. This was a natural emphasis because disempowered people are often unable to exercise their political rights or obtain essential resources. Therefore, empowerment efforts focused on obtaining rights and resources to redress inequities.

Now, some empowerment theorists have begun to acknowledge that empowerment also means taking control of your own life and making your own decisions, and this clearly requires accepting responsibility for yourself and for others. Therefore, the emphasis is now shifting to seeking a balance between developing individual autonomy and developing a viable community, as well as achieving a balance between individual rights and personal and social responsibilities. This shift is a major emphasis, for example, in the new "Communitarian" movement (see Barber 1992; Etzioni 1993b).

8. Resources. For most theorists, increasing empowerment means increasing access to essential resources. The category of resources includes all of the nonmaterial psychological and social resources, and the material resources needed to meet human needs and interests. What constitutes essential resources depends to some extent on the culture and society, the prevailing ideology or social theory, and other personal and political factors.

Political rights and resources are often discussed together in the empowerment literature, but they are listed as separate components here because they are distinctly different concepts and their pursuit may involve the classic value conflict between freedom and equality. It is difficult to achieve both simultaneously. For example, capitalist societies have traditionally chosen to emphasize individual freedom as the paramount value, whereas communist societies have emphasized social and material equality.

One of these values may be achieved without the other. For example, long after Southern Blacks in the United States won the right to vote, they continued to live in poverty in many areas. On the other hand, in some authoritarian regimes, such as Singapore or China, the basic material resources necessary to sustain life may be available and even plentiful but the political rights are suppressed. Significant personal empowerment assumes access to resources as well as the exercise of political rights and responsibilities.

Empowerment: Power and Powerlessness

Before we consider the matrix of empowerment components and empowerment theorists, one crucial question remains—what about the concept of power? What is the relationship between power and empowerment? Power is the root word in empowerment and a core concept in the social sciences, especially in political science. A few theorists have defined empowerment as the process of gaining power (Rummel 1976; McClelland 1975; Solomon 1976). But these are the exceptions. Most empowerment theorists have avoided the concept of power. For example, in an extensive survey of the empowerment literature, Dorothy Torre found that "the empowerment literature avoids specific discussion regarding the relationship between power and empowerment" (1986, 39). What would account for this puzzling tendency to avoid the concept of power by those concerned with trying to understand the related concept of empowerment? A major explanatory factor seems to be the very different connotations associated with the two terms "power" and "empowerment." On the other hand, the concept of empowerment as we have discussed has an overwhelmingly positive image with scholars, politicians, and the general public in America. Empowerment is associated with positive American cultural values, such as autonomy, human growth and development, social justice, self-actualization, peace, and altruistic behavior. Empowerment is viewed as a personally transforming process by which people gain greater control over their lives and create alternatives to domination.

The concept of power, however, generally has a negative image among empowerment theorists, mediators, and with the general public. One of the best known and most influential formulations of power appears in Robert Dahl's classic definition: "A has power over B to the extent that he can get B to do something that he otherwise would not do" (1957, 203). But if A has power over B, then B is correspondingly disempowered or dependent. Thus the concept of *power over* is associated with other negative concepts, such as domination, coercion, authority, and dependency on others. These concepts are an anathema, especially to many of the scholars, practitioners, and advocates of personal and political empowerment. This discomfort with or even revulsion to the concept of power is also shared by those who do community mediation and those who write about mediation. For example, in her study of Quaker community mediation, Jennifer Beer points out that "for many CDS [Community Dispute Services] mediators . . . power itself, in any form, is the great evil" (1986, 104).

How is power related to empowerment? Are they polar opposites, two sides of the same coin, or totally different concepts? The concept of power is related to, but it is not synonymous with, empowerment. For example, powerful people are not necessarily personally empowered according to the definition used here. For example, an individual may have inherited great wealth that provides the potential to dominate others and get much of what they might want to have, and yet have low self-esteem and low self-efficacy and lack the other personal competencies associated with empowerment. Conversely, empowered people are not necessarily powerful in the sense that they have the capability or desire to dominate others. It is possible, for example, to be highly empowered psychologically with high levels of self-esteem and self-efficacy and develop sophisticated political awareness but still not possess significant political or economic power.

On the other hand, different types of power conceptually overlap with empowerment and are integral to the empowerment components discussed earlier. For example, self-esteem, self-efficacy, knowledge, and skills may be considered to be basic components of "social" power. Additionally, an individual's political awareness, the cooperative relationships formed as a result of social and political participation, their exercise of political rights and responsibilities, as well as access to vital resources, provide basic factors for "political" power.

Rollo May (1972) has distinguished four different types of power relationships. First is the most negative type of power, the *exploitative* and *manipulative* use of power, or what is called power *over.* Second is the *competitive* use of power, or power *against.* The third type of power is *nutrient,* or power *for.* Finally, May describes the concept of *integrative* power, or power *with.* A key distinction that May makes is between "constructive" and "destructive" power. He argues that power *over* is destructive, while power *against* has both constructive and destructive aspects, and power *for* and power *with* are both classified by May as constructive.

The empowerment literature that does mention the power concept generally refers to either power *for* or power *with.* The notion of power *for* or *nutrient* power is associated with traditional models of education and many of the "helping" professions, such as social work, mental health, and medical services, and it usually is based on a concern for others. While power *for* is usually well-intentioned, there is a real risk that it can become a variant of power *over.* For example, the traditional "medical model" with its "professionals" providing services to "clients" is generally considered to be disempowering by empowerment advocates. These professional "experts" have most of the power in the expert-client relationship, and they make decisions for their clients that may be medically beneficial but psychologically or socially detrimental in that they may tend to increase the clients' dependency on the professional and on continued access to medical services.

For these reasons, many empowerment advocates would agree that only *integrative* power (Boulding 1989), or power *with* is truly empowering. This type of power emerges out of continuous dialogue and ongoing collaboration for problem solving and conflict resolution. It assumes mutual respect, mutual growth, and mutual benefits. It is sometimes called "synergistic power" (Craig and Craig 1979; Katz 1984), "right power" (Ferguson 1980), or a "win/win" orientation. Designing situations and settings that are characterized by this type of positive power relationship would greatly enhance opportunities for personal and political empowerment.

The Matrix of Empowerment Components and Theorists

The empowerment components discussed by empowerment theorists are presented in Table 4.1. The rows of the matrix refer to articles and books on empowerment by social science and mediation theorists. The first twenty rows represent the various views on empowerment found in the social science literature. The next six rows represent views on empowerment found in the mediation literature. The last row of the matrix contains the results from a survey of active community mediators that presents the collective views of fifty HNJC mediators on empowerment.

The matrix columns contain the eight components relevant to individual empowerment. The ninth column includes the concept of *disempowerment* or *powerlessness*, which is mentioned often by theorists attempting to define empowerment. Rappaport, for example, suggests, "Empowerment is easy to define in its absence: powerlessness, real or imagined; learned helplessness; alienation; loss of a sense of control over one's own life. It is more difficult to define positively only because it takes on a different form in different people and contexts" (1984, 3).

The concept of disempowerment/powerlessness is included here to extend the conceptual analysis. Three measures of disempowerment are included in the empirical analysis to provide a measure of divergent validity.

Content analysis was used to delineate the pattern of the empowerment components considered to be important by the different theorists. Their definitions of empowerment and other selected writings relevant to empowerment were assembled and coded. Each definition and text was coded for the eight empowerment components as well as for references to the concept of disempowerment. Components that are *explicitly* mentioned by each theorist are coded with the notation "x" in Table 4.1. Components that are only *inferred* from the text or whose meanings are ambiguous (for example, where the type of participation discussed is not clear), are coded with an "*" in the matrix. A

Table 4.1
Empowerment Characteristics

THEORISTS/ MEDIATORS	SELF ESTEEM	SELF EFFICACY	SKILLS KNOWLEDGE	POLITICAL AWARENESS	SOCIAL PARTICIPATE	POLITICAL PARTICIPATE	POLITICAL RIGHTS	RESOURCES	POWER LESS
Biegel			X	X	X		X	X	
Checkaway & Norsman	X	X	X	X	X	*	X	X	
Chesler & Chesney	X	X	X	X	X	X	X	X	X
Fawcett et al.	X	*	X	X	X	*	X	X	X
Freire	X	X	X	X	X	X	X	X	X
Gaventa	*	X	X	X	X	X	X	X	X
Gutierrez	X	X	X	X	X	X	*	X	X
Katz		*	*	*	X	*	*	X	
Kent	X	X	X	X	X	X	X	X	X
Kieffer	X	X	X	X	X	X	X	X	X
Maton & Rappaport		X			X			X	
O'Sullivan		X	X	X	*	X	*	X	X
Parsons	X	X	X	*	X		X	X	X
Rappaport	X	X	X		X	*	X	X	X
Riger	X	X	X	X	X	*	X	X	X
Rivera	X	X	X	X	X	*	*	X	X
Serrano-Garcia		X	X	X	X	X		X	
Solomon	*	*	X	X	X		*	X	X
Torre	X	X	X	X	X	X	*	X	
Zimmerman & Rappaport	X	X	X	X	X		X	X	
Adler, Milner & Lovaas	*	*	X	*	X	*	*	X	*
Slaton & Becker			X	*	X	X	*	*	X
Beer	*	X	X		X			*	X
Davis & Salem	*	*	X		X			X	
Moore			X		X				
Shonholtz	X	X	X	*	X	*	*	X	*
HNJC Mediators	X	X	X	*	X	X	X	X	

X = Explicit Mention   * = Implied

blank cell in the matrix indicates that there was no mention of that component in the material surveyed. It should be noted that this analysis is limited to only the material cited in the references. It is quite possible that some of these writers may have expanded on their views of empowerment in other written works that were not included here.

When read horizontally across the rows, the matrix shows how each theorist has conceptualized or defined the term "empowerment." The central meaning of their views on empowerment are captured well by the matrix, and many of their definitions can be essentially reconstructed from the matrix with little loss of meaning.

Social Science Theorists. Three authors in the social sciences have been particularly influential in the development of empowerment theory. The first is Paulo Freire, a Brazilian educator and development theorist widely known to students of liberation education, economic development, and empowerment. The second writer, Charles Kieffer, conducted an early qualitative study of empowerment and leadership participation in grass-roots organizations that is widely cited in the empowerment literature. The third scholar, Julian Rappaport, is one of the most influential proponents of empowerment in the field of community psychology.

As the matrix indicates, all three scholars mention the eight empowerment components in their writings. Most of the other social science scholars included in this study frequently cite at least one of the three theorists, and they seem to have derived many of their views on empowerment from the writings of Freire, Rappaport, and Kieffer. Thus, it is not surprising that many of these writers share a similar view of empowerment even though they come from different disciplines.

A vertical reading of the table shows the frequency with which references to the specific components of empowerment appear in their writings. For the sake of brevity, in my discussion of this matrix and the calculation of percentages, I have not distinguished between those who explicitly mention a component and those who make inference to it. The reader will have to consult the table to make those distinctions. The two components of *resources* and *social participation* are included in their analysis of empowerment by 100% of the authors. The resources component includes having access to a wide variety of psychological, social, and material goods, including community services. People are often considered to be powerless or disempowered primarily because they lack access to needed resources. Becoming empowered, and gaining control over one's life and environment, means gaining access to vital resources. Therefore, it is not surprising that access to or control of needed resources is considered by all of the theorists as essential to the empowerment process. Some type of social participation is also included as a major component by all of the theorists, since it is viewed as the primary strategy for obtaining resources and developing the other components of empowerment, such as self-efficacy, knowledge, and skills.

The *self-efficacy* and *knowledge and skills* components are mentioned by nineteen out of the twenty writers (95%). Self-efficacy provides the positive attitude essential for taking effective action, and knowledge and skills supply the tools and tactics needed for active social participation in order to obtain resources. These three components are closely linked and are considered to be basic to the empowerment process by nearly all of the theorists.

The central importance of some aspect of political *awareness* and the exercise of *political rights* is recognized and discussed by eighteen (90%) of the authors. *Political participation* is mentioned by fifteen (75%) of these writers. This seems to indicate that many of those concerned with increasing political rights and political awareness believe that the existing political system is not sufficiently responsive to the political rights of the disempowered and that there is a need for political action of some type in addition to social participation. The last column in the matrix indicates that about two thirds (65%) of the theorists are concerned about powerlessness. Furthermore, most of these same theorists recognize the importance of political awareness, political participation, and political rights to personal empowerment.

The *self-esteem* component is mentioned by fourteen (70%) of the authors. This still constitutes a majority of the empowerment theorists and indicates their beliefs about the importance of the individual's self-worth in the empowerment process. However, the empowerment theorists surveyed here seem to consider the concept of self-esteem to be somewhat less essential to the empowerment process than some of the other components, including the other psychological attitude of self-efficacy, which was mentioned prominently by 95% of the writers.

Mediation Theorists. An analysis of the meaning of the empowerment concept in the mediation literature is somewhat more problematic. Although empowerment is considered to be a core value of community mediation ideology, few of the mediation researchers have attempted to define explicitly what they mean by empowerment. Unlike the social science theorists discussed above, few of the mediation theorists indicate any familiarity with the social science literature on empowerment, and none of them cite the three influential social science theorists, Rappaport, Kieffer, or Freire. The mediation theorists listed in Table 4.1 are among those who have written most frequently and clearly on the relationship of mediation to empowerment. Their views are discussed earlier, so I will only summarize them here.

Peter Adler, Karen Lovaas, and Neal Milner (1988) have distinguished two views of empowerment based on an analysis of a selection of community and agency mediation program materials. They focus particular attention on an analysis of Shonholtz's writings. Raymond Shonholtz (1984), founder of the San Francisco Community Boards, has written and spoken at length about how community mediation empowers disputants, mediators, and the community. Within the community mediation group Shonholtz is the most widely known and most influential voice on the importance of personal and community empowerment. Christa Slaton and Theodore Becker (1981) share similar views about the importance of mediator and disputant empowerment, but they are especially interested in the potential of grass-roots community mediation as a vehicle for social-political transformation. Jennifer Beer (1986) also considers disputant and mediator empowerment to be an important benefit of community mediation.

Albie Davis and Richard Salem (1984) and Christopher Moore (1986) are primarily concerned with the empowerment of disputants, and based on their writings analyzed here, they are not directly concerned with mediation's potential for social-political transformation. However, they provide sufficient detail to discern what they consider to be the major characteristics of disputant empowerment.

Table 4.1 indicates that the empowerment components of *knowledge and skills*, *social participation*, and *resources* are seen by 100% of the mediation writers as essential to their view of empowerment relevant to the mediation process. This is nearly identical to the finding for these components in the social science literature. However, unlike the social science theorists discussed above, the mediation theorists are more specifically focused on the knowledge and skills of conflict resolution, social participation in community mediation activities, and access to the resources of dispute resolution services. Community mediators are trained intensively in mediation skills, such as active listening and negotiation, and they acquire specialized knowledge about conflict dynamics and how to conduct the mediation process.

Mediation advocates argue that the mediation process is empowering for the disputants because compared to the formal legal system, community mediation provides the necessary information and skills that people need to communicate, problem-solve, and craft their own agreements to resolve their disputes. Thus, especially for the mediation theorists, knowledge and skills are the basic and most important empowerment components for both disputants and mediators.

The social participation and resource connection is clear. Community mediation is a form of social participation that provides psychological and social resources for mediators and disputants. Community mediation programs are examples of what Berger and Neuhaus (1977) have called "mediating" structures, which use collaborative problem solving to resolve community conflicts. According to the literature on citizen participation (Heller et al. 1984), frequent involvement in community activities may empower the participants.

Self-esteem and *self-efficacy* are both mentioned by four out of the six mediation writers (66%, compared to 70% and 90%, respectively, for the social science group). The importance of mediator roles and the community mediation ideology in the development of mediator self-esteem and self-efficacy was discussed in detail in earlier chapters. The idea of empowering disputants to make their own decisions, to solve their own problems, and to author settlement agreements that are fair and mutually agreeable is part of the ideology of mediation. Along with this goes the idea of treating the disputants with dignity and respect and avoiding the dependency orientation fostered by traditional medical and social service organizations. The concept of *powerlessness* is also mentioned by four of the writers (66%).

The most striking comparison between the social science theorists' and the mediation theorists' views of empowerment concerns the political components of empowerment. The mediation writers mention *political awareness, political participation,* and *political rights* in only half of the cases (50%, compared to 90%, 75%, and 90%, respectively, for the same characteristics in the first group). Even the 50% figure is inflated in that much of the mediation program material analyzed by Adler, Lovaas, and Milner relevant to empowerment consists of analysis of Shonholtz's views, and so in affect his view on political characteristics is given double weight in the matrix.

As Rappaport has pointed out, empowerment is a very complex idea "because it has components that are both psychological and political" (1985, 17). Most of the mediation research writers who are concerned with empowerment appear to emphasize the "psychological" and "social" aspects of empowerment. They emphasize the importance of learning new dispute resolution skills, the value of social participation, gaining access to resources, and developing more positive attitudes toward the self and the community. Their primary empowerment concern is with the need for personal psychological and social transformation and not with developing political awareness. Most of the mediation theorists do not link individual conflicts with a political analysis of deep-rooted societal causes.

On the other hand, the mediation writers who are aware of and concerned with political components of empowerment and see the need for political transformation are often those with a political science background, such as Becker, Slaton, and Milner. While some have argued that community mediation may raise critical consciousness by revealing the structural roots of individual conflicts (Scimecca 1987, 32), other scholars dispute the claim that community mediation provides a political education for the disputants (Rothschild 1986).

Most of the community mediation theorists (Beer, Davis, and Salem, and Moore) who champion the value of empowerment do not tend to associate it with political awareness, political participation, or political rights. Compared to the social science group, the majority of the mediation authors associate the concept of empowerment primarily with knowledge and skills, self-esteem, and self-efficacy. In other words, most community mediation theorists are interested in empowerment in the sense of personal transformation instead of political transformation. Thus the mediation theorists seem to have a narrower or more focused view of empowerment.

As this book goes to press, three new books have just been published that emphasize disputant empowerment as the primary objective of community mediation. There was not sufficient time to include them in this conceptual analysis, but they demonstrate that the personal empowerment and transformation projects have not yet been abandoned (Bush and Folger 1994; Folger and Jones 1994; Shailor 1994).

Mediators' Views. How do the HNJC mediators view the concept of empowerment? How do their views of empowerment compare to those of the two groups of theorists just discussed? Seventy-two experienced community mediators were surveyed and asked several questions, including: (1) What does the term "empowerment" mean to you? (2) Do you believe that community mediation is empowering? (3) If yes, how is mediation empowering for: (a) the disputants, (b) the mediators, (c) the community, (d) you personally?

Most of the community mediators were familiar with the term "empowerment" and had some ideas about how it was linked to the kind of mediation they were doing. In fact, for many of them one of the major motivations for becoming a mediator was the belief that community mediation had the potential to empower themselves and others in the community. To those HNJC mediators surveyed, empowerment has a variety of positive meanings, including the following:

1. Giving others the power to make their own decisions and control their direction.

2. Equality, the ability to act, to take control of one's situation/life. To give someone strength.

3. Knowing what the game is, what the rules are, and what your position is, and finally knowing it's your game.

4. To give another the ability to influence activities and actions through education, training, and skills development.

5. Self-determination, actualization.

6. To offer skills and knowledge to allow others to make decisions, and to enable them to take control of their lives.

7. Providing the structure and modeling the skills that allow people to take positive action on their own behalf; placing the power to achieve meaningful outcomes into the hands of those who have the most vested interest in achieving them.

8. Helping people to help themselves. I think this really applies to mediators. I don't feel disputants are truly empowered.

9. Empowering people in our society to take hold of their own problems and resolve them themselves. People lose power referring the resolution of disputes to lawyers.

10. Having the knowledge and freedom to make decisions.

11. Helping others achieve their goals by recognizing and expanding their resources; seeing that the power is shared to achieve common objectives as well as individual objectives.

12. Being in control of your inner and outer self, determining your own direction and purpose.

This sampling of the mediator comments provides a feel for the mediators' views on empowerment in their own words. It is clear that many of them have well-developed ideas about what empowerment is about and why community mediation is empowering for themselves and the disputants. In order to make a comparison of the mediators' views on empowerment with the views of the theorist groups, I did a content analysis of all of the mediator survey results to determine specifically which components of empowerment the community mediators were most familiar with and concerned about.

In the mediators' views on empowerment, the *self-efficacy* component is mentioned most frequently. It appears consistently in their comments in various aspects (i.e., being in control, the ability to act, having the power to make decisions) in 70% of their responses. The *social participation* component (i.e., helping people, enabling others, educating people) appears in 45% of the mediator responses, and the importance of developing conflict resolution *knowledge and skills* for disputants and mediators is mentioned in 40% of the mediator statements.

The community mediators appeared to be either unaware of, or far less concerned with, the other empowerment components. The *political rights, self-esteem,* and *resources* components were mentioned by only 10% of the mediators, and the importance of *political awareness* appeared in only 7% of the mediator responses. As was the case with the mediation theorists, there is no indication of the importance of *political participation* for empowerment. *Political awareness, political rights,* and the concept of *powerlessness* were not specifically mentioned by any of the mediators.

As with most of the mediation theorists, the community mediators are primarily concerned with the "psychological" and skills aspects of empowerment and with empowerment specifically relevant to conflict resolution. This commonly shared perspective on empowerment is not surprising, because many of those who research and write about mediation are still, or have been, mediator practitioners. Many of the mediation theorists are also involved in the development and promulgation of the community mediation ideology that links mediation and empowerment. Therefore, the community mediators and the mediation theorists share common experiences and an ideology that shapes their perspectives on empowerment.

In summary, this content analysis of the empowerment literature has delineated the major empowerment components that capture the primary aspects of empowerment for mediators and social scientists. It indicates where their conceptions of empowerment overlap and where and how they diverge. In the later chapters on research design, these empowerment components provide a guide for operationalizing the empowerment concept.

Reconstruction and Definition

Following Sartori's (1984) guidelines, the next step in the conceptual analysis process was to reconstruct the empowerment components into a general definition of empowerment that would be parsimonious but adequate to serve the needs of theorists and practitioners. Consider the following definition:

Empowerment is the process of gaining mastery over one's self and one's environment in order to fulfill human needs.

This statement succinctly captures the essential qualities of personal empowerment. It indicates that the key attributes of an empowered individual are mastery of the self as well as mastery of the environment. It answers the question "Empowerment for what purpose?"—to fulfill human needs. Elaborating on the supporting conditions for the empowerment process combines the empowerment components discussed earlier in a meaningful sequence.

The empowerment process links individual *attitudes* (i.e., self-esteem and self-efficacy) and *capabilities* (i.e., knowledge and skills and political awareness) to enable efficacious *individual and collaborative* actions (i.e., social and political participation) in order to attain personal and collective sociopolitical *goals* (i.e., political rights, responsibilities, and resources).

Empowerment: A Theoretical Framework

This definition suggests the development of the theoretical framework for empowerment represented in Figure 4.1. Only the major relationships salient to this study are highlighted in the figure. As the arrows in Figure 4.1 indicate, the individual's attitudes and capabilities enable participation in various types of collaborative behavior that in turn empowers the participants. The application of empowerment theory to this study is represented in the mediator-empowerment model, which is described below.

The theoretical framework illustrates the interrelationship of the empowerment components. As Figure 4.1 indicates, **attitudes** and **capabilities** are the key attributes of individual empowerment. The self-esteem and self-efficacy components define a positive self-concept that is basic to an individual's psychological empowerment. Knowledge and skills, and political awareness are the capabilities or personal competencies required for social and political empowerment that enable an individual to survive and accomplish goals. It is

Figure 4.1
Empowerment Theory

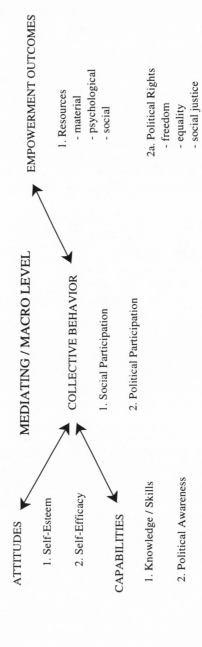

theoretically possible for an individual to have high levels of self-esteem and self-efficacy and yet have few personal competence skills and little political awareness. Although attitudes and capabilities appear to be positively correlated, such an individual may be considered to be "psychologically" empowered and mentally healthy and happy but may not really be capable of, or interested in, taking individual or collective action to achieve social or political objectives. A reclusive artist, for example, might be such an individual.

Conversely, an individual might develop high levels of political awareness and believe strongly in the need for major political transformation, and yet have low self-esteem and doubt his self-efficacy in social and political situations. It may be argued that such an individual is potentially effective but lacks sufficient psychological empowerment and the participatory skills needed to take action. An example of such an individual might be an "ivory tower" scholar. Theorists and activists who view meaningful empowerment as the ability to take effective political action might consider this person to be politically disempowered. On the other hand, the development of critical consciousness about political conditions and structures is regarded by some empowerment theorists as the first and the most important step in developing "political" empowerment.

As illustrated by the arrows in Figure 4.1, **social and political participation** are linked to individual attitudes and capabilities. Those who have developed higher levels of self-esteem and self-efficacy as well as highly developed knowledge and social skills are more likely to be socially and politically active than individuals who have low self-esteem, low levels of self-efficacy, and poorly developed social and communication skills.

Possessing social skills as well as knowledge about community needs and the availability of resources, enhances the individual's possibilities and probabilities for participation in community events and organizations. Developing increased political awareness might facilitate involvement in community organizing activities, or conducting environmental campaigns to close nuclear plants, or save whales or other endangered species. Individuals with highly developed political awareness may be more likely to participate in more political activities than other less politically sophisticated individuals, who may be equally active in the community but are involved in some type of social participation.

What motivates some individuals to participate in social and political activities? Different individuals are driven by different motives at different times, but the pursuit of human needs is the engine that drives the empowerment process. Humanistic values, such as social justice, freedom, equality, diversity, and transcendence, are intimately linked to empowerment and distinguish it from other concepts such as power. These values give shape and meaning to empowerment goals and provide ethical guidelines. Whenever possible these needs should be met in ways that are empowering for all of those involved in the process. This implies the importance of maximizing opportunities for full participation for all, for self-help in a mutual assistance context, and for tolerance for diversity.

Human needs, represented in the framework by political rights, responsibilities, and resources, are a powerful source of explanation for human behavior at all levels from interpersonal to international relations (Burton 1990b; Clark 1993). The existence of human needs makes human society both possible and necessary. The interaction of people in their pursuit of needs satisfaction in social settings underlies and gives meaning to politics. All individuals have needs that they strive to satisfy, either by working within the existing political system or by working to bring about political transformation. As indicated in Figure 4.1, individuals striving to fulfill their needs interact with other individuals attempting to do the same. In this sphere of social and political participation opportunities exist for conflict or collaboration. To obtain the **empowerment outcomes** represented in Figure 4.1—political rights and responsibilities, and psychological, social, and material resources—individuals will often collaborate in various social and political settings.

This social and political participation may in turn empower individuals by making them feel more confident and competent, thus enhancing their self-esteem and self-efficacy. There may also be an increase in the individual's level of knowledge about themselves and their environment, an increase in social and political skills, and perhaps the development of "critical consciousness." As participation brings the individuals more opportunity to exercise their political rights and responsibilities, and to access community resources, their level of activity and commitment to groups and community associations may further increase. Gaining increased access to rights, responsibilities, and resources may correspondingly increase self-esteem and self-efficacy. As this causal reciprocity between the various empowerment components develops, a synergistic empowerment process is set in motion for the individuals involved in it.

This theoretical framework shows the potential for linking micro and macro levels to develop an ecological theory of empowerment relevant to interpersonal and global behavior. The "mediating" level refers to small groups (families, churches, and voluntary community organizations) that mediate between the individual and the larger social structures of government and business and provide settings where empowerment may occur. The macro level refers to larger government and business organizations, such as states, nations, and corporations. Different types of social and political participation cut across these levels.

There is a conceptual gap in the social science literature between the micro and macro levels that has been difficult to bridge. Psychologists study individual idiosyncrasies, and international relations theorists focus on abstract macro entities called nation-states. Interdisciplinary communication is almost nonexistent, but fundamentally it is individuals that drive world society. As individuals participate in groups and social networks of relationships to pursue their needs, we can build from the level of the individual to macro-level collectivities. This framework can enable analysts to examine all social relationships that constitute political behavior at the community, national, or international levels.

This is only one among many possible approaches to the study of human behavior, but it appears to have potential for explaining behavior at several levels and providing guidance to reflective practitioners and policy-makers. In addition to theoretical fertility and empirical usefulness, empowerment theory has the ideological appeal to stimulate the interdisciplinary and cross-cultural research needed to develop a richer and more useful understanding of human behavior.

THE EMPOWERMENT PROCESS

The purpose of this chapter was to answer three related questions: What is empowerment?, How do individuals become empowered or disempowered?, and What is the linkage between the mediation process and the empowerment process? In order to address the first question, a conceptual analysis beginning with lexical analysis and ending with the development of a theoretical framework for empowerment was carried out. We are now ready to apply this framework to answering the second and third questions.

Paths to Empowerment

How, or in what ways, do people become empowered? In the process of answering the first question about *what empowerment is*, I have briefly alluded to *how it happens*. There is not one optimal path to empowerment. The approach taken depends on each individual's unique needs, the relevant cultural values, the available resources for empowerment, and other factors. While the focus of this study is on developing citizen empowerment through collective, collaborative types of social participation and political participation, it is of course possible to enhance personal empowerment through autonomous or individualistic behavior such as reading, thinking, or writing.

But the most effective personal empowerment strategies should address the development of the empowerment attitudes and capabilities described in this chapter. For example, psychological counseling, studying self-help books, or participating in self-help mutual support groups can be useful approaches to developing greater self-esteem and self-efficacy. Skills and practical knowledge can be acquired through life experience, by reading books, by participating in human development seminars and training workshops or by pursuing academic goals. Freire's (1970) model of "liberation education" and other consciousness-raising approaches can be used to develop greater political awareness in individuals and groups.

Since the focus of this study is on the linkage between social participation, particularly in community mediation, and citizen empowerment, the recent research on citizen participation in community settings and empowerment is most relevant. Grass roots political action and participatory research offer two powerful strategies for individual and group empowerment. In one of the most interesting studies of grass roots empowerment, Charles Kieffer (1984) conducted in-depth interviews with fifteen individuals who had emerged as local leaders in grass-roots citizens organizations. Kieffer identified three key aspects of participatory competence that could be developed through grass-roots leadership: (1) development of a positive sense of self-competence and self-concept, (2) construction of an analytical understanding of the social and political environment, and (3) cultivation of resources, both personal and collective, for social action. These aspects of participatory competence are similar to the empowerment components of self-efficacy, self-esteem, political awareness, and resources identified in this study.

According to Kieffer, grass roots empowerment is a lengthy process that has four specific phases. First is the *entry* stage where the disempowered individual realizes that there is an immediate threat of some sort to himself or his family, and he therefore becomes involved in political activities to counter the threat. Second is the *advancement* phase, where the individual establishes ties with an enabling and supportive peer group and becomes more critically aware of the external causes of his problems and of the interrelations of social, economic, and political structures. Third is the *incorporation phase*, which is characterized by the maturation of the self-concept, the development of strategic ability, and critical comprehension. The final *commitment* phase is characterized by the continuous application of empowerment skills and abilities to change the environment and to enable others to empower themselves in a similar process. Based on his study of these grass roots leaders, Kieffer claims that the complete empowerment process normally takes three or four years to fully accomplish.

In their book, *To empower people* (1977), Peter Berger and Richard Neuhaus, two theorists associated with the conservative think tank, the Heritage Institute, suggest a more conservative path to empowerment. They argue that public policy should seek to empower people by increasing their opportunities for involvement in various community organizations, such as churches, neighborhood groups, and service organizations. These organizations mediate between the individual and the larger social structures of government and business, thereby decreasing alienation and withdrawal from community life. According to Berger and Neuhaus, these "mediating structures" can provide citizens with valuable opportunities for learning new skills, developing a sense of efficacy, and improving their community life.

In their study of community psychology, Heller et al. (1984, 372) also argue the merits of citizen participation for empowerment. They contend that participation "allows citizens to provide input into the programs and policies which affect them. It has the potential of increasing participants' feelings of control, and allows them the opportunity to develop or select programs which match their needs and values. As such it represents a process for empowering people."

Recent empirical research supports this view linking community participation and empowerment. A study of different community service organizations, service clubs, and self-help groups found that "greater participation in community activities and organizations is associated with psychological empowerment" (Zimmerman and Rappaport 1988, 745). This line of empirical research on citizen participation and empowerment is at an early stage. It will be necessary to look at a variety of settings and different types of participation to learn more about the specific conditions that are most favorable for empowerment.

My research is a study of citizen participation and empowerment that in many ways builds on and extends the theoretical and empirical work done by Kieffer, Rappaport, and others by studying the empowerment process in a community mediation setting. By consciously striving to build a cumulative body of knowledge about this linkage we can most effectively use our resources to develop a coherent interdisciplinary base for empowerment theory building.

Mediation as an Empowering Setting

Different community settings will vary in their empowerment potential, depending on a number of factors, including: the organizational culture, the ideology, membership characteristics, communication patterns, problem-solving style, and the opportunities for participation in decision making. Community mediation would seem to be an especially supportive setting for empowerment in that mediation ideology, training, and practice may contribute to the development of a mediator's self-esteem, self-efficacy, knowledge, and skills. In addition, mediation ideology specifically stresses the importance of empowerment as an outcome of the mediation process. The citizen volunteer mediators report a high degree of satisfaction with being mediators, and with the opportunities for learning valuable skills and acquiring knowledge that may contribute to their income, status, and personal power in other community and professional settings.

Community mediation has the potential to meet the mediator's needs for power, achievement, and affiliation (see McClelland 1975). The mediator's use of power in the mediation process and its relationship to the empowerment of the mediator was discussed earlier. The mediator's affiliation needs may be met by being part of the new community justice movement, by being accepted into the community of mediators, by working closely with co-mediators, and by the praise and gratitude of the disputants.

Achievement needs may be derived from a feeling of mastery over the mediation process, and the accomplishment of helping others to overcome seemingly intractable problems and reach mutually satisfying agreements. In addition to helping others, achieving their own personal growth and reaching new competency levels is important to most of the mediators.

The Mediator Empowerment Model

What specific aspects of the mediation experience might be empowering? The Mediator-Empowerment Model (Figure 4.2) illustrates the potential linkage between the different types of mediation participation and mediator empowerment. This model is directly derived from the empowerment theory framework set forth in Figure 4.1. For example, the mediator figure embedded in the concentric circles in the Mediator-Empowerment Model relates to the individual attitudes and capabilities discussed in the empowerment theory framework. The community mediation experience, including the training, mediation sessions, and leadership activities is considered to be a form of social participation that provides dispute-resolution services to the community and may empower the mediator. The mediator-empowerment outcomes represented in the model are a subset of the empowerment outcomes represented in Figure 4.1

The figure in the concentric circles represents a new citizen volunteer prior to becoming involved in community mediation. As Figure 4.2 shows, each citizen mediator brings to the mediation experience a certain level of personal empowerment based on the development of their personal attitudes, knowledge and skills, and political awareness. Much of this personal empowerment has been developed as a result of prior and current social and political experiences with family, friends, support groups, work, community, and political groups. In order to ascertain the existing psychological empowerment profile for each volunteer *prior* to their participation in mediation training, baseline data on empowerment was collected at this point before training began. Numerous empowerment measures (described in the next chapter) were used to tap the self-esteem, self-efficacy, skills, and political awareness aspects of empowerment for each citizen before becoming a community mediator.

The Mediator-Empowerment Model represents the mediation experience primarily in terms of three possible types of organizational participation, including (1) mediator training, (2) mediation practice, and (3) organizational leadership activities. Every prospective HNJC mediator, regardless of their background or professional expertise in related fields such as law or counseling, must participate in the intensive mediation training before actually mediating cases. Some of the mediators will also become involved in leadership participation in the mediation center. The arrows in Figure 4.2 show the progression of the community mediator through these three phases of the mediation experience.

Figure 4.2
Mediator-Empowerment Model

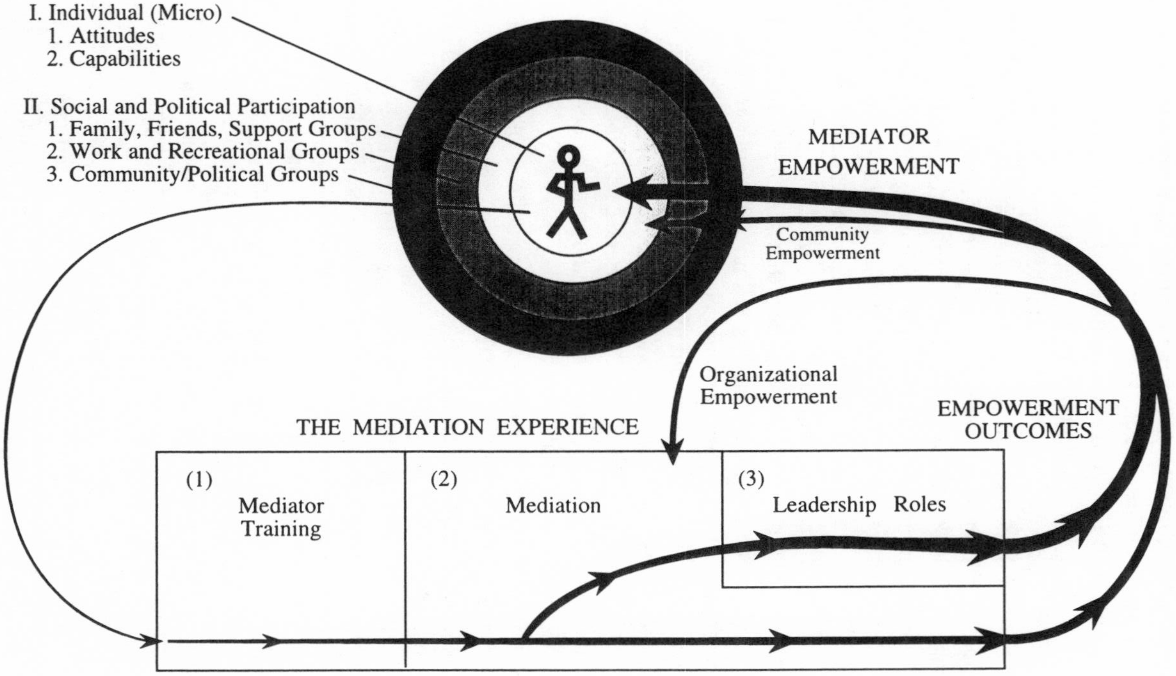

I. Individual (Micro)
   1. Attitudes
   2. Capabilities

II. Social and Political Participation
   1. Family, Friends, Support Groups
   2. Work and Recreational Groups
   3. Community/Political Groups

MEDIATOR
EMPOWERMENT

Community
Empowerment

Organizational
Empowerment

EMPOWERMENT
OUTCOMES

THE MEDIATION EXPERIENCE

(1) Mediator Training

(2) Mediation

(3) Leadership Roles

The increased personal empowerment that may result from these mediation activities is represented by the empowerment outcome arrows in Figure 4.2 that emerge from the mediation experience diagram and return to the figure within the concentric circles, illustrating the possible empowering effect of mediation participation on the individual mediator. Thus a possible feedback cycle is created as the mediator becomes empowered and continues to mediate and use his personal empowerment to facilitate the empowerment of others.

The possibility of organizational empowerment is represented in Figure 4.2 by the empowerment outcome arrows that return to the community mediation setting. This illustrates the prospect that empowerment effects may also feed back into the community mediation organization, transforming it into an even more empowering setting for HNJC staff and citizen volunteers (see Vogt and Murrell 1990 for a discussion of empowered organizations).

The possibilities for community empowerment are represented in Figure 4.2 by the empowerment outcome arrows that are shown returning to different social, work, and political groups within the community with which the mediator interacts. This arrow represents the linkage argued for by community mediation advocates who contend that the empowering effects of community mediation on mediators and disputants may "spill over" to the community or be transferred to the individual's family, friends, and other community settings, thus improving the quality of life in families and the community and accomplishing sociopolitical transformation.

While these hypothesized transformational effects of community mediation on both the mediation setting and the community are represented in Figure 4.2 for the sake of theoretical completeness, they are not addressed in the empirical analysis.

The HNJC mediation experience begins with fifty to sixty hours of intensive **training** that emphasizes many of the kinds of practical knowledge and skills that have been identified as key characteristics of an empowered individual. For example, as described earlier, aspiring mediators learn and practice new communication, problem solving, negotiation, conflict resolution, and teamwork skills. They learn about conflict dynamics and the emotional problems facing families going through the divorce experience, and they may learn something about themselves in the process. The trainees' self-esteem and self-efficacy are positively affected by the support and praise they receive from the training faculty and their peers, and by the use of specifically designed empowering educational techniques. Empowerment ideology is introduced during the training, and it stresses using a power *with* approach to empower disputants. Thus, empowerment attitudes and capabilities may be impacted by mediation training. To determine if there were any changes in personal empowerment as a result of the training, data on empowerment was collected both before training began and again at the end of the training period for each participant.

Mediation practice may reinforce or extend the mediators' level of personal empowerment. It is often suggested by social practitioners that helping others benefits one's self (see O'Connell 1983). In addition, becoming accepted as a member of the mediation community and belonging to a movement that they believe benefits mankind may enhance self-esteem. Knowledge and skills are reinforced and refined by doing the work of conflict resolution and by attending ongoing advanced workshops. Their perceptions of self-efficacy may be positively affected by the opportunities afforded to help others deal with their problems, and to craft fair and mutually acceptable agreements.

Leadership is the third type of mediation participation. It provides opportunities to learn additional planning, budgeting, and decision-making skills and to participate in organizational governance and program development decisions. Again as a result of this type of participation, one might expect to find an accompanying enhancement of self-esteem and self-efficacy for those in leadership positions.

In summary, the research question that guides the empirical analysis which follows is: Are mediators empowered by mediation training, mediation practice, and leadership of the organization? This Mediator-Empowerment Model provides the rationale for the research design described in the next chapter.

5

Research Design and Empowerment Measures

The research design described in this chapter compares the three mediator groups: *Trainees*, *Mediators*, and *Leaders*. This chapter also describes the research participants, the data-collection procedures, and the instrument developed to measure mediation empowerment.

RESEARCH APPROACH

Given the present state of knowledge about community mediation and empowerment, this research was considered to be exploratory. Therefore formal hypotheses tests would be inappropriate at this point. As Selltiz argues, "[I]n the case of problems about which little knowledge is available, an exploratory study is usually most appropriate" (1964, 52). Kerlinger points out that the exploratory study seeks to describe what *is* rather than to predict relationships, and it further attempts to "discover significant variables, discover relationships, and lay the groundwork for later rigorous testing of hypotheses" (1973, 406). While formal hypotheses tests are not considered to be appropriate for this study, specific data patterns can be expected to emerge if the mediation experience empowers those individuals who participate in it. These expected data patterns are discussed below.

RESEARCH DESIGN

Development of a research design requires numerous, often difficult research decisions about the choice of available models, methods, and modes of analysis.

Research design also requires inevitable compromises between what would be ideal scientifically, and what is possible given real world constraints such as time, funding, and accessibility to data.

The choice between using a laboratory experiment or a field research approach for this project was one of the most fundamental research decisions. Both approaches have inherent strengths and weaknesses (Locke 1986; Gordon et al. 1986, 1987; Greenberg 1987). In general, the laboratory is best suited to test theories in a very controlled setting, and the field setting is best used to describe and understand the natural world as it is (Berkowitz and Donnerstein 1982). The choice between these two approaches depends on several factors, such as the purpose of the study, the nature and duration of the phenomenon of interest, and the resources available to the researchers.[1]

A major purpose of this study was to describe the real world setting of community mediation and to learn more about the citizens who volunteer to serve as mediators. I was not interested in studying college sophomores role-playing mediators in a laboratory setting. Since the intent here was to understand more about the psychological, social, and political implications of community mediation programs, an active community mediation center was the preferred research setting for this project.[2]

The choice between using experimental or non-experimental research designs was another key decision. Researchers who are primarily concerned with explanation and causality prefer the classic randomized experimental model because of its power to control for threats to internal validity. In the experimental model, subjects are chosen from the target population and then randomly assigned to experimental groups or control groups. The experimental model is quite effective in ruling out the possibility that factors other than the experimental intervention have caused any observed changes in the subjects of the experiment, and therefore it increases one's confidence about making causal inferences (Campbell and Stanley 1963).[3]

However, in doing social action research projects, such as this study, there are usually many practical impediments to using the "pure" experimental model in real world settings like the HNJC. First, the costs of using the experimental model are high. Second, the research procedures are intrusive. Third, the operation and service delivery of the organization being studied can be seriously disrupted. In most social agency settings, program mission and priorities are paramount, and therefore research design compromises are often necessary in doing applied research. For all of these reasons, Peter Rossi (1985), a leading scholar of evaluation research, suggests that a first go-round with "soft" techniques, such as correlational, ex-post-facto, or one-group before and after designs can show whether a service-delivery program warrants further study.

Only if the initial reconnaissance phase of the research project detects positive effects is it worthwhile moving to a more costly controlled experiment approach. Similarly, Cook et al. (1985) recommends that researchers start with a sequence of steps that emphasize *external* validity at the early stages of a research project to establish parameters of generalizability, before moving on to those stages that emphasize *internal* validity.

Even if the random assignment of participants to experimental and control groups were not problematic for the reasons discussed above, its use here is not considered to be desirable given the purposes of this study. My concern is not with determining causal inference at this point or with studying how the mediation experience might affect people randomly assigned to it in a laboratory setting. My purpose is to describe how a real community mediation center actually functions, and the resulting psychological, social, and political implications for participating individuals and the surrounding communities. For example, the mediator-selection procedure actually used by the HNJC organization includes both mediator self-selection, as well as organizational staff screening, in order to maximize those characteristics considered desirable by the staff for community mediators. This selection process is quite different of course from the random assignment to mediation training that might be appropriate for an experimental research program.[4]

For these reasons a "pure" experimental model was ruled out, and a quasi-experimental research design was developed that compares the three mediator groups (see Figure 5.1). (Note that in order to clarify that I am referring specifically to one or more of the three research groups, the first letter of each group [i.e., *Trainees*, *Mediators*, and *Leaders*] will be capitalized and the complete word will be italicized.) The *Trainees* were given a pre-test using the Volunteer Mediator Survey (VMS, described below) before training began, and then they were given a post-test after completing training with the VMS.

The experienced *Mediators* who have previously gone through a similar training program and who have been active HNJC mediators for one or more years were administered a version of the VMS survey, which includes additional questions relating to their mediation experiences, what they believe they may have gained from doing mediation, and whether they have used their mediation skills to deal with conflict in other areas of their lives, such as disputes in the family or workplace.

The third group of experienced mediators is similar to group two, but in addition these mediators have also chosen to participate in a variety of HNJC leadership activities. The *Leaders* group also completed the version of the VMS survey administered to the other experienced mediators.

These three comparison groups represent three different levels and types of mediation participation: (1) mediation training only (*Trainees*), (2) mediation training and one or more years of participation as a mediator (*Mediators*), and (3) mediation training with one or more years of mediation experience as well as organizational leadership experience (*Leaders*).

The research design developed for this study is not as strong as an experimental model would be with regard to internal validity in that it does not control

Figure 5.1
Research Design

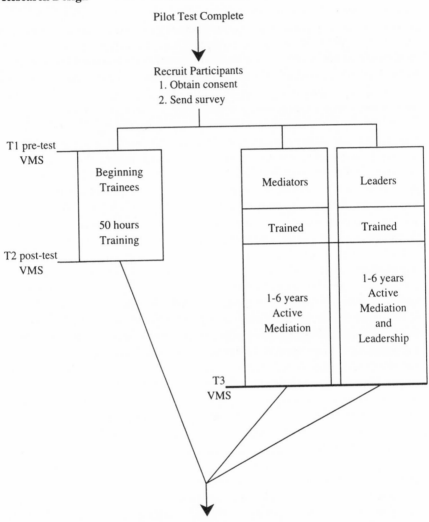

Pilot Test Complete

Recruit Participants
1. Obtain consent
2. Send survey

T1 pre-test
VMS

Beginning
Trainees

Mediators

Leaders

50 hours
Training

Trained

Trained

T2 post-test
VMS

1-6 years
Active
Mediation

1-6 years
Active
Mediation
and
Leadership

T3
VMS

Data Collection and Analysis

for many of the possible rival explanations for empowerment that might act in congruence with, or counter to, the effects of the independent variables. However, the research model used in this study does have several practical advantages that offset its limitations. First, it has better external validity than a laboratory experiment would have. Second, it is less costly than an experimental approach. Third, it is feasible to carry out within the constraints of an applied natural community setting. This design is also likely to yield useful theoretical insights and to generate specific hypotheses for future research on empowerment in mediation or in other settings.

Research Participants

Given the small size of the HNJC mediator training groups, which averaged twenty to thirty participants in each session, all of the *Trainees* from two consecutive training sessions were invited to participate in this study in order to generate a large enough sample for meaningful data analysis. Fifty *Trainees* (95% of the trainees involved in the two sessions) participated.

All of the *Mediators* in the mediator pool, as well as all of the current HNJC mediator *Leaders*, were also invited to participate. It was not possible to collect pre-training baseline data for these two groups, but since all of the experienced *Mediators* and *Leaders* were recruited from the same local population and by the same recruitment techniques as the new *Trainees* groups, it was assumed for the sake of the data analysis that the members of the three research groups were similar enough that the pre-test scores of the current *Trainee* groups could also be used as a rough baseline measure for the *Mediator* and *Leader* groups. Ideally of course, if it were possible to do a long-term study of mediation participation and empowerment, it would be most desirable to begin with a group of new *Trainees* and then follow them over a period of several years as they completed their mediation training and went on to become experienced mediators and leaders of the organization. But given the practical constraints of time and funding, this approach was not possible and compromises were necessary.

There were fifty participants in the *Mediator* group and twenty-two participants in the *Leader* group. The demographic data characteristics of these three mediator groups are presented and compared in the following chapter.

Data-Collection Procedures

The *Trainees'* names were provided by HNJC staff from the list of applicants selected for upcoming training sessions. Each applicant was contacted by phone by the researchers and informed that the general purpose of this research was to learn more about the community mediation process and about the volunteer mediators themselves. The procedures to be used in the study were described, and they were invited to participate on a voluntary basis and assured that any personal data would be kept confidential and would not be reported in the research findings. Those prospective *Trainees* who agreed to participate in the study were mailed an information packet containing a cover letter, which repeated the same information conveyed by phone, a research participation consent form, and the VMS questionnaire, along with instructions for completing the survey and returning it to the researchers. The survey was completed by each participant, returned by mail or brought to the mediation training site, and turned in to the researchers before the training began. Ninety-five percent of the individuals accepted for mediation training volunteered to participate in the research project and completed the pre-training survey materials. Several weeks later, immediately after completing the training, the new mediators received the second version of the VMS survey along with a stamped self-addressed envelope. They were asked to complete the post-training survey and to return the forms within two weeks to the research staff. All but two of those individuals who completed the pre-test also completed the post-test and returned it within two weeks.

Participants for the other two research groups were selected from the HNJC mailing list of currently active mediators, and those mediators who were acting in a leadership capacity were identified. There were over 100 active mediators and about twenty-five leaders on the lists. Since the population was small for both groups, all of the names on the lists were called by the researchers. Many were not available, but of those contacted, 87% of the *Mediators* and 95% of the *Leaders* consented to participate in the research project. As with the *Trainees*, they were informed in general about the purposes of the study and were invited to participate in the research project. Those members of the two groups who agreed to participate in the study were mailed a research packet similar to the one sent to the *Trainees*, along with a stamped, self-addressed return envelope. A basic mailout and telephone follow-up procedure was conducted with both of the mediator groups, which resulted in a very high level of completion and return of materials.

Throughout this research process the researchers were quite careful to ensure that the term "empowerment" was not used in either the survey questionnaire or in any of the accompanying materials, nor was empowerment mentioned in discussions of this study with any of the research participants in order to minimize possible bias and contamination of research results.

According to Earl Babbie (1973, 265), a leading expert on survey research, a survey return rate of 50% is considered adequate, 60% is good, and 70% is considered to be very good. The return rate in this study for *Trainees* was 95% for the pre-test and 90% for the post-test. The return rate for the *Mediators* was 85%, and the return rate was 88% for the *Leaders*. This high rate is especially unusual given the considerable amount of time (over two hours) and effort required to fill out the lengthy survey questionnaire. The high return rate and the completeness of the forms returned are at least partially explained by the uniqueness of the study participants. Their cooperation was highly motivated by their strong belief in the value of community mediation and by their desire to learn more about the process and practice of mediation and about themselves as mediators.

INSTRUMENT DESIGN AND CONSTRUCTION

While several data-collection methodologies, such as participant observation, interviews, and content analysis were used in this study, survey questionnaires were chosen as the primary method for data collection because of their inherent advantages of economy, speed, standardization of data, and the amount of data that can be collected in a cost-effective manner (Babbie 1973, 259–279).

The VMS survey questionnaire developed for this study combined some existing psychological scales used to measure constructs associated with empowerment along with some new measures developed specifically for this research. Instruments with acceptable levels of reliability and validity were selected from research on self-esteem, self-efficacy, alienation, and empowerment. Some of the instruments were adapted to meet the research objectives of this study. New items were designed to address concerns specific to this study that were not dealt with satisfactorily by existing scales. These additional questions tap the participants' expectations and beliefs about mediation, power, and empowerment, as well as their personal philosophy and the possible transfer of mediation skills and knowledge to other social or work settings in the community.

A large number of psychological scales were used for this study in order to capture some of the complexity of the empowerment concept. The VMS questionnaire strives for a robust combination of variety and balance by using a mix of different scale types and formats.

Other demographic and social data collected for this study includes the participants' age, marital status, sex, employment status, income level, occupation, level of education, political affiliation, ethnicity, and data on other types of community participation.

The VMS design went through several stages of development. The initial VMS questionnaire draft was first *pre-tested* by administering it to a small group of twenty-five mediators, non-mediators, and researchers who would not be participating in the main study. The results were analyzed and discussed with the pre-test participants. As a result of the feedback from the pre-test participants, the questionnaire was then revised and enlarged.

The next stage of the research was a *pilot test* of the VMS questionnaire and the data collection and data analysis procedures. Actually, several pilot tests were carried out in other similar community mediation programs on the "neighbor" islands in Hawaii. These mediation programs were ideal for the purposes of pilot testing for several reasons. First, they were geographically separated from the Honolulu Neighborhood Justice Center program and therefore the mediators from those programs had little or no contact with HNJC mediators. Second, these "neighbor" island programs were modeled after the HNJC program, and their mediator training sessions were conducted by HNJC trainers. Therefore, they used identical mediation training materials and followed the same mediation model, processes, and techniques.

With the cooperation of program staff from these other community mediation programs, mediator trainees were tested before and after completion of their training. This pilot study enabled further refinement of the research design, development of the final VMS questionnaire, and a walk-through of the data-collection steps to test and debug procedures. Data collected from the pilot study was analyzed to validate the psychological scales, to refine the data analysis procedures, and to establish the formats to be used for the statistical tables.

Empowerment Measures

The Volunteer Mediation Survey was designed to cast a wide net to capture those aspects of empowerment most relevant to mediators. The dependent variables in this study include eleven measures of individual empowerment, such as self-esteem, general self-efficacy, political efficacy, political awareness, group cooperation, perceived competence, desirability of control, and three locus of control measures. These scales were selected to measure many of the empowerment components discussed in chapter 4.[5]

In addition to the empowerment measures, three measures of disempowerment (powerlessness, normlessness, and social isolation) were included in the analysis to enhance discriminant validity. Highly empowered individuals should have negative scores on all three of these measures. All of these scales are described below.

While empowerment is a key concept in political science, community psychology, and many other fields, a review of the literature revealed only one attempt to design an instrument to specifically measure personal empowerment. Torre (1986) used what she called a structured conceptualization strategy to develop three scales that measured distinct aspects of empowerment.[6] The first scale, called *Self-Esteem/Self-Efficacy*, was designed to measure ability, confidence, and autonomy. It has thirteen items such as: "I am an important member of my community," and "I can do most of the things I set out to do."[7]

The second scale, *Group Cooperation*, has ten items. It taps attitudes about working collaboratively with others with items such as: "In order to accomplish important goals, people must join groups who share their goals," and "It is just as important to help others become fulfilled as it is to help oneself."

The third scale, *Political Awareness*, with fourteen items, assesses one's attitudes towards political power, social justice, and the need for social change. It contains items such as: "This country would be a better place if all people understood how the political system really works," "It is a good idea for people to question the behavior of people in powerful positions," "If people hope for a more just world, they must learn how, and why, they are oppressed," "Power should be more equally shared between people," and "Before the United States can truly guarantee people freedom, social change must occur."

All three of these scales used a five-point Likert format. Torre's test results to assess the validity of the three scales were encouraging, but must be viewed judiciously because of the small samples used in her pilot tests. However, since this appeared to be the only instrument developed thus far to specifically measure individual empowerment, these scales were included to assess their reliability with a different population and larger samples.

Eight additional psychological scales were included in this analysis to supplement Torre's scales and to tap into other aspects of empowerment. The concept of self-efficacy is considered by most theorists to be central to psychological empowerment, and so the next three scales were chosen to distinguish different aspects of the concept. Craig and Magiotto (1982) developed two scales that distinguish between internal political efficacy and external political efficacy. The general concept of political efficacy that has been employed in studies of political behavior refers to "the feeling that individual political action does have, or can have, an impact upon the political process, i.e., that it is worthwhile to perform one's civic duties."[8]

But Craig and Maggiotto argue that conceptually the general definition of political efficacy actually contains two distinct and important components, which are political effectiveness and system responsiveness. Therefore, their *Internal Political Efficacy* scale with five items assesses individuals' perceptions that they understand the political system and have the competencies to take political action. The items include: "I feel like I have a pretty good understanding of the important political issues which confront our society," and "People like me are generally well qualified to participate in the political activity and decision making in our country."

Their *External Political Efficacy* scale, with nine items, is concerned with the individual's beliefs about the responsiveness of political leaders and institutions, rather than about the individual's own abilities to take effective political action. External political efficacy is related to feelings of political trust and includes items such as: "There are plenty of ways for people like me to have a say in what our government does," and "Politicians are supposed to be servants of the people but too many of them try to be our masters."

In developing and testing these two scales, Craig and Maggiotto found that those individuals who possess a strong sense of themselves as effective political actors but tend to view the political system as unresponsive to their needs are likely to have a favorable orientation toward political protest and violence. This kind of relationship is more likely to occur in anti-democratic settings, and it may provide favorable conditions for the mobilization of political discontent.

While these two efficacy scales were designed to tap specific aspects of efficacy, Tipton and Worthington (1984) have developed another scale to measure *Generalized Self-Efficacy* (GSE, ten items). This generalized scale is designed "to measure 'people's' expectations that they can perform competently across a broad range of situations which are challenging and which require effort and perseverance" (545).

Alfred Bandura's (1986) well-known self-efficacy theory suggests that an individual's level of self-efficacy will help to determine the activities he chooses to participate in, the effort he expends in those activities, and his perseverance in the face of adversity. One of the most interesting questions raised about self-efficacy concerns the specificity or pervasiveness of mastery. Does the self-efficacy an individual experiences in one situation transfer to other related or unrelated situations, or is self-efficacy highly situation specific?

The Tipton-Worthington GSE scale was designed to assess the belief that one can cope effectively in a broad range of situations, and it includes items such as: "I am a very determined person," and "Nothing is impossible if I really put my mind to it." The authors contend that:

> when faced with adverse circumstances, people bring with them specific expectations about how they can perform in that particular kind of situation (specific self-efficacy, SSE) as well as some expectations about their abilities to handle adversity in general (GSE). It is hypothesized that SSE would account for the greater part of the variance when the situation is clearly defined and familiar to the individual, whereas GSE would account for more of the variance when the situation is more ambiguous and less familiar to the individual. (548)

Construct validity for the GSE was supported by studies of a simple self-determination task and a behavioral self-modification project (see Tipton and Worthington 1984).

Locus of control is another important and well-established construct that is linked to self-efficacy. High locus of control refers to strong expectations that individuals can exert control over their lives. On the other hand, low locus of control refers to the converse beliefs that one's destiny is largely controlled by three external forces: either by fate, by chance, or by powerful others.

In order to investigate the relationship between locus of control and participation in social action, Levenson (1974) revised Rotter's (1966) original and often used I-E scale into three new scales to more clearly distinguish between internal control, chance control, and control by powerful others. Each of these scales has eight items in a six-point Likert format. The items refer specifically to the individual rather than to people in general. Sample statements from the *Internal Control, Chance Control,* and *Powerful Others* scales, respectively, include: "My life is determined by my own actions," "When I get what I want, it's usually because I'm lucky," or "My life is chiefly controlled by powerful others" (Levenson 1974, 381).

Levenson found that a belief in chance was negatively related to an individual's involvement in anti-pollution activities, with the high *Chance* scale scorers being less involved. Her factor analysis of data collected on college students confirmed the multidimensionality of the locus of control measures. A replication of the Levenson study by Walkey (1979) clearly confirmed the three-factor structure underlying Levenson's questionnaire and demonstrated close agreement with her findings on scale characteristics and relationships.

It should be noted that for use in this study, I "reverse-scored" the *Chance Control* and *Powerful Others* sub-scales so that a *high* score on these measures reflects a *low* belief in the effects of chance and powerful others. In other words, a high score on these two scales indicates high expectations that one can exert control over one's life.

The *belief* that people can exercise control over their own lives as measured by the locus of control scales can be further distinguished from the *motivation* to control the events in one's life as measured by the *Desirability of Control* scale developed by Burger and Cooper (1979). According to Burger and Cooper, those individuals who have a high desire for control tend to be assertive, decisive, and active, and usually seek out leadership roles (383).

The twenty-item scale developed by Burger and Cooper uses a seven-point Likert format and contains items such as: "I enjoy political participation because I want to have as much of a say in running government as possible," "I would prefer to be a leader rather than a follower," "I enjoy being able to influence the actions of others," and "I enjoy having control over my own destiny."

In discussing the possible differences between the locus of control and desire for control constructs, Burger and Cooper suggest that it is possible to argue for either a positive or a negative relationship between them. "A 'wishful thinking' or 'cognitive consistency' hypothesis would lead us to predict that people who find personal control highly desirable feel personally effective. A 'sour grapes' or 'reactance' hypothesis would predict low personal control leading to high desirability. That is, an individual may desire personal control because he/she perceives little internal control in his/her life. It seems, then, that knowing a person's position along one dimension tells us little about the other" (386).

Statistical confirmation of their conceptual analysis was provided when an empirical analysis demonstrated that the *Desirability of Control* scale had discriminant validity from Rotter's locus of control scale. Studies that Burger and Cooper conducted on learned helplessness and hypnosis provided construct validation for the *Desirability of Control* scale.

In addition to the concepts of self-esteem and self-efficacy, the research on empowerment discussed earlier indicates the importance of developing certain skills and competencies that facilitate an individual's involvement in social and political participation. As the individual's level of participation increases, a major benefit of these social and political activities is that additional skills and competencies are acquired and refined through participation. They in turn enhance the individual's level of personal empowerment in a synergistic feedback process (Kieffer 1984).

In a study of the factors related to an individual's decision to participate in community development efforts, Florin and Wandersman (1984) developed a four-item, four-point Likert *Perceived Competence* scale to measure perceived competencies in such areas as public speaking, leading groups, influencing others, and organizational abilities. According to the authors, these competencies provide important skills for effective community participation, and the perception that one has developed these skill competencies also reflects a self-efficacy expectation that facilitates participation.

The eleven scales just described are designed to measure many of the aspects of psychological empowerment related to self-esteem and self-efficacy, as well as individuals' beliefs about their skills that are relevant to empowerment and social-political participation.

In addition to the eleven empowerment measures, the three "disempowerment" scales were included in the empirical analysis to provide discriminant validity for the empowerment scales and because of the conceptual linkage between powerlessness and empowerment.

Dean (1961) developed a twenty-four item *Alienation* scale consisting of three sub-scales. The first sub-scale, labeled *Powerlessness*, includes items like, "We are just cogs in the machinery of life." The second scale, called *Normlessness*, includes "Everything is relative, and there just aren't any definite rules to live by," and the *Social Isolation* scale includes, "Sometimes I feel all alone in the world." These well-validated scales have been used in many studies with different populations and have consistently demonstrated high reliability (Dean 1969). In the literature, individual empowerment is often contrasted with feelings of powerlessness and the condition of disempowerment. Thus, I would expect that these three measures of disempowerment will be negatively correlated with the eleven empowerment measures.

Finally, two additional scales were included in this study to control for the possible effects of response bias that results when research respondents choose the responses that they perceive to be socially desirable, instead of selecting the items that reflect their true beliefs or preferences (Mueller 1986). For this purpose, I used the five-item *Sociability* scale designed by Buss and Plomin (1975), "I make friends very quickly," which measures a desire to be with others, and Jackson's (1967) *Social Desirability* scale (16 items), "I always try to be considerate of the feelings of my friends," which measures a need for social approval.

EXPECTED DATA PATTERNS

While this exploratory research project is not concerned with formal hypotheses testing for reasons discussed earlier, it is useful to suggest the data patterns that should be expected if there is a positive relationship between types of mediation participation and increases in mediators' personal empowerment.

Direction of Scores

If the mediation training is empowering for the participants, the *Trainees* would be expected to have higher positive empowerment scores after they complete the training that they had before beginning the process ($T_2 > T_1$, where T_1 is pre-training and T_2 is post-training). Following the same logic, the experienced *Mediators* group should score higher on the empowerment scales than the *Trainees* do after they have completed training if the experienced *Mediators'* practical experience in doing mediations has had an empowering impact on them ($M > T_2$, where M is the experienced *Mediators* after one or more years of mediation practice). It was also expected that the *Leaders* group would score higher on most of the empowerment measures or that they would be empowered on different measurement components than the other two groups ($L > M > T_2$, where L refers to experienced mediators who also perform leadership tasks).

Magnitude of Scores

It was expected that even if mediation participation does empower mediators, the magnitude of the score increases from one type or stage of participation to the next would be modest at best, and furthermore that score increases would occur on only a few of the empowerment scales used here. There were several reasons for expecting to find only small score changes. First, it would be unrealistic to expect large score changes in this study considering the small and inconsistent kinds of changes that typically occur in the research findings on other social action programs. For example, in their studies of numerous public and private social action programs, Gilbert, Light, and Mosteller (1977, 185) report only a few studies that demonstrated positive effects. As the authors pointed out, "Even innovations that turned out to be especially valuable often had small positive effects—gains of a few percent, . . . or larger gains for a small subgroup of the population treated." But, as they contend, "Because even small gains accumulated over time can sum to a considerable total, they may have valuable consequences for society" (185).

Second, it should be noted that in the Gilbert, Light, and Mosteller studies, their research sought to measure how well such social action programs accomplished their *primary* mission. Whereas, in this study the primary mission of the organization being studied, as articulated by the Honolulu Neighborhood Justice Center documents, is providing community mediation services, not empowering mediators. If mediator or disputant empowerment does occur it would be considered to be a desirable outcome. However, it is a secondary consequence of delivering mediation services to the community. Therefore, under these circumstances it should be expected that increases in mediator empowerment would show an even smaller effect in the HNJC program than it would in another community mediation program that focused on mediator empowerment as a primary outcome, and therefore specifically planned program objectives linked to program tasks and activities to enhance mediator empowerment.

A third reason for expecting small effects in this study is related to the personal characteristics and life experiences of the research population. HNJC mediators volunteer for the program, and then they must undergo an intensive screening process before they are selected as trainees. Both their self-selection as citizen volunteers and the subsequent organizational screening process may significantly affect the magnitude of empowerment score changes that can be realistically expected. First, it is quite likely that the type of individuals who perceive themselves to be problem-solvers and would volunteer to be the mediators of others' disputes are already relatively highly empowered. In this regard, the literature on political participation suggests that low self-esteem (Carmines 1978) and feelings of inefficacy (Rosenberg 1988) inhibit social and political participation. Second, the HNJC screening process is designed to further select for attributes associated with personal empowerment, such as personal competence, flexibility, and concern for others. Those finally selected as prospective mediators are probably much more empowered than members of the general populace, and therefore they would be expected to score highly on most of the empowerment scales *even before* taking mediator training. If most of these people selected for mediator training are relatively highly empowered even before beginning the mediator training process, only small increases in empowerment scale scores can be expected to occur as a result of training.

A fourth reason to expect marginal score increases in personal empowerment relates to the frequency and importance of mediation activities in the day to day life of most volunteer community mediators. It should be realized that while mediation may be important to most of the volunteers, it is still a relatively small part of their lives, with most of them contributing only a few hours per month to HNJC activities. Given these circumstances, how profound an effect can community mediation activities be expected to have on increasing their level of personal empowerment?

Finally, there is always a methodological concern about how effectively self-report instruments, such as those used in this study, tap the beliefs and attitudes of interest. There are many potential sources of error in the analysis, and thus it is possible that empowerment may be occurring, but the instruments are not sufficiently sensitive to capture the effect.

In summary, considering a number of factors, such as the small program effects found in well-conducted research on other social action programs, the personal characteristics and selection of the mediators, and the limitations of the research design and instrumentation, only small gains in empowerment scores are expected, even if mediation participation has a powerful potential for empowering mediators. Therefore, any positive gains in empowerment scores may be considered important.

At this juncture we are ready to examine more closely the data on mediators and empowerment and to determine which of the expected data patterns will be confirmed by data analysis.

NOTES

Copies of the VMS instrument may be obtained by contacting the author.

1. Laboratory experiments have many advantages. They facilitate manipulation of experimental events, permit the researcher to exercise control over extraneous sources of variance that could influence the dependent variables, and are particularly suited to situations where the frequency and duration of the variables studied is likely to be limited. Therefore, laboratory research provides a powerful technique for demonstrating causal relationships between variables (Jones 1985, 282).

However, the virtues of laboratory experiments have not gone unchallenged (Locke 1986). They suffer from a lack of external validity due to the artificiality of the laboratory setting (Kerlinger 1973, 380) and the lack of representativeness of the populations used, such as the reliance on college sophomores as subjects (Caulder, Phillips, and Tybout 1981). It is argued that these problems limit the generalizability of laboratory research findings to the real world (Gordon, Slade, and Schmitt 1986).

2. The research focus here was on studying the actual community mediation experience. The duration and complexity of that experience does not lend itself to the constraints of the laboratory setting where the typical laboratory experiment lasts one to two hours and involves two to three independent variables and two to three dependent variables (Fromkin and Struefert 1976). The main research question here is, Does the mediation experience of community mediators empower them? This emphasis requires observation of real mediators in a natural mediation setting.

If, on the other hand, the research was concerned with studying what *can* happen, rather than what *does* happen, laboratory studies that are best for addressing threats to internal and construct validity would have an advantage. For example, the research question might be, How *can* people be empowered, and what interventions are most effective for this purpose?

3. Experimental research design is not uncritically accepted. Many researchers feel that randomization has been oversold (Cronbach 1982). Two major arguments that are especially relevant to this study are made against randomization. First, it is an ideal that is almost impossible to achieve in social settings. Second, randomization is a misguided ideal, since some threats to internal validity may be so implausible that the application of good judgment and reasoning alone is fully adequate for an acceptable interpretation.

4. Since this study draws from the entire population of mediators instead of using a random sample, the utility of statistical significance tests must be considered. Some researchers argue that when random sampling and randomization are absent, statistical inference is illegitimate. Others contend that tests of significance might be appropriate based on arguments about a hypothetical universe of volunteer mediators (Hagood 1969), or that statistical inference is legitimate in this case because the observations may be subject to measurement error (Gold 1969).

There is a persistent debate in the methodology literature about the utility of significance tests in experimental and non-experimental research (Morrison and Herkel 1970; Oakes 1986). Earl Babbie (1973, 428), for example, argues:

A. Tests of significance make sampling assumptions that are virtually never satisfied by research designs.

B. They assume the absence of nonsampling errors, a questionable assumption in most empirical measurements.

C. In practice they are too often applied to measures of association that have been computed in violation of the assumptions made by those measures (for example, product-moment correlations computed from ordinal data).

D. Statistical significance is too easily misinterpreted as "strength of association," or substantive significance.

In addition to these difficulties, it should be noted that in exploratory research such as this study tests of significance have less utility than in confirmatory research. As Lipset et al. (1956) have argued, tests of significance are irrelevant to exploratory research because unlike the case of confirmatory research a decision with regard to a hypotheses is not required.

5. These measures were selected for three reasons. First, they have face validity with many of the empowerment characteristics discussed in chapter 4. Second, they have shown acceptable levels of reliability in previous studies discussed below. The reliability levels from previous studies are Self-Esteem/Self-Efficacy (.88), Group Cooperation (.74), Political Awareness (.85), Internal Political Efficacy (.72), External Political Efficacy (.82), General Self-Efficacy (.84), Perceived Competence (.76), Desirability of Control (.80), Internal Control (.78), Chance Control (.78), Powerful Others (.77), Powerlessness (.78), Normlessness (.73), and Social Isolation (.84).

Third, most of these measures have been developed for, or used in, other studies of participation and/or empowerment. Zimmerman and Rappaport (1988), for example, used many of the same measures to examine the relationship between psychological empowerment and participation in a variety of community activities and organizations. Using the same measures, whenever appropriate, in studies of the relationship between different types of participation and empowerment will facilitate comparison of findings.

6. A fourth empowerment scale was developed by Torre, but it was not included in this study because it had a low reliability score (.62) and the scale items lacked sufficient face validity with the empowerment characteristics relevant to this study.

7. Torre's final version of this scale was untitled, but in the previous draft it was titled "Locus of Control, Perceptions of Self-Efficacy and Self-Esteem." The scale title used in this paper is mine, and it is based on an evaluation of the scale items. While the scale was developed by a multi-stage empirical procedure, it is somewhat conceptually problematic because it contains items that refer to similar, but not synonymous, concepts such as self-esteem, self-efficacy, and locus of control. Therefore, I have supplemented it with other measures that more clearly delineate these concepts. I have also named the next two scales, which were untitled in their final form. In a prior draft of both scales, Torre calls them, "Group Support, Group Action and Helping Others" and "Awareness and Support of Action Aimed Toward Social Change."

8. From Campbell et al. 1954, 187, quoted in Craig and Maggiotto.

6

Mediation Participation and Empowerment

DATA ANALYSIS

The data analysis for this project consists of several stages, which are displayed in Figure 6.1. The initial pre-analysis stage consisted of data checking and cleaning procedures. Data visuals and data tables were used to plot each raw data distribution and to inspect the location, spread, and shape of the distributions in order to determine which statistical techniques were most appropriate. Item analysis techniques and measures of reliability were used to analyze the empowerment measures and to create scales.

The first stage of the preliminary analysis (shown on the left side of Figure 6.1) used descriptive statistics and comparative analysis in order to understand the similarities and differences between the three mediator groups. The analysis began with a description of mediator characteristics. Means, standard deviations, and frequency distributions were calculated for all of the items in the demographics section of the Volunteer Mediator Survey (VMS) questionnaire in order to develop a profile of each group of volunteer mediators. The three groups were compared with each other and then with similar data on the disputants and the general population of Hawaii residents.

The second stage of the preliminary analysis (shown on the right side of Figure 6.1) generated an empirical profile of the empowerment measures. First, a correlation matrix of empowerment indices was calculated to determine the extent to which these empowerment measures share some common variance and the extent to which they measure distinct phenomena. For example, it is likely that scales such as self-efficacy and desire for control are at least

Figure 6.1
Data Analysis Flow Chart

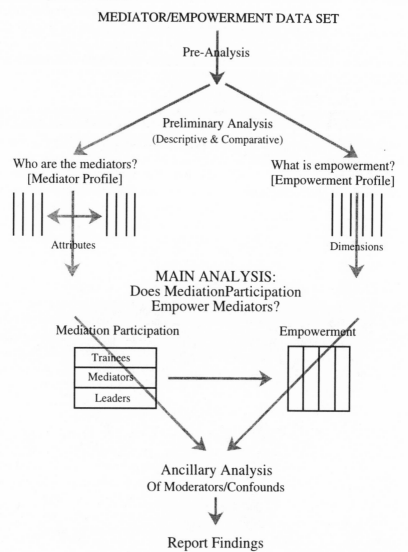

MEDIATOR/EMPOWERMENT DATA SET

Pre-Analysis

Preliminary Analysis
(Descriptive & Comparative)

Who are the mediators?   What is empowerment?
[Mediator Profile]   [Empowerment Profile]

Attributes   Dimensions

MAIN ANALYSIS:
Does MediationParticipation
Empower Mediators?

Mediation Participation   Empowerment

| Trainees |
| Mediators |
| Leaders |

Ancillary Analysis
Of Moderators/Confounds

Report Findings

moderately correlated. Factor analysis was then used to delineate the dimensionality of the empowerment construct.

The main stage of the analysis focused on the proposition that mediation participation empowers mediators. The three comparison groups—*Trainees*, *Mediators*, and *Leaders*—were compared across the fourteen indices of empowerment and disempowerment. The main analysis used multiple analysis of variance (MANOVA) to test for any group differences across all of the empowerment measures, and then a subsequent univariate analysis of variance (ANOVAS) was done for the most significant dependent variables.

To check for the possibility that response bias affects group differences, Social Desirability and Sociability measures were entered as co-variants in the (MANCOVA) analysis. A discriminant function analysis was then conducted to describe underlying dimensions that might distinguish among the three groups. A detailed description of each stage of the analysis, as well as the major findings, is presented below.

PRELIMINARY ANALYSIS: MEDIATOR AND EMPOWERMENT PROFILES

Mediator Characteristics

The Volunteer Mediator Survey (VMS) questionnaire was used to collect demographic data on the three mediator groups (fifty *Trainees*, fifty *Mediators*, and twenty-two *Leaders*). The characteristics of the three groups are presented in Table 6.1. The empowerment scores of the three mediator groups are compared in the main data analysis stage, and so it is also worthwhile to compare their demographic characteristics at this point, since the individual's demographic characteristics may have an influence on their empowerment scores. For example, those with high levels of education may be more highly empowered than those who are similar in other characteristics, but are less educated.

The mediators' characteristics are also compared to some of the characteristics of the disputants who use mediation services, and to similar census data on Hawaii residents in general, in order to gain additional perspective on the question of who these mediators are and how similar they are to other Hawaii citizens. Many community mediation programs claim that their volunteer mediators are quite similar to those who bring their disputes to the mediation center for resolution. Is this the case at HNJC?

The Total column in Table 6.1 combines the three mediator groups into an aggregate of 122 cases. As indicated, there are slightly more women than men in the combined mediator group (51.6% to 48.4%). The HNJC training staff attempts to recruit equal numbers of men and women in order to have sufficient male mediators available for the male-female divorce mediator teams, but the staff usually has difficulty finding enough men. This is a problem for many other community mediation centers. In most mediation centers there are significantly more female mediators.

The last column shows that in the disputant group, men outnumber women (56.4% to 43.6%). These statistics are based on a data base of over three thousand disputants served by HNJC over a period of ten years. It is interesting

Table 6.1
Mediator Characteristics

CHARACTERISTICS	N=50 TRAINEES	N=50 MEDIATORS	N=22 LEADERS	N=122 TOTAL	N=3018 DISPUTANTS
1 **GENDER**	cell %	cell %	cell %	cell %	cell %
Male	44.0	50.0	54.5	48.4	56.4
Female	56.0	50.0	45.5	51.6	43.6
2 **MARITAL STATUS**					
Married	58.0	56.0	50.0	55.7	-
Divorced	18.0	14.0	22.7	17.2	-
Single	10.0	4.0	9.1	7.4	-
3 **AGE** (Mean Years)	45.2	46.9	46.8	46.2	36.0
4 **EMPLOYMENT**					
Employed	80.0	86.0	90.9	84.4	80.4
Unemployed	2.0	2.0	0.0	1.6	14.9
Retired	8.0	4.0	4.5	5.7	4.8
5 **OCCUPATION**					
Managerial/Professional	28.0	42.0	50.0	34.9	-
Tech/Sales/Admin Support	36.0	22.0	13.6	29.1	-
Service	6.0	6.0	4.5	5.8	-
Military	4.0	4.0	0.0	3.5	17.7
Lawyers	8.0	12.0	13.6	9.9	-
Counselors/Psychologists	12.0	6.0	18.2	11.0	-
6 **INCOME**					
<$9,000	4.0	0.0	0.0	2.3	-
9,001-16,000	2.0	2.0	0.0	1.2	-
16,001-25,000	10.0	8.0	9.1	9.9	-
25,001-35,000	20.0	18.0	13.6	18.7	-
35,001-50,000	22.0	30.0	13.6	22.7	-
50,001-75,000	24.0	32.0	36.4	28.5	-
>$75,001	18.0	10.0	27.3	16.9	-
7 **EDUCATION**					
BA or BS degree	16.0	22.0	13.6	15.7	-
MA or Law degree	50.0	50.0	59.1	51.2	-
PhD, MD or EdD	6.0	6.0	27.3	8.7	-
8 **POLITICAL PREFERENCE**					
Conservative	8.0	12.0	4.5	8.7	-
Liberal	38.0	42.0	40.9	39.5	-
Moderate	42.0	38.0	31.8	39.5	-
Radical	4.0	0.0	9.1	3.5	-
Non-Political	6.0	6.0	4.5	5.8	-
9 **ETHNICITY**					
Black	2.0	2.0	0.0	1.7	3.6
Caucasian	52.0	70.0	86.4	61.6	48.3
Chinese	12.0	0.0	4.5	7.6	6.5
Filipino	2.0	0.0	0.0	1.2	12.5
Hawaiian	4.0	0.0	4.5	2.9	4.1
Japanese	12.0	18.0	0.0	12.8	14.7
Portuguese	2.0	0.0	4.5	1.2	2.7
Multi-Ethnic	12.0	8.0	0.0	9.3	7.5

that more women volunteer to be mediators but that evidently more men volunteer to have their disputes resolved by mediation. Perhaps this simply means that in general men are more involved in conflict situations and that women are more willing to be peacemakers.

Most of the mediators are married (55.7%), while 7.4% of them have never been married, and 17.2% of them are divorced. Their mean age is 46.2 years, and it ranges from twenty-three to seventy-six years of age. Marital status data were not available for Hawaiian residents or the disputants, but the disputants are on average about ten years younger than the mediators. Their mean age is 36.0 years and age range is eleven to ninety-two years. The younger disputants are usually involved in the juvenile restitution program or family mediations. Note that the percentiles in the table do not always total to 100% because of rounding error, missing data, and because some of the data-collection categories in the VMS questionnaires that had low numbers were omitted from the table to keep the table reasonably concise.

The volunteer mediators are primarily employed in the managerial/professional occupations (34.9%), with a high proportion of them employed as mental health counselors (11.0%) and lawyers (9.9%). Accurate comparable occupational data was not available for the general Hawaiian population or for the disputants, but the number of professionals in the ranks of the mediators is extremely high. As a group, the mediators are therefore correspondingly highly educated: 15.7% of them have B.S. or B.A. degrees, 51.2% have M.A. or law degrees, and 8.7% of the mediators have earned Ph.D., M.D., or Ed.D. degrees. Thus, 75.6% of the volunteer mediators have four or more years of college. This is in significant contrast with the general population of the state, where only 21.7% of Hawaii residents have four years or more of college. Data on education was not available for the disputant group.

The political preferences of the volunteer mediators are strongly liberal or moderate, with 79% of them about equally divided between both political categories. This is not surprising considering that Hawaii is a strongly Democratic state with organized labor as the primary political interest group. Data on political preference was not available for the disputant group.

The citizen mediators are predominantly Caucasian, with 61.6% of the total, and Caucasians also make up almost half, or 48.3%, of the disputant group. But since Caucasians comprise only about 23% of the multicultural Hawaii state population, Caucasians are highly over-represented in both the disputant and mediator groups. In contrast, the Japanese also comprise about 23% of the Hawaii state population, but only 12.8% of the HNJC mediators and 14.7% of the disputants are of Japanese descent. Chinese are also underrepresented, with 14% in the general population but only 7.6% of them working as mediators, and 6.5% coming to mediation as disputants. The Filipinos, which are a fairly recent immigrant group in Hawaii, are well represented at HNJC as disputants (12.5%) but poorly represented as mediators (only 2% of *Trainees*, and 0% as *Mediators* or *Leaders*).

These racial imbalances in the mediator population exist despite HNJC's persistent efforts to recruit racially balanced training groups. Many community mediation programs located in multicultural neighborhoods believe that it is desirable to try to match disputants with mediators of the same ethnic background, and HNJC attempts to do so whenever possible.

There is a major difference in the income levels of mediators and disputants. Only 14.2% of the disputants claim to have an income exceeding $30,000 per year (not displayed in table), whereas over 68% of the mediators earn more than that each year. Furthermore, 16.9% of the mediators make over $75,000 per year. Clearly, with regard to socioeconomic status, the volunteer mediators have a very different profile from the people who come to the mediation center to resolve their disputes.

How do the three mediator groups compare to each other? The *Trainee* group and the *Mediator* group are quite similar across most of the demographic characteristics. The *Trainee* group does reflect the recruitment efforts to increase ethnic diversity, with more Chinese, Filipino, Hawaiian, and Japanese mediators compared to the other two groups. The percentage of Caucasians is lower in the *Trainee* group but is still over-represented with 52%.

The *Leader* group, however, has some obvious differences compared to *Trainees* and other *Mediators*. The *Leaders* are more predominantly white, with 86.4% Caucasian (compared to 52% for *Trainees*, 70% for *Mediators*, and 48.3% for disputants), and more male, with 54.5%. The *Leaders* also have much higher incomes than the other mediators, with 27.3% earning in excess of $75,000 per year (compared to 18% of *Trainees*, 10% of *Mediators*, and 0% of disputants earning in excess of $75,000). The *Leaders* have achieved more advanced academic degrees, with 59% having M.A. or Law degrees and 27% having earned Ph.D., M.D., or Ed.D. degrees, compared to 6% with the most advanced degrees in the other two groups. This data demonstrates two things quite clearly. First, volunteer mediators, at least in this community mediation center, differ from the disputants in some very important ways, especially in socioeconomic characteristics. Second, those who play leadership roles in the organization are wealthier, mostly Caucasian, and better educated than the other mediators.

Finally, and of special significance to this study, the data profile of the mediators indicates that they are the kind of individuals who are likely to have a relatively high level of personal empowerment, aside from any empowerment benefits that are derived from their participation in mediation. Their level of personal empowerment may be based largely on their demographic characteristics, especially those characteristics such as level of education, occupation, and income, all of which are highly correlated with high levels of personal empowerment in other studies of empowerment.

The Empowerment Measures

Reliability and Item Analysis. As shown in Figure 6.1, the second stage of the preliminary analysis focused on the empirical question, *What is empowerment?* I used item analysis, correlation analysis, and factor analysis techniques to explore this question and to generate an empowerment profile.

All of the empowerment and disempowerment scales used in this study have demonstrated desirable psychometric qualities in previous studies. However, a scale's reliability can vary somewhat depending on the research population's characteristics and other factors. Therefore, in order to assess the scale reliability for the mediator population, I calculated Cronbach alphas (Mueller 1986, 57–64) for each of these measures. As shown in Table 6.2, the alphas scores were high for most of the scales, ranging from a high of .89 for the Political Awareness measure, to .60 for the Social Isolation measure. Many of the alphas calculated for this study are actually higher than the scores reported for them in the original studies from which many of these scales were derived. Even the lowest alphas reported in Table 6.2 are considered to be acceptable since this study compares group means across all of the measures, and an alpha of .60 or higher is acceptable for this purpose (see Mueller, 83).

The Intercorrelations of All Indices. To determine the amount of shared variance between the indices, I ran correlations on all of the measures prior to doing the factor analysis. The correlation matrix for the indices of empowerment and disempowerment is presented in Table 6.3. As shown in the table, the positive correlations range from .15 to .66, with an average correlation of .35. The highest correlations are found between General Self-efficacy and Internal Control and Self-esteem/Self-efficacy, and between Perceived Competence and Self-esteem/Self-efficacy. As was expected the three disempowerment measures (Powerlessness, Normlessness, Social Isolation) are negatively correlated with all of the eleven empowerment measures.

The highest negative correlations occur between the Powerlessness measure and Self-esteem/Self-efficacy, Chance Control, and Powerful Others. The overall pattern of correlations in Table 6.3 indicates moderate correlations between the empowerment and disempowerment measures. Thus as expected, while these measures do share some common variance, they also measure distinct aspects of the empowerment construct.

The Factor Analysis of Empowerment Indices. An exploratory factor analysis is useful at this point in the analysis in order to ascertain whether the observed correlations among the empowerment variables can be explained by the existence of a smaller number of hypothetical variables. Factor analysis provides an expedient way of determining the minimum number of factors that can account for the observed covariation. It is also useful as a means of exploring the data for the purposes of possible data reduction.

I conducted a principal-components analysis of the eleven empowerment indices, which reduced them to only three factors. The first factor dimension accounted for 46% of the variance in all eleven indices. The three factors taken together accounted for 65% of the variance. The first three factors were then rotated to both a varimax orthogonal solution as well as to an oblimin oblique solution. Both varimax and oblique solutions are presented in Table 6.4., but only loadings of .50 or higher are reported in order to keep the table concise.

Table 6.2
Reliability Measures for All Instruments

	MEASURES	CRONBACH ALPHAS	NUMBER OF ITEMS
1	Self-Esteem / Self-Efficacy	0.88	13
2	Group Cooperation	0.84	10
3	Political Awareness	0.89	14
4	Political Efficacy - Internal	0.73	5
5	Political Efficacy - External	0.86	9
6	General Self-Efficacy	0.87	6
7	Perceived Competence	0.69	4
8	Desire for Control	0.85	20
9	Internal Control	0.80	8
10	Chance Control	0.77	8
11	Powerful Others	0.74	8
12	Powerlessness	0.66	9
13	Normlessness	0.66	5
14	Social Isolation	0.60	7
15	Sociability	0.80	3
16	Social Desirability	0.64	10

The empowerment variables that load most highly on the first factor in the varimax solution are Chance Control (.81), General Self-Efficacy (.78), Internal Control (.77), Self-Esteem/Self-Efficacy (.60), and Powerful Others (.57). This first factor contains the general self-efficacy and locus of control measures as well as the combined self-esteem/self-efficacy measure. However, the internal political efficacy and external political efficacy measures do not load on this factor. They appear separately on the other two factor dimensions.

Recall that the *Chance Control* and *Powerful Others* locus of control scales were reverse scored so that a high score on these measures reflects a low belief that chance and powerful others control one's life. *General Self-Efficacy* measures people's expectations that they can perform competently across a broad range of situations that are challenging and that require effort and perseverance. *Internal Control* refers to the expectation that individuals can exert control over their lives. *Self-Esteem/Self-Efficacy* measures attitudes of self-worth and personal competence. Altogether these measures represent an individual's beliefs about achieving *mastery over one's self and one's environment*—which is identical to the definition given earlier in chapter 4 for individual empowerment. Therefore, I have named this first factor dimension **Mastery**.

Table 6.3
Correlations of Empowerment (11) and Disempowerment (3) Indices: All Groups

MEASURES	SE/SE 1	GC 2	PA 3	PEIN 4	PEEX 5	GSE 6	PC 7	DC 8	IC 9	CC 10	PO 11	PLN 12	NLN 13	ISO 14
1 Self-Esteem Self-Efficacy (SE/SE)	1.00													
2 Group Cooperation (GC)	.52	1.00												
3 Political Awareness (PA)	.43	.50	1.00											
4 Political Efficacy Internal (PEIN)	.38	.15	.30	1.00										
5 Political Efficacy External (PEEX)	.33	.39	.25	.25	1.00									
6 General Self-Efficacy (GSE)	.62	.43	.27	.21	.21	1.00								
7 Perceived Competence (PC)	.62	.43	.27	.46	.24	.49	1.00							
8 Desire for Control (DC)	.50	.47	.51	.42	.27	.57	.53	1.00						
9 Internal Control (IC)	.55	.55	.34	.20	.33	.66	.40	.53	1.00					
10 Chance Control (CC)	.50	.42	.16	.19	.33	.49	.30	.48	.58	1.00				
11 Powerful Others (PO)	.50	.39	.29	.32	.35	.40	.31	.43	.41	.57	1.00			
12 Powerlessness (PLN)	-.57	-.47	-.19	-.28	-.46	-.43	-.26	-.35	-.42	-.54	-.53	1.00		
13 Normlessness (NLN)	-.45	-.39	-.33	-.36	-.37	-.28	-.24	-.41	-.32	-.49	-.43	.54	1.00	
14 Social Isolation (ISO)	-.43	-.27	-.07	-.17	-.26	-.37	-.24	-.26	-.36	-.40	-.25	.43	.39	1.00

Table 6.4
Factor Analysis of Empowerment Indices

EMPOWERMENT MEASURES	VARIMAX ROTATION			OBLIMIN ROTATION		
	#1	#2	#3	#1	#2	#3
1 Chance Control	.81			.87		
2 General Self-Efficacy	.78			.81		
3 Internal Control	.77			.78		
4 Self Esteem/Self Efficacy	.60			.54		
5 Powerful Others	.57			.55		
6 Political Awareness		.85			.89	
7 Group Cooperation		.68			.63	
8 Political Efficacy - External		.55			.53	
9 Political Efficacy - Internal			.85			.87
10 Perceived Competence			.73			.69
11 Desire for Control			.51			

The variables that load highly on the second factor dimension are Political Awareness (.85), Group Cooperation (.68), and External Political Efficacy (.55). *Political Awareness* assesses the individual's attitudes toward political power, social justice, and the need for social change. *Group Cooperation* taps attitudes about working with others in order to achieve individual and collective goals and to fulfill psychological, social, and physical needs. *External Political Efficacy* assesses the individual's beliefs about the responsiveness of their political leaders and institutions. This second factor, which I have named **Political Awareness/Participation**, links the individuals' level of critical consciousness beliefs about the accessibility and responsiveness of the political system with their willingness to collaborate with others in working for common goals.

Internal Political Efficacy (.85), Perceived Competence (.73), and Desire for Control (.51) load highly together on the third factor, which I have named **Leadership**. *Internal Political Efficacy* measures the individuals' perception that they understand the political system and that they have the personal competencies needed to take efficacious political action. *Perceived Competence* measures the individuals' perceptions that they have developed the essential skills associated with leadership, such as public speaking, leading groups, influencing others, and organizational abilities. Those individuals who score high on the *Desire for Control* scale tend to be assertive, decisive, and active, and they seek out leadership roles. In other words, individuals who score high on these three measures believe that they understand the political system, that they have mastered the skills and knowledge required for effective leadership, and that they have the strong desire to lead others.

The oblimin rotation results also displayed in Table 6.4 confirm the stability of the underlying factor structure revealed by the varimax solution. The empowerment variables again load on three factor dimensions in nearly identical order to the varimax solution. The Desire for Control measure still loads together with the same two variables in the oblimin rotation, but it does not appear in Table 6.4 because its factor loading drops to (.41) and (.50) was the cutoff level for inclusion in the table.

In summary, the preliminary data analysis produced a comparative profile of the three volunteer mediator groups' social, economic, and demographic characteristics. Next, an exploratory factor analysis of the eleven empowerment indices revealed that there were three underlying factor dimensions of empowerment, which were named **Mastery**, **Political Awareness/Participation**, and **Leadership**.

This empirical analysis supports the theoretical analysis of empowerment presented in chapter 4 and provides a foundation for the main analysis. The findings of the preliminary analysis will also be useful in interpreting the findings of the main analysis.

MAIN ANALYSIS: MEDIATION PARTICIPATION AND EMPOWERMENT

We are now ready for the main analysis, which compares the three mediator groups across all of the empowerment measures in order to investigate the proposition that *mediation participation empowers mediators*. First, we will look at the effects of the training experience on mediator empowerment, then at the effects of mediating disputes, and finally at the possible empowering effects derived from participating in leadership activities.

Training and Empowerment

Does the HNJC mediation training enhance the *Trainee*'s level of personal empowerment? Based on the results of the analysis of variance the answer is yes. To answer this question, in the main analyses I tested for the expected mean differences in the empowerment and disempowerment measures between the pre-training survey and the post-training survey. A multivariate analysis of variance (MANOVA) across the fourteen measures was significant ($F = 14.64$; $df = 14,1372$; $p < .01$). The univariate results, in terms of the means, standard deviations, and the ANOVA results, for the pre- and post-training assessments, are reported in Table 6.5. As this table clearly indicates, *all* of the empowerment measures, as well as *all* of the disempowerment measures, differ significantly between the pre-training and post-training time periods (represented in the table by 1s and 2s, respectively).

Table 6.5

Means, Standard Deviations, and ANOVA Results for Trainees on Empowerment (11) and Disempowerment (3) Measures

	MEASURES	[1] TRAINEE PRE-TEST	[2] TRAINEE POST-TEST	GROUP COMPARISON	F	VARIABLE FUNCTIONS CORRELATION
1	Self-Esteem Self-Efficacy	52.64 [4.31]	56.40 [4.8]	2>1	a 16.98	0.63
2	Group Cooperation	38.14 [3.28]	42.88 [4.91]	2>1	a 32.24	0.89
3	Political Awareness	54.74 [5.33]	59.96 [6.74]	2>1	a 18.45	0.68
4	Political Efficacy Internal	26.28 [4.30]	28.46 [4.18]	2>1	a 6.61	0.41
5	Political Efficacy External	45.34 [8.08]	48.84 [8.22]	2>1	b 4.61	0.32
6	General Self-Efficacy	31.62 [4.62]	35.44 [5.6]	2>1	a 13.86	0.57
7	Perceived Competence	11.88 [1.27]	12.72 [1.67]	2>1	a 8.02	0.44
8	Desire for Control	102.16 [9.03]	112.58 [13.99]	2>1	a 19.57	0.68
9	Internal Control	37.20 [3.17]	40.36 [5.59]	2>1	a 12.10	0.53
10	Chance Control	36.10 [3.91]	39.50 [5.39]	2>1	a 13.00	0.54
11	Powerful Others	35.52 [4.27]	38.86 [4.88]	2>1	a 13.26	0.56
12	Powerlessness	22.58 [3.29]	20.66 [3.67]	2>1	a 7.58	-0.42
13	Normlessness	11.98 [2.85]	10.06 [2.99]	2>1	a 10.83	-0.49
14	Social Isolation	19.48 [3.33]	17.90 [3.25]	2>1	b 5.76	-0.37
		N = 50	N = 50			

a   b
p<.01   p<.05

Canonical Correlation=.63
Variance Explained=.40

The scores on all of the empowerment measures increased, indicating that the *Trainees* experienced increased levels of self-efficacy, self-esteem, and perceived competence in participation skills. They also demonstrated an increase in positive attitudes toward group participation and in the level of political awareness. This significant increase in empowerment scores greatly exceeded the expectations discussed earlier.

As expected, the *Trainees'* scores on the three disempowerment scales declined between the pre-tests and post-tests, indicating that they showed a strong decline in feelings of powerlessness, normlessness, and social isolation after mediation training. These findings also greatly exceeded the expectations for the effect of training on disempowerment.

To test for the possibility that response bias or need to affiliate were accounting for some of the observed differences, the *Trainee* data on the Social

Desirability and Sociability measures was entered as covariates in a multivariate analysis of covariance (MANCOVA). The overall result still remained significant (F = 14.14; df = 14,1344; p <.01), indicating that response bias or need to affiliate were not significant factors in the analysis. When the univariate ANOVAs were examined, all fourteen of the measures continued to be significantly different.

Next, I conducted a discriminant function analysis in order to more fully describe and understand the underlying dimensions that were distinguishing between the pre- and post-test assessment. As shown in Table 6.5, only one discriminant function was found. It accounts for 40% of the variance (canonical correlation = .63). The most effective variables in distinguishing between the pre- and post-training measures were Group Cooperation, Political Awareness, and Desire for Control.

Were there any differences in empowerment effects observed between the female and male *Trainees*? Again, the answer given by the analysis was yes. The outcomes of the multivariate analysis of variance (MANOVA) was significant (F = 2.064; df = 14,1344; p <.01), indicating that there were differences on at least some of the measures. None of the univariate ANOVAs were significant at the p < .01 level, but the Internal Political Efficacy, Perceived Competence, Chance Control, and Political Awareness measures were significant at the p < .05 level. The mean scores for all four of these measures were slightly higher for the male *Trainees*.

Mediation and Empowerment

If doing mediation and leadership activities are empowering for the mediators, we would expect that the mean scores for both the *Mediators* and the *Leaders* on the empowerment measures would be higher than the scores of the *Trainees*, who have just completed their mediation training but who have not yet had either the opportunity to work as mediators or to serve in leadership roles in the mediation organization. What do the results of the data analysis show? Are the *Mediators* and *Leaders* higher on all or most of the empowerment measures?

In this stage of the analysis, the results are somewhat more mixed. The MANOVA results for the *Trainee, Mediator,* and *Leader* groups were significant (F = 7.21; df = 28,1666; p < .01). When the Social Desirability and Sociability measures were introduced into the model as covariates, the MANCOVA remained significant (F = 7.63; df = 28,1634; p < .01).

Table 6.6 reports the means, standard deviations, ANOVA results, and the comparisons for all three of the mediator groups on all of the empowerment and disempowerment measures. The findings here are not nearly as clear as those shown in Table 6.5, where there was a decisive increase in the score of every empowerment measure and a significant decline in all disempowerment scores between the pre- and post-tests for *Trainees*.

Table 6.6
Means, Standard Deviations, ANOVA Results, and Comparisons of All Groups on Empowerment (11) and Disempowerment (3) Measures

	MEASURES	[1] TRAINEES PRE-TEST	[2] TRAINEES POST-TEST	[M] MEDIATORS	[L] LEADERS	GROUP COMPARISON	F
1	Self-Esteem Self-Efficacy	52.64 [4.31]	56.40 [4.8]	54.10 [4.5]	54.23 [5.9]	2>L>M>1	b 3.07
2	Group Cooperation	38.14 [3.28]	42.88 [4.91]	38.96 [4.07]	38.00 [4.46]	2>M>1>L	a 14.10
3	Political Awareness	54.74 [5.33]	59.96 [6.74]	54.70 [6.19]	58.91 [7.02]	2>L>1>M	a 8.35
4	Political Efficacy Internal	26.28 [4.30]	28.46 [4.18]	26.60 [5.72]	29.64 [3.89]	L>2>M>1	a 3.49
5	Political Efficacy External	45.34 [8.08]	48.84 [8.22]	43.42 [9.76]	45.36 [6.02]	2>L>1>M	a 5.52
6	General Self-Efficacy	31.62 [4.62]	35.44 [5.6]	31.32 [5.8]	31.59 [7.20]	2>1>L>M	a 7.64
7	Perceived Competence	11.88 [1.27]	12.72 [1.67]	11.64 [1.94]	12.09 [1.93]	2>L>1>M	a 4.76
8	Desire for Control	102.16 [9.03]	112.58 [13.99]	101.68 [11.37]	105.46 [10.66]	2>L>1>M	a 10.08
9	Internal Control	37.20 [3.17]	40.36 [5.59]	37.64 [4.27]	35.96 [3.35]	2>M>1>L	a 8.37
10	Chance Control	36.10 [3.91]	39.50 [5.39]	37.02 [3.82]	36.32 [4.16]	2>M>L>1	a 6.01
11	Powerful Others	35.52 [4.27]	38.86 [4.88]	36.02 [4.65]	37.14 [5.45]	2>L>M>1	b 4.67
12	Powerlessness	22.58 [3.29]	20.66 [3.67]	22.40 [3.78]	22.54 [4.98]	2>M>L>1	b 3.58
13	Normlessness	11.98 [2.85]	10.06 [2.99]	11.94 [2.54]	11.32 [2.46]	2>L>M>1	a 6.17
14	Social Isolation	19.48 [3.33]	17.90 [3.25]	19.60 [2.66]	19.23 [3.34]	2>L>1>M	a 4.91
		N = 50	N = 50	N = 50	N = 22		

a   b
$p<.01$ $p<.05$

In fact, as Table 6.6 shows, the mean score for the experienced *Mediators* was actually *lower* across *all* empowerment measures than was the mean scores for the *Trainee* group at the end of their mediation training. Furthermore, the mean score for the *Mediators* on the three measures of disempowerment was *higher* than that of the post *Trainees*, indicating higher levels of disempowerment for those who are active *Mediators*. These findings are opposite to what one would expect to find if practicing mediation, added to the personal empowerment mediators gained from mediation training.

Interestingly, the *Mediators* are also slightly lower on five of the empowerment measures, including external political efficacy, general self-efficacy, perceived competence, desire for control, and political awareness, than the scores on those measures recorded for the *Trainees before* they began the mediator training. In addition, the *Mediators* have a higher score on the social isolation scale than the *Trainees* did before beginning training. These findings are contrary to what would be expected if mediation participation increased personal empowerment. Either mediation is actually disempowering for many of the experienced mediators or as a cohort they must have been less empowered than the present group of *Trainees* before they became involved in community mediation.

Leadership and Empowerment

The results for the *Leader* group are somewhat mixed (see Table 6.6). As expected, the *Leader* group scored higher than the other experienced *Mediators* on most of the empowerment measures, except for internal control, chance control, and group cooperation. But in comparing all four group mean scores for the pre- and post-*Trainees* and *Mediators*, the *Leader* group had the highest score on only the Internal Political Efficacy measure, which taps the individuals' perception that they understand the political system and that they have the personal competencies to take effective political action. On all of the other empowerment and disempowerment measures, the post-*Trainee* group had the highest scores, as indicated in the group comparison column.

DISCUSSION OF THE MAIN ANALYSIS RESULTS

If all three types of mediation participation have empowering effects on the mediators, we would expect to find increasing levels of empowerment as individuals progress through their mediation experience from mediation training to mediating conflicts, and in some cases to participating in leadership activities. Thus, it was expected that *Trainees* would have higher positive empowerment scores after completing the training than they had before beginning the training ($T_2 > T_1$).

Also, it was expected that the *Mediators* would have higher empowerment scores than the *Trainees* had after completing their training ($M > T_2$), and it was expected that the *Leaders'* scores would be higher than the empowerment scores of the other two groups. Therefore, if empowerment increases as the mediators progressively participate in mediation activities, the expected data pattern for a comparison of the empowerment levels for all three groups should be ($L > M > T_2 > T_1$).

However, as discussed in chapter 5, it was also expected that the empowerment score increases at all levels would be small at best even if mediation participation was empowering. Furthermore, it was expected that increases might occur on only some of the empowerment scales used in this study even if mediation is an empowering experience.

For the *Trainee* group, the results of the data analysis confirmed the *direction* of the expected data patterns in that *all* of their empowerment scores had increased immediately after completing mediation training. However, the *magnitude* of the increases in the empowerment scores for *Trainees* between pre-test and post-tests greatly exceeded expectations, since only modest increases were predicted for the reasons discussed above. These substantial increases occurred on all of the empowerment scales used in this study, which also exceeded expectations for the *comprehensiveness* of the empowerment effect, since increases were expected on only a few.

While the direction of the expected increases for *Trainees* was confirmed for all of the empowerment measures, and the predictions for the magnitude and comprehensiveness were exceeded, the expected pattern for experienced *Mediators* when compared to *Trainees* was not confirmed, and the expected pattern for *Leaders* was only partially confirmed. What factors might explain these differences? Each finding is discussed in turn below.

The *Trainees*

For the *Trainees*, the expected data patterns were overwhelmingly supported. When the mean empowerment and disempowerment scores were compared between the pre-training survey and the post-training survey, *all* of the measures differed markedly. Scores on all eleven empowerment measures *increased* substantially, indicating increased levels of Self-Efficacy, Self-Esteem, and Perceived Competence in participation skills. There was also an increase in positive attitudes toward Group Cooperation and Political Awareness. As also expected, the scores on all three of the disempowerment scales *declined* substantially, indicating a diminishment in feelings of powerlessness, normlessness, and social isolation.

The magnitude of the differences between the pre- and post-measures, as well as the finding of significant gains across all of the empowerment measures, greatly exceeded expectations in that only modest gains on some of the measures had been expected for reasons set forth in chapter 5. If this study had employed an experimental design, with random assignment to experimental and control groups, threats to internal validity would have been controlled and these results would be quite persuasive. But even with this quasi-experimental design, the findings are so substantial in magnitude that they strongly suggest that mediation training does indeed empower the participants in significant ways.

This outcome of significant empowerment across all measures may result from several factors specific to the training experience. First, the mediation training workshop is quite intensive, with over fifty classroom hours as well as hours of additional homework assignments compressed into a four-week period. As a result of this "immersion" experience, *Trainees* are inculcated with the empowering skills, attitudes, and behaviors expected of mediators. Second, the HNJC staff exposes them to the language of empowerment, and they employ training techniques, such as small group work, dialogue, and role play, all of which are basic to models of empowering education (see Kindervatter 1979).

Third, the HNJC training staff is strongly supportive throughout the training. They treat *Trainees* with respect and attempt to make workshop participants feel as if they are a valued part of the HNJC mediation community. Fourth, the *Trainees* are genuinely enthusiastic about the value of mediation and believe that mediation will empower themselves as well as those who bring their disputes to the mediation center. *Trainee* comments made after completing the training (see chapter 3) indicate that they are well aware of the importance of empowerment and that they believe strongly that they have been empowered by the training experience. Since they were administered the post-training questionnaire immediately after completing the workshop, it is not surprising that the attitude measures would reflect their strong positive feelings about themselves and their beliefs about empowerment, which were expressed in the mediator comments.

The *Mediators*

While the training sessions clearly have a strong empowering impact on the *Trainees*, the findings for the *Mediator* group do not concur with the expected data patterns. These findings appear to be contrary to the expectations that flow from the research proposition that doing mediation will empower the mediators. They also appear to be contrary to the analysis of mediator roles and strategies presented in chapter 2, which provided a number of arguments linking mediator behavior and their use of power in mediation to the development of their personal empowerment. The mean scores for the *Mediators* are lower across all of the empowerment measures than the mean scores for the *Trainee* groups at the end of their mediation training, instead of being higher as expected. In addition, the mean scores for the *Mediators* on the three measures of disempowerment are higher than those of the post-*Trainees*, a finding that is also opposite to expectations.

Furthermore, the *Mediators* scored slightly *lower* on five of the empowerment measures including external political efficacy, general self-efficacy, perceived competence, desire for control, and political awareness than the *Trainees* did *before* beginning training. What might explain this finding? First, it is possible that many of those in the *Mediator* group were initially far less empowered than those in the *Trainee* group, and they still haven't developed high levels of personal empowerment. Another possible explanation may relate to the timing of the pre-training survey of the *Trainees*. In this regard it should be noted that while the *Trainees'* empowerment scores were assessed before beginning training, they had already been through a rigorous recruitment and selection process. This process included reading community mediation material, viewing films on mediation, and interviews with HNJC staff. It is possible that this selection process might have had some empowering effect on the volunteer mediators even before they began the training workshops.

What might explain the other contrary findings? There are at least three logical possibilities. First, it may be that doing mediation does in fact empower mediators but that due to methodological limitations of the research design, or empowerment measures, data collection, or statistical analysis, the data analysis findings did not reveal the empowerment effects. Second, it may be that, contrary to the claims of mediation ideology discussed earlier, mediating disputes has little or no effect on empowering mediators. After all, none of those claims has been empirically verified before, since this is one of the first empirical studies on mediator empowerment. Third, and contrary to the claims of many community mediation advocates, it is possible that mediating disputes may actually be *disempowering* for some mediators. I will first consider the possibilities that mediation has no empowerment effect, or that it may actually be disempowering, and then I will discuss how various methodological limitations might affect the empirical findings.

The finding that the experienced *Mediators'* scores are lower than the post-training scores of the *Trainees* may indicate the possibility that the psychological empowerment associated with the training is intense, but short lived, and that doing the actual mediation work does not provide the mediator with any additional psychological empowerment. It is likely that the high expectations and high levels of enthusiasm experienced in mediation training fades quickly for many of the mediators. This phenomenon is commonly observed in other types of human development training, where the attitudes and behaviors that are developed in the intense workshop environment tend to revert to well-established habit patterns when participants return to their normal life style and work environment.

Thus, the post-training empowerment measures given immediately after completion of training may be tapping a powerful but short-lived training effect that will naturally decline somewhat over time for all, or at least for many, of the *Trainees.* When the scores of *Mediators* are contrasted to those of post-*Trainees*, the *Mediators* appear to be less empowered in comparison. But if the *Trainee* groups in this study were to be retested a year later, it is possible that their empowerment scores might be similar to those of the experienced *Mediators* in this study.

However, in addition to a natural decline in psychological empowerment over time after the training, it is conceivable that doing mediation might actually contribute to a decline in a mediator's level of psychological empowerment. Doing mediation might be *disempowering* for several reasons. First, the reality of actually doing mediation may be a major disappointment for some of the *Trainees* who have developed unrealistically high expectations about the mediation experience and empowerment that are not fulfilled once they begin to mediate. If they encounter problems with learning and using the mediation model, or if they have a negative experience early on as they begin to mediate, they may feel personally incompetent and suffer a subsequent loss of self-esteem or self-efficacy. In fact, it is possible that mediation may turn out to be a frustrating or disappointing experience for some of these individuals compared to their early high expectations.

Second, due to organizational scheduling difficulties for some of the trainees, there may be a lengthy period of time between the completion of their training and their first mediation session that could exacerbate this prospect of an unsatisfactory mediation experience. During the time period between completion of mediation training and engaging in the first real mediation, anxieties about their mediation performance may develop, and the hard-earned skills learned in the training workshop may get rusty. In addition after these new mediators begin to mediate, many of them may mediate very infrequently due to their own schedule and priorities or the preferences of HNJC staff who schedule mediation sessions. Those mediators who put little time or effort into the mediation activity are unlikely to develop a high level of mediation competency or to derive significant empowerment benefits from doing mediation.

Third, the significant differences between the mediation training experience and the mediating experiences in terms of the time, intensity, or commitment required for each of them may affect the levels of resultant empowerment realized by the participants. As described earlier, the mediation training workshop packs fifty hours of intensive effort into the short time frame of just a few weeks. In contrast, an average mediation session lasts only about two or three hours, and even the most active mediators usually do only one mediation session per week. It is quite possible that two hours or less per week of mediation or any other potentially empowering activity may be insufficient to enhance the psychological empowerment of most individuals. And so while both the training workshops and the mediation experiences are designed to shape and develop the various skills and attitudes relevant to community mediation, they are very different kinds of experiences in many important ways, and they may therefore have different impacts on the levels or types of empowerment inculcated in the participants.

Fourth, when training is completed, trainees usually leave the workshops with a strong sense of social bonding, friendship with other mediators, and community with each other that fulfills their affiliation needs. They are enthusiastic about becoming active members of the HNJC organization and being part of the community mediation movement. This feeling of camaraderie and affiliation may not last long after completing training, however, because many of them soon discover that they are unlikely to ever see the people they trained with and came to know and like. The mediator pool sometimes has over 200 members, and the HNJC mediation model often uses only a single mediator for many types of simple neighbor-neighbor, juvenile restitution, or small claims cases. The only possibility for working with other mediators as a team is the pairing of mediators in female-male dyads, which are used only for divorce mediation cases. Therefore, the scheduling and procedures for pairing of mediators means that female mediators will never get to mediate with their other female friends, and of course the same is true for the male mediators. Mediators who decide to mediate their cases at night or on weekends, as most of them who are employed do, will have only minimal interaction with the fulltime HNJC staff or with other core volunteers who usually work normal daytime schedules. Therefore, the majority of HNJC mediators have little opportunity to see or socialize with each other once they have completed their mediation training, except for infrequent social events.

This HNJC program situation contrasts sharply with that of other more grass roots community mediation programs, like the San Francisco Community Boards, which stress the central mission of enhancing the empowerment of both disputants and volunteer mediators and facilitating community building. In order to build commitment and a strong sense of community within the program, the Community Boards program mediates all of their cases with three- to five-member panels, and keeps their volunteers heavily involved with other types of outreach and governance activities in addition to mediation.

This loss of a sense of community affiliation and friendships that were developed during their mediation training, as well as a feeling of being under-utilized and unappreciated, are common complaints from HNJC mediators who are not very active. These frustrations that develop over time after training could result in the loss of much of the empowerment benefits that were derived from their training. Thus for these reasons, it is likely that at least for some of the community mediators, their actual experience with doing mediation and belonging to a community mediation program has little positive empowering effect, or may in some cases even be disempowering for them.

Let us now consider the remaining possibility that mediation is generally an empowering experience for mediators but that the evidence of mediator empowerment has been masked by methodological limitations of this study. Plausible explanations for this possibility stem from the research assumptions made and the research design and procedures used. In every empirical analysis, numerous research decisions must be made that may affect the final results. There is no perfect research design. Inevitable constraints of time, funding, and data accessibility condition the research decisions, and compromises are made that result in limitations on the validity of the study, the power of the statistical analysis, and the generalizability of the findings.

In this study, for example, research decisions had to be made about selecting the appropriate unit of analysis. Should the study focus on the empowerment of mediation disputants, the mediators, the mediation organization, or empowerment of the community? Then decisions were made about what aspects of individual empowerment to focus on (i.e., attitudes, skills, awareness, or behavior), how to collect data or measure empowerment (i.e., questionnaires, interviews, observations, or physiological measures), how to develop the measure (i.e., construct new scales or adapt existing measures), where to perform the study (i.e., laboratory or field), and what kind of research design would be most appropriate. This series of research decisions that were explained and justified in chapter 5 can significantly affect the outcomes or research findings.

The research design, for example, had several limitations. First, the *Trainee* group part of the study used a pre-post one-group design. This study would have been strengthened by the random assignment of participants to the training group and to a control group. In an ideal experimental research design, the two trainee and control groups would have been tracked for several years as the members of the experimental group were trained and participated in mediation and HNJC leadership activities, whereas the control group members would not have been involved with mediation. Empowerment data might have been collected on all mediation participants and the control group members every three to six months to ascertain their comparative levels and intensity of personal empowerment at that point in time. While this kind of "pure" experimental model has advantages, it also has limitations, and it is difficult to use in real-world research for reasons discussed earlier.

For this study, data was collected on the experienced *Mediators* who had been active for a year or more after training and on those experienced mediators who had also been active in HNJC training and other leadership activities. There was of course no baseline data available for these two mediator groups who had been active with the HNJC for at least one year. Therefore, for the purposes of this study, it was assumed that since the *Mediators* and *Leaders* had been recruited and selected by the same procedures as the new *Trainees*, and they had similar demographic characteristics to the *Trainees*, and had gone through a similar training experience, the new *Trainee* post-training scores could also be used as an estimated base line for the *Mediator* and *Leader* groups. In other words, it was assumed that the *Mediator* and *Leader* groups would have had similar empowerment levels after completing their mediation training as did the present group of new *Trainees*.

This simplifying assumption is of course somewhat problematic. If the experienced *Mediators* had had the same empowerment scores after training as the new *Trainees* did, and if doing mediation over time subsequently increased their levels of psychological empowerment, then the mean empowerment scores for *Mediators* should be higher than the scores of post *Trainees*. But this is not the case, the *Mediators*' scores are lower.

On the other hand, it is possible that the *Mediators* actually had *lower* mean empowerment scores at the end of their training than did the current group of

Trainees, either because they were less empowered as a group before beginning training, or because they were less empowered by their training. If they had lower post-training scores, then it is possible that they could have increased their level of empowerment by mediating, but not sufficiently to raise their *Mediator* scores to the same level as the post-*Trainee* scores of the new *Trainees*. In this case, a comparison of post-*Trainee* and *Mediator* scores would not reveal the possible empowerment gains realized from mediating, and the outcome would therefore be misleading because of the assumption that the two groups started out at the same level of empowerment. The additional empirical finding that the *Mediators* actually had slightly lower scores on some of the empowerment measures than did the *Trainees before* their training, gives some support to the possibility that their empowerment baseline scores before the training were not the same.

Third, there are differences within the groups that make comparison between them problematic. All of the participants in the recent *Trainees* group have shared exactly the same training experience. In that sense there is uniformity with regard to mediation experience within the group. The *Mediator* group, however, contains individuals who have widely varying amounts and types of mediation experience. For example, one mediator may have been mediating for only a year and may only mediate a one-hour juvenile restitution case each month, whereas another mediator may have been highly active for three or more years and on average mediates a complex three-hour divorce session each week. These may be extreme comparisons, but the point is that while within the *Trainee* group the training experience is quite similar, the *Mediators'* group is comprised of individuals with very different types and levels of mediation experience. Consequently, it is possible that within the *Mediator* group there are some individuals with high levels of personal empowerment that may be related to their extensive and frequent mediation experience, and still other individuals with little mediation experience and relatively low levels of personal empowerment. While highly active *Mediators* may be highly empowered by their participation, the relatively underutilized and inexperienced mediators may show little or no empowerment effects or, as discussed above, they may be disempowered by their inactivity or feelings of inadequacy. In short, in the calculation of *Mediator* group mean scores, the relatively few "core" mediators with high levels of empowerment may be canceled out by many more relatively inactive mediators with low levels of empowerment. Therefore, these differences in the homogeneity of mediation experience between the two groups make comparison of the empowerment effects derived from training and mediation participation problematic.

Fourth, in addition to the limitations in research design there are other plausible possibilities. Few studies have attempted to measure psychological empowerment related to community mediation. I have operationalized empowerment by measuring specific attitudes, particularly self-esteem and self-efficacy. In doing so, I used the best existing instruments I could find and ran an item analysis to test their reliability for this research population. However, it is possible that the empowerment effect associated with doing mediation may not be sufficiently captured by the questionnaires used in this study. Using other attitude measures, or employing another data-collection technique, such as in-depth interviews or behavioral observation, may be more effective in detecting evidence of psychological empowerment.

Fifth, it should be noted that empowerment is a complex concept encompassing a variety of attitudes, beliefs, skills, and behaviors. It may be that participation in training, mediating, and leading activities all have somewhat different empowerment effects on different individuals. The empirical part of this study has focused primarily on measuring empowerment attitudes. I did not attempt to directly measure other key aspects of individual empowerment, such as skills, specialized knowledge, or behavior. On one hand, it is possible that the training workshops may impact and shape empowering attitudes much more than do mediating and leadership experiences. On the other hand, participating in mediation and leadership roles and activities may primarily consolidate and refine various empowering communication, problem-solving, and conflict resolution skills, or they may facilitate the development of positive behavioral changes in the mediation setting that may transfer to other important areas of the individual's social or work life. In other words, there may be important kinds of personal empowerment occurring that have not been detected or measured by this research design.

Finally, it is also possible that doing mediation may provide a new sense of empowering purpose or life mission for some of these community mediators that partially balances other negative factors or influences in their lives that are creating disempowerment effects. This may especially be the case for many of the retirees who are among the most active HNJC mediators. Without the positive personal fulfillment that mediation provides, many of these people might with increasing age become progressively disempowered. In other words, perhaps the empowerment derived from involvement with mediation helps to balance the loss of personal empowerment that is inevitable for many individuals with increasing age. Mediator comments discussed earlier indicate that many of them believe that mediation has made an important difference in their lives.

Therefore, for all the reasons just discussed, it may be that there are powerful types of empowerment taking place for many of the *Mediators* that were not revealed by the limitations of this exploratory empirical analysis.

The *Leaders*

The research findings for the *Leader* group partially met expectations. As expected, the *Leaders* scored higher than did the other *Mediators* on most of the empowerment measures, including Internal Political Efficacy, Perceived

Competence, and Desire for Control. These empirical results for the *Leaders* are compatible with the factor analysis results, which revealed a **Leadership** dimension, with the same three measures loading highly on it. Therefore, we would expect those in the *Leader* group to score highly on these three measures.

However, the *Leaders* had lower scores than the *Mediators* on the Internal Control and Chance Control measures. In the factor analysis these two variables loaded highly on the **Mastery** dimension. Perhaps this implies that *Leaders* are more concerned about control issues than non-leaders and that they are more pessimistic or anxious about the influence of chance and other factors on personal control. Perhaps they seek out leadership roles as a means to compensate for this anxiety. Interestingly, the *Leaders* also had the lowest score of the three groups on the Group Cooperation measure, which may indicate that they have more of a power *over* others rather than a power *with* others orientation and this may also relate to their leadership style.

In comparing all three groups' mean scores, the *Leaders* had the highest score on Internal Political Efficacy, which assesses an individual's perception that they understand the political system and they have the competencies to take action. On all other measures the post-*Trainee* scores were slightly higher.

Why did the *Leaders* score lower than the post-*Trainees* on most of the empowerment measures? Again, we can only speculate about the possible explanations. Since most of the *Leaders* are also active mediators, much of the reasoning used above to explain the differences between the scores of the *Trainees* and the experienced *Mediators* and the variances from the expected results would apply here as well.

There may also be additional factors directly relevant to their leadership activities. First, it is possible that leadership participation in a community mediation organization may not be empowering for all of the individuals involved because of the nature of the leadership activities or their frequency. As with the other experienced *Mediators* there is a great deal of variation within the *Leaders* group. Some individuals are highly active at the top levels of organizational leadership, while others who were classified in this study as *Leaders* may serve on a committee that meets infrequently. Those who are highly active in the organization may be highly empowered by their leadership activities, and those who are much less active may be affected little, if at all. Ideally, if the population of leaders in the HNJC was substantially larger, leaders could have been grouped according to the type of governance activity they are involved in (i.e., board membership, committee members, or training staff) and their frequency of participation. There might be significant differences in the levels and types of empowerment that occur between these more homogeneous groups.

Second, just as with the other *Mediators*, the *Leaders* may in fact be psychologically empowered, or empowered in other ways that have not been measured, but the empirical findings do not reveal the empowerment effects because of the methodological limitations discussed above.

Why do the *Leaders* have higher scores on many of the empowerment measures than the other *Mediators* do? First as discussed earlier, leadership roles in community mediation or other kinds of community organizations may provide the *Leaders* with additional opportunities, incentives, or resources for empowerment compared to those with ordinary membership status. The *Leaders* have the opportunity to learn more and to exercise decision-making and governance skills within the HNJC organization. They enjoy higher status and recognition and may get more respect within the mediation community and in the outside community, and many of them are active and well-known in the larger state and national mediation movement. As core members of the organization the *Leaders* are much more involved in the HNJC community than the majority of regular members who simply mediate disputes.

Second, however, it should also be remembered that the *Leaders* are citizen volunteers who partially self-select for their leadership roles, and they therefore are likely to have been more psychologically empowered than other non-leader mediators even before they become involved in leadership activities. Third, compared to the other mediators, the *Leaders* have significantly higher scores on many of the socioeconomic characteristics like education and income that other empirical studies have strongly associated with high levels of personal empowerment. These personal characteristics may account somewhat for the higher empowerment scores for *Leaders*.

7

The Future of Community
Mediation and Empowerment

What have we learned about the linkage between mediation participation and personal empowerment, and what are the next steps in theory development and empirical research? What is the probable future of the community mediation movement and the implications for personal and political transformation?

EMPOWERMENT AND MEDIATION

The empirical analysis focused on mediation's ideological claims that mediation participation is empowering. I looked specifically at the psychological empowerment of citizen mediators in a large urban community mediation setting. The major purposes of this study include; assessing the linkage between mediation and citizen empowerment, discovering significant variables and relationships, laying the groundwork for more rigorous testing of hypotheses, and generating insights for future research, practice, and policy. At this point I will summarize what has been learned and suggest a future research agenda. After a brief discussion of psychological empowerment, I will suggest what impact, if any, the mediation experience has on social and political aspects of citizen empowerment.

Empowerment Components: Psychological, Social, and Political

Psychological Empowerment. Empowerment is a complex concept with many components. I have differentiated theoretically between three types of personal empowerment: psychological, social, and political. But for the empirical analysis I focused only on psychological empowerment and selected thirteen instruments that measured different aspects of the self-esteem and self-efficacy concepts. Three volunteer mediator groups representing three different types of mediation experience, were compared across all of the psychological measures. I found that mediation training demonstrated a strong empowerment effect that greatly exceeded expectations. The *Trainee* group exhibited significant increases on all of the psychological empowerment measures at the end of the training sessions. The intensity and impact of the training experience assessed by the empowerment measures was supported by the *Trainees'* comments on post-training surveys. They reported feeling empowered, euphoric, and enthusiastic as a result of the training experience. Thus, the impact of the mediation training had a more powerful effect on psychological empowerment than was anticipated. However, the empowerment measures were administered within a week of completing the training, and there is no way of knowing how long this powerful empowerment effect lasts for the *Trainees*, or what factors might prolong or dampen the empowerment effect.

For future research, studies might be done at different time periods following training in order to answer these questions. It would also be useful to study mediation training in different mediation program settings to see if similar empowerment impacts occur, when training varies in duration, intensity, or substance. Research must also begin to unpack the training experience in order to understand what factors or aspects of training affect personal empowerment. This kind of information would be helpful for designing more empowering mediation training workshops as well as for improving empowering interventions used in other social and political settings.

The psychological empowerment findings for the *Mediators* and *Leaders* as measured by the instruments used in this study were more mixed and difficult to interpret. As discussed above there are research design limitations that make it difficult to untangle the psychological effects for leaders and mediators. It should also be noted that the training experience is very different from actually doing mediation and leadership activities. The training is a much more focused, intensive activity specifically designed to produce desired attitudinal changes and enhance skill development. In comparison, doing mediation and governance activities is an enjoyable but sporadic form of experiential learning for most of the mediators. The core mediators and leaders are very active members of the organization and perhaps benefit more from the experience. Other mediators may have infrequent contact with the mediation center. In this study both active and inactive mediators were grouped together. The *Mediator* and *Leader* groups are not large enough to subdivide into groups by level of activity or other factors that might affect the degree or type of psychological empowerment.

There are theoretically many ways to improve the research design used here and perhaps clarify these findings, but most of them are prohibitive in terms of cost and other implementation factors. A strong experimental design with control groups and random assignment of subjects to *Mediators* and control groups could be used to control variables and enhance validity. But the true experimental design is normally considered too expensive and too intrusive to use in action research projects and in social service agency settings. It would also be desirable to do a follow-up study in the same research setting to study the original *Trainee* group after two or three years when many of them are likely to be active mediators or even leaders of the organization. Unfortunately, with the high dropout rate for volunteer mediators, there are unlikely to be enough of the original *Trainees* still active after two or three years to provide a sufficiently large study group.

Research could be conducted in a laboratory setting designed to simulate as closely as possible the conditions of mediation training, mediation practice, and organizational governance with college sophomores or other typical subjects role-playing mediators. Such an approach might yield useful insights about the effects of participation in simulated training exercises and in role-playing of mediators and leaders. However, it is difficult to generalize from the laboratory experiment findings to the real world due to external validity problems. If one is really interested in how existing community mediation programs affect the citizens who volunteer to be mediators, then it is best to study how those actual mediation programs operate, and observe people who actually volunteer to be mediators and leaders of community programs.

In summary, mediation training appears to strongly enhance some aspects of psychological empowerment. While mediation and leadership may also enhance psychological empowerment, the results of this empirical analysis are difficult to interpret on this potential linkage. More research is needed. But at this point we should remember that empowerment is a complex concept with many other components of interest to mediation advocates, transformationalists, and other scholars. How would we expect that participation in community mediation would affect the other social and political aspects of personal empowerment?

Social Empowerment. As Figure 4.1 shows, the third empowerment component consists of knowledge and skills. "Knowledge" includes basic literacy, self-knowledge, and specialized knowledge relevant to social and political participation, such as knowledge about conflict dynamics and conflict management processes. "Skills" include problem solving, planning, brainstorming, and listening. I have characterized these kinds of skills and knowledge as "social empowerment" because when combined with the psychological empowerment attitudes of self-esteem and self-efficacy, these capabilities enable an individual to participate efficaciously in social activities.

The empirical analysis might have focused on social empowerment instead of psychological attitudes. It didn't for two reasons. First, most of the other empirical studies of community participation and empowerment have been conducted by community psychologists, and they have focused on psychological empowerment. I wanted to use similar measures in order to facilitate comparison across studies and build some cumulative knowledge about community participation and personal empowerment. Second, instruments are readily available that measure self-esteem and self-efficacy and that have been tested in community participation studies.

If instead of, or in addition to attitudinal measures, the acquisition of knowledge and skills were used as a measure of personal empowerment, would mediators be considered to be empowered by training, or by mediation and leadership activities? The primary purpose of training is to teach the mediation process and skills. Mediation training consists of fifty to sixty hours of intensive instruction in specialized knowledge about conflict dynamics and the mediation process. In addition, trainees are given opportunities to learn a variety of mediation skills, including establishing rapport, asking specialized questions to elicit different kinds of information, specialized listening skills, and agreement writing. Many mediators also gain self-knowledge about their own biases and preferences, what they have a talent for, or other aspects of self-knowledge as a result of their mediation experience. Therefore, it is clear that trainees are strongly "socially" empowered in terms of acquiring new knowledge and skills that are useful in mediation and other personal and professional interactions.

Experience in mediating conflicts extends and refines the mediator's knowledge and skills beyond what is learned in training. In some ways the acquisition of knowledge and skills for mediation is similar to pilot flight training. At first, pilot trainees study lessons in a flight manual and later may log time in a flight simulator on the ground. As a result they acquire specialized knowledge about aerodynamics and develop and practice basic flight skills. But they are not yet full-fledged pilots. Only after they have logged a certain number of hours in the air with an instructor and then later in solo flight do they refine the knowledge and skills needed to be considered an experienced pilot. In the same way, a mediator continues to develop valuable knowledge about conflict dynamics and the mediation process while refining mediation skills for some time after mediation training by first co-mediating and then solo mediating various kinds of disputes. Therefore, mediating increases social empowerment in that it increases the mediator's knowledge about conflict behavior, and refines and enhances conflict-resolution skills for many years after mediation training has been completed.

The leaders must also learn about planning, fund-raising, budgeting, group decision making, and other kinds of specialized knowledge and governance skills relevant to their roles as organizational leaders. Therefore, as a consequence of acquiring new knowledge and valuable leadership skills in addition to the knowledge and skills required for the mediation role, the leaders also gain increased "social" empowerment.

In short, if knowledge and skills are used as the measures of personal "social" empowerment, those individuals who experience mediation training will increase their levels of "social" empowerment in addition to increasing psychological empowerment. If after completing mediation training they continue to participate in community mediation, they will undoubtedly continue to increase and refine their knowledge and skills, further increasing their "social" empowerment. Finally, those who become organizational leaders will acquire even more and different kinds of specialized knowledge and skills about organizational governance, and will again further increase their level of "social" empowerment.

Political Empowerment. What about the other capability component called political awareness? This component includes four aspects of specialized knowledge relevant to political effectiveness, such as understanding what is, and what will be (i.e., political analysis and prediction), what should be (i.e., political vision), and how to get there from here (i.e., political planning and strategy). Political awareness, in combination with self-esteem, self-efficacy, and knowledge and skills, enables an individual to participate effectively in political activities and therefore constitutes "political" empowerment. Does mediation participation enhance the mediator's "political" empowerment in any way? It might be argued that some aspects of mediation ideology are political in that it offers a critique of the formal legal system and suggests that it is preferable to resolve conflict whenever possible at the informal community level using citizen volunteers. This anti-court, anti-lawyer ideology is communicated in the mediation training of many community mediation centers, and the critique is known, if not always accepted, by most mediators and leaders in community mediation centers. To the extent that this critique provides an analysis of a part of the political system, it can be said to enhance political awareness. It focuses attention on the limitations of the existing system and suggests that community mediation should be encouraged as a supplement to, or perhaps in some cases as an alternative to, the formal legal system.

It is also possible that some of the most perceptive mediators and leaders could, as a result of their experience with various kinds of social conflict, begin to detect underlying patterns of conflict causation, or become curious enough to do research on the roots of social conflict. But most community mediation programs do not directly or consciously attempt to educate volunteer mediators about the possible structural causes of the conflicts they deal with. Conflicts are handled on a case-by-case basis. Disputants bring their personal conflicts with family, neighbors, landlords, and others to the mediation center to be resolved. They do not come seeking a political education, and most mediators make no attempt to raise their political consciousness or to educate them about the possible structural causes of their conflicts.

A few of the community mediation programs such as the San Francisco Community Boards (SFCB) suggest that mediation can expose the root causes of social conflict and that conflict can provide an opportunity for political education, community building, and social transformation. Therefore, the SFCB mediation panel was comprised of three to five community members, and the mediation hearings were supposedly open to the public so that anyone in the neighborhood could attend them and learn more about the underlying causes of community conflict.

But a recently published critical study of the SFCB contends that the mediation hearings were rarely attended by anyone not directly involved in the conflict, and there was no real attempt to use conflicts as an opportunity to analyze root causes of conflict or to provide a political education about the need for social transformation. Indeed, the study contends that conflicts were de-politicized. The disputants were encouraged to express their feelings to each other, to resolve their conflict, and to restore harmony to the community. This "harmony model" discouraged political analysis and focused on personal conflict and the need to get along with one's neighbors and not on the need for social transformation (see Merry and Milner 1993). This study of SFCB, which has long been regarded as the exemplar of the social transformation project, suggests that even "grass-roots" community mediation programs do little to directly enhance the political empowerment of disputants or mediators. In short, if mediators are politically empowered as a result of the training, mediation, or leadership activities, the effect is unintended and incidental to other aspects of personal empowerment.

Social and Political Participation. What about the next two components of empowerment—social and political participation? Community mediation is considered to be a form of social participation that may impact other types of social and political participation. On one hand, as a result of mediation participation, volunteer mediators may increase their levels of self-esteem, self-efficacy, and knowledge and skills and therefore be willing and able to become involved in other kinds of social and political activities. These activities may in turn further enhance personal empowerment and contribute to political transformation. Conversely, volunteer mediators may become so immersed in mediation activities that they lose interest or lack the time for other types of social and political participation. To study the relationship between mediation participation and other types of social and political participation, it would be necessary to survey mediators about their other social and political activities before and after becoming mediators.

Empowerment Outcomes. Finally, what about the other empowerment outcomes? How might rights, resources, or responsibilities be affected by mediation participation? First, using mediation involves taking personal responsibility for conflict for both the disputants and the mediators (see Shonholtz 1993a). The mediators' experiences may increase their capabilities and willingness to take responsibility or control in other areas of life, in personal relationships, at work, in the community, or as active citizens in a democracy. Second, increases in personal empowerment resulting from mediation participation may enable individuals to struggle to maintain and enhance their rights as citizens.

Resources include both material and nonmaterial resources that meet people's needs. Access to both kinds of resources could be enhanced through mediation participation. Material resources may be enhanced as a result of contacts made, or a personal network developed as a result of participation in community mediation. Skills developed through mediation may increase career opportunities and financial income. Nonmaterial resources such as psychological and social support can result from new friendships, increased social standing, and acceptance in the community of mediators. In the SFCB study discussed earlier (DuBow and McEwen 1993), the volunteer mediators mentioned that their acceptance as members of the SFCB mediation community was one of the most important and valuable benefits of their mediation participation.

In summary, based on the results of the empirical analysis, as well as the survey analysis of mediators and the participant observation of mediation training, mediating, and governance, it must be concluded that mediation participation *does* empower the mediators in several important ways. In this study, psychological empowerment was strongly enhanced by the mediation training experience. Mediation and leadership experience may also positively affect psychological empowerment, although not as strongly or extensively as the training effect. The knowledge and skills component of "social" empowerment was not included in the empirical analysis, but it is clearly enhanced by mediation training in which increasing knowledge and skills relevant to mediation are the primary training objectives. Mediating disputes and leading the organization also result in the additional development and enhancement of each participant's knowledge and skills. Finally, political empowerment is only indirectly impacted, and it is probably not increased to any great extent by mediation participation even in those community mediation programs that espouse an ideology of social transformation.

Other Research. Additional recommendations for future research are suggested by insights developed as a result of this research. First, this study could be extended by doing follow-up research on the HNJC mediators to fill in research gaps and to clarify the present findings. In-depth interviews with mediators from each group and program staff could be conducted to find out more about their perceptions of personal empowerment. Second, a natural follow-up would be a comparison study of mediation disputants to determine if they too are empowered by their participation in the mediation process as claimed by mediation ideology. If disputants are empowered, how is their empowerment similar to or different from the empowerment of mediators? Third, a study of the impact of community mediation programs on community empowerment might use mediator interviews on the transfer of empowerment skills to other settings and groups in the community. Additional data on community empowerment might be collected from the mediators' families, social networks, and workplaces.

Fourth, it would be useful to look at a wide variety of mediation programs and other types of settings where empowerment may occur. Since mediation training had the most impact on individual empowerment it could provide the research focus in comparing different mediation programs. Training programs in nonmediation organizations as well, would be an interesting unit of analysis to determine the specific aspects and techniques of training that are effective for maximizing personal empowerment.

Fifth, higher levels of personal empowerment, or different types of empowerment, might develop in settings that encourage widespread participation in decision making and provide a variety of flexible roles for participants that enable personal control, growth, and learning. For example, the two related factors of organizational culture and organizational leadership may affect the prospects for personal empowerment. Democratic governance encourages widespread participation in decision making and would be more empowering than an autocratic management style. Similarly, transactional leadership focuses on effective, routine management of the organization, whereas transforming leadership (see Burns 1978 and Couto 1993) focuses on empowering followers. Most community mediation programs use a transactional leadership style that would result in less empowerment for citizen volunteers.

It is clear that research on mediation and empowerment is still in the early stages. This book fills a research gap, and poses some questions that have not been widely explored by other researchers who tend to focus on the mediation process, techniques, strategies, and effectiveness (see Wall and Lynn 1993). The primary concern in this study is with mediation as an *empowerment process*, rather than as a *conflict resolution process*. Instead of looking at how mediators *affect* the mediation process, I have focused on how mediators are affected *by* the mediation process, and how they may have been affected by mediator training and organizational leadership. This study also considers how mediators may be affected by mediation ideology, with its central theme of empowerment, and it responds to Tomasic's (1982) challenge for further empirical study of mediation's ideological claims. The emphasis here is not on the legal implications, but rather on the possible broader social and political impacts of community mediation.

Mediation Praxis and Policy

What are the implications of this research for community mediation advocates and practitioners? This study strongly suggests that mediation training increases personal empowerment for citizen volunteer mediators. But, is the empowerment of mediators generally viewed as a desirable outcome? If mediator empowerment is considered to be desirable, how can it be enhanced through changes in training, mediation practice, organizational culture, and leadership?

As discussed earlier, most community mediation programs emphasize a service delivery mission, and the empowerment of participants or the community is given far less importance. In fact, attempts to empower the mediation participants and the community may be widely perceived as conflicting with the program's service delivery goals, such as providing access to dispute resolution services to the largest number of clients and achieving the highest percentage of agreements in a cost-effective manner. Mediating in ways that would be maximally empowering for disputants and mediators may be more time consuming than moving expediently through the process, less effective than focusing on getting agreements signed, as well as more costly. If a community mediation program is evaluated and funded by government or foundations largely on the basis of the numbers of clients and the number of successful agreements concluded, then a concern for empowerment could distract from those objectives and thus be counter-productive for the continued funding or even survival of the program.

On the other hand, the empowerment of mediators may actually facilitate achieving service objectives if empowerment is shown to be a positive factor that contributes to mediator effectiveness, increases mediation quality assurance, and enhances mediator recruitment and retention. While no research has been done on these questions, it could be argued that highly empowered mediators would be better mediators given the correspondingly higher levels of confidence and competence that comes with increased personal empowerment.

If mediation programs could provide some evidence that volunteer mediators were empowered by doing mediation service for the community, mediator recruitment might be enhanced and turnover might be lowered, thereby providing substantial benefits to the community mediation program. First, the prospects for, and possibilities of, empowerment would be enhanced by making empowerment a conscious goal and mission of community mediation programs. Second, they would be further enhanced by clarifying the meaning of empowerment, by purposely planning for it, designing for it, and evaluating for it.

Policy-makers and funders concerned with ascertaining the costs and benefits of community mediation for individuals, the community, and society might ask: What are the social and political implications of mediator empowerment for social change or social control?

THE FUTURE OF COMMUNITY MEDIATION

What is the probable future of the community mediation movement, and what are the implications for personal empowerment and political transformation? As discussed earlier there are at least three different models of community mediation: the court adjunct model, the social service agency model, and the grass roots community model. In addition, three different ideological projects have been distinguished in the mediation movement: the service delivery, the human growth or personal empowerment, and the social transformation project (see Harrington and Merry 1988).

Even though the community mediation movement in America is only about twenty years old, there has long been an ongoing debate primarily between the "reform" groups and the "transformational or communitarian" groups about the future of community mediation and which model and ideological projects should or will prevail. In general, the "reformers" favor the court adjunct and social service agency mediation models, and the service delivery and sometimes human growth projects. The "transformationalists" favor the grass-roots community mediation model, and the social transformation and personal empowerment projects.

This debate is complex, and some individuals attempt to bridge both camps, but in broad terms it suggests two very different directions for the future development of mediation that have wide-ranging implications for the future of the formal legal system and transformational politics. On one hand, the reform group, which consists of many of the lawyers and other dispute resolution professionals associated with mediation, believes that the primary mission of community mediation should be the provision of high-quality dispute resolution services that supplement the formal court services, relieve court congestion, and provide dispute resolution tools that are appropriate for disputes that should not be handled by the courts. This group argues that as mediation grows and matures there must be more emphasis given to the quality of service that is provided and that the courts and other funders of community mediation programs have a right and a responsibility to monitor mediation services and provide accountability to the public and users of mediation services.

They argue that in order to ensure the quality and uniformity of mediation services it is necessary to develop and apply professional standards for mediation practice. For example, John Burton and Frank Dukes have argued that, if the field of conflict resolution is to progress and succeed, it is time to move beyond the limited training and minimum qualifications and pragmatism, which "enables unlicensed 'skills' to be practiced with impunity" and to develop and apply professional standards. They contend that while pragmatism is "a natural and inevitable phase in the development of practice" it should be viewed as "a temporary expedient." They warn of the danger that pragmatism can be self-perpetuating, and once established it can move "from being defined as uninformed 'meddling' . . . to being defined as positive 'science' " (Burton and Dukes 1990, 19).

This debate over the need to develop standards and qualifications for mediators and whether or not to certify mediators has been carried on at every professional meeting for more than a decade (see Gentry 1994). Proponents of certification argue that other legal and social service professionals, such as lawyers, social workers, and marriage and family therapists are licensed or certified and mediators should be also. They insist that this is especially true of those conducting divorce mediation because of its complexity and potentially devastating financial and psychological impact on the adults and children involved.

Consequently, this reform group generally favors greater institutionalization, professionalization, and bureaucratization of community mediators. The use of amateur volunteer citizen mediators would be replaced in complex cases and those cases involving paying clients, by lawyers and professional mediators who are well paid for their services, or by highly trained "professionalized" volunteers. The reform group generally favors the court adjunct mediation model or community mediation programs that are closely tied to the courts and dependent on the courts for client referrals and major funding. This group primarily supports the service delivery project and in some cases also favors the human growth project or at least uses the ideological rhetoric of personal empowerment as a symbolic resource (see Harrington and Merry 1988). The social transformational ideological project is not on the mediation agenda for this group. They are either unconvinced of the need for social transformation or have a strong vested interest in status quo maintenance.

Therefore, there is a clear conflict between those who favor the institutionalization and professionalization of mediation and the second group composed mostly of community grass roots activists and other transformationalists. This group generally favors the ideological projects of social transformation and personal empowerment. They support the development of "pure" community mediation models, such as the San Francisco Community Boards as a community-based and community-controlled form of "popular justice" independent of the formal legal system. They are suspicious of the motives of those they believe are attempting to "capture," "colonize," or "co-opt" community mediation. The transformationalists argue that we must resist the efforts of the formal court system to dominate and subvert "the processes of informal justice," the efforts of lawyers and other professionals to profit from community mediation, and the efforts of the power elite who seek to maintain the oppressive systems and institutions that are viewed as "root causes" of much of the societal conflict and violence.

In this struggle for control of the American community mediation movement and the hearts and minds of mediators, which group will prevail. What are the likely implications of the probable and possible future of community mediation? In order to suggest the probable future of the American community mediation movement, I will consider a number of historical and recent developments. First, I will consider the developmental pattern of other historical and contemporary social movements. Next, I will look at the development of community mediation, or popular justice, and its relationship to the formal legal system in other countries and cultures. Third, I will discuss the apparent empirical trends in the development of American community mediation and the views of theorists who have observed and studied the mediation movement from its beginning in the 1970s.

Finally, I will discuss the findings of a recently published case study of the San Francisco Community Boards. For this discussion, I will draw extensively from two pivotal attempts to assess the probable future of community mediation. The first is an article by Theodore Becker (1986) entitled "Conflict and paradox in the new American mediation movement." The second is a book edited by Sally E. Merry and Neal Milner (1993) called *The possibility of popular justice*, which attempts to assess the future of community mediation almost ten years after Becker's analysis of the struggle between the forces of "status quo and social transformation." Both Becker and Merry and Milner focus on the San Francisco Community Boards (SFCB) as the pre-eminent model for the transformational community mediation movement. Becker eloquently articulates the widespread image of the SFCB during the 1980s, what it stood for, and how it operated. Merry and Milner, with the advantage of ten years of hindsight and extensive data from a major evaluation of the SFCB, provide a very different assessment of what the SFCB was about in the early years and what it represents today.

But first I will briefly discuss the development patterns of other social movements and their struggle to survive and resist co-optation by powerful forces.

Social Movements

Are the patterns of development observed in studies of other kinds of social movements relevant for understanding the probable future of the community mediation movement? I would suggest that sociological research on social movement organizations (Weber 1946; Michels 1962) provides insights about what might be expected to happen to the American community mediation movement. Social movement organizations normally evolve through several developmental stages. In their early stages of development social movements begin as informal loose-knit groups concerned with specific issues or problems such as consumer rights or nuclear energy. As a new social movement begins to develop a stable base in society it usually becomes more bureaucratic and develops more conservative goals as a means of maintaining itself and gaining financial support from government and mainstream funders. In order to survive

and grow, these developing organizations generally abandon their early oppo-
sitional stance on issues that might alienate institutional funders so that they
can obtain resources to sustain the organization. While this process may not be
inevitable, it is usually difficult to maintain the original ideological vision that
inspires the emergence of most social movements.

In *The politics of transformation*, Betty H. Zisk (1992) studied a spectrum
of local peace and environmental activists and found similar patterns. She
compared "transformational" groups that work from the grass roots level up
and endeavor to make basic changes "in the way we conduct our politics, our
economics and our social relations," with "incremental" groups who tend to
"work for step-by-step change within the existing structure" (1992, 5). When
Zisk compared the success of the two types of groups (measured by goal
achievement, membership growth, favorable media coverage, and optimistic
perceptions of group success), she consistently found that the transformational groups fared poorly in comparison with their incrementalist counter-
parts. In other words, those who work within the system rather than trying
to resist will tend to survive and thrive. Thus, studies of the developmental
patterns of other social movement organizations suggest that the prospects
for the "reformist" agenda for community mediation are strongly favored
over the "transformationalist" vision of the future.

Trends in Community Mediation

What patterns of development have been observed when informal conflict
resolution movements have been studied in other cultures or historical contexts?
What is their relevance for understanding the future of the American mediation
movement? After a brief look at what has happened to popular justice movements in other countries and cultures I will consider the emerging trends in
American mediation.

Forms of mediation or popular justice have been used for hundreds of years
in Western cultures, including Europe and the United States (see Auerbach
1983), as well as non-Western cultures in Africa, Asia, and Oceania. How
successful have these movements been? Some interesting conclusions have
been drawn by Sally Engle Merry, an anthropologist and leading theorist on the
American mediation movement. In a recent survey of the conditions under
which popular justice flourished or languished in other cultures, Merry con-
cludes, "Popular justice has a basic temporality, a historically formed and
changing quality. In this respect, it differs from the formal legal system, which
typically has far greater continuity and stability. . . . Popular justice established
in opposition to the state tends to die out or be colonized by state law, while
popular justice established by the state itself gradually becomes formalized and
incorporated into state law." (Merry 1993, 31–32).

Is this tendency observed in other times and cultures for popular justice to die out, to be colonized by state law, or incorporated into state law to be the inevitable fate of community mediation in America? Jerold S. Auerbach (1983) answers this question affirmatively in his widely read book *Justice without law* (1983). His conclusion is based on a historical survey of informal justice in America beginning in the Colonial period and progressing to the present day. According to Auerbach, arbitration and mediation were the preferred alternatives to the formal legal system among the Quakers in Philadelphia, the Chinese in San Francisco, the Scandinavians in Minnesota, Jews in Manhattan, and other immigrant ethnic groups. Businessmen also sought to elude lawyers and the courts by using informal modes of dispute settlement. While informal approaches were at times widely practiced, Auerbach's analysis shows that they were continually absorbed by the formal legal system usually through the introduction of standards, formal procedures, and the participation of lawyers and judges in these processes.

In analyzing this struggle over the future of mediation, Theodore Becker concluded nearly a decade ago that "for the time being, the American conflict resolution movement has been substantially overwhelmed by the force and forces of the legal system, professionalization, bureaucracy, and interest-group politics." As a theorist and practitioner interested in mediation's potential for "people empowerment" and "as an instrument for socio-political transformation," Becker was disappointed with the trends he perceived (Becker 1986, 110).

An analysis of more recent mediation movement trends support Becker's earlier observations. As the American community mediation movement grows and expands into new areas of dispute resolution, it is moving increasingly in the direction of greater institutionalization and professionalization. Mediation services are evolving from generic conflict resolution processes, used to deal with fairly simple neighborhood disputes and small claims cases, to increasingly more sophisticated models designed for specific types of conflict, such as complex divorce and child custody cases, condominium disputes, public policy disputes over environmental and other complex issues, and international commercial mediation. These specializations in the field of mediation require highly trained mediators with increasingly specialized knowledge and sophisticated negotiating skills and thus seemingly favor the increasing use of professional mediators and lawyers. Alternatively, some community mediation centers attempt to "professionalize volunteer mediators" by increasing their training requirements and instituting monitoring systems for ensuring greater quality assurance and accountability.

This increasing emphasis on developing more sophisticated conflict resolution techniques, as well as the vital importance of getting written agreements that are a common yardstick used for measuring the success of mediation, militates against the concern for increasing individual empowerment or community empowerment as important values for community mediation programs (see Lowry 1993, 117).

The strong emphasis given to service delivery emerges clearly in the Dispute Resolution Forum (December 1988) interviews with directors of six of the largest mediation centers in the United States, including the director of the HNJC. When asked to talk about their program successes, they mentioned factors such as the growing caseloads, the number of agreements concluded, the number of clients served, the number of volunteer mediators who were trained, their ability to maintain or increase funding levels, and their close relationships with the state and local formal courts system. Sufficient funding is always a problem for community mediation agencies, even for the larger mediation programs. Most of the large funders like the courts and private foundations, are primarily concerned with the number of cases processed and agreements reached. Program evaluations designed to measure mediation program success have also tended to emphasize service delivery variables and client satisfaction. Data on the number of cases processed and agreements concluded, as well as assessments of client satisfaction, are relatively easy to collect and to understand.

The "reform" movement has strong support from legal, academic, and political institutions such as the American Arbitration Association, Harvard Law School, and the George Mason University Postgraduate Program in Conflict Management (see Sandole 1985). Powerful and highly visible public figures like former Chief Justice Warren Burger and former Attorney General Griffin Bell were early advocates of mediation and other judicial reforms. Professional mediation organizations such as the Society of Professionals in Dispute Resolution (SPIDR) and the National Institute for Dispute Resolution (NIDR) provide forums and sponsor meetings to explore the development of professional standards and procedures for mediator certification (see Gentry 1994). These individuals and organizations provide legitimacy, funding, clients, and other resources to the reform movement in mediation. In short, all of the emerging trends appear to support the reformist agenda for increasing the certification and professionalization of mediation.

The San Francisco Community Boards—A Model of Transformational Mediation? In contrast, the transformational movement has had greater difficulty in attracting funding and clients, and according to Becker has therefore been "confined to a scattered few 'community based' or 'home grown' programs. The major success story of a 'community' project is the Community Boards Program of San Francisco" (Becker 1986, 119). As discussed earlier, the SFCB has long been regarded as the exemplar of the "transformationalist" model of mediation. This unique program, with the leadership of its charismatic Director Raymond Shonholtz, developed and promulgated the social transformational ideology project. It resisted the control of the formal legal system. It sought clients by community outreach, not by referral from the courts, which is the major client source for most other community mediation programs. The SFCB sought funding from private foundations and conflict resolution training fees to avoid dependency on court funding and thereby resist court control. For these reasons, the SFCB has been held up as a model of how transformational community mediation could and should be done.

The SFCB appears to be a vehicle for personal empowerment, community building, social transformation, and a viable example of a truly empowered organization and citizen democracy in action. As Becker points out in discussing the SFCB, "The key to a successful, community-style mediation program, one that is truly non-institutional, non-hierarchical, non-professional, and decidedly democratic in theory and practice, is to *educate* the disputants, staff, and ordinary citizens who wish to learn the art and science of peacemaking and democratic organization. Shonholtz sees education as a major 'bridge' and catalyst in developing the 'democratic dimension' of community" (Becker 1986, 120).

Based on Shonholtz's numerous ideological writings and descriptions of SFCB, an image was created and widely believed that this was a unique transformational program with a well-developed philosophy and ideology, which was reflected consistently in all aspects of the organizational culture, leadership style, program operation, public education, public discourse, and the way in which the mediation process was organized and practiced. For example, it was believed that SFCB's "uniqueness stems from its adherence to the theory that mediation training and the practice of mediation is a way to help develop a socio-political community awareness." Furthermore, it was believed that the SFCB "actively promotes and practices the values and benefits of decentralized, democratic organizational processes in its work." Unlike most other community mediation programs the "idea is not to process as many cases as possible, but to return the power of conflict resolution to individual citizens in a community setting" (Becker 1986, 119).

Public education about conflict, and the "root causes" of conflict, as well as skill building, community building, democratic self-governance, and broad and full citizen participation in "civic activity" were believed to be the core mission of the SFCB. It was generally believed that these values were reflected in practice. In contrast to many other community mediation centers with ties to the courts that emphasized the number of clients served and getting agreements signed, it was believed that SFCB focused on empowerment and "consciousness raising" through direct efforts to educate disputants and the community in order to enable social transformation. According to Becker (1986), a major ingredient of SFCB mediation practice "is to teach the disputants that in many circumstances there are external factors directly responsible for their predicament. These may be economic, social, political, or a combination of all three. Community mediation, properly practiced, can help alert the disputants to the role these factors play in creating the problems. The program can also assist the parties in organizing themselves so as to combat their mutual enemies instead of one another" (1986, 120).

It was widely believed that this public education function of the SFCB was exemplified by and facilitated by its unique and innovative mediation procedures. SFCB used large mediator panels of five mediators, who reflected the ethnicity of the disputants wherever possible (the norm in other mediation centers is one or two mediators). These mediation sessions were supposedly open to the public in order to educate the community about conflict causes and patterns (most programs have closed, private sessions).

This idealized image of the SFCB as a kind of "Camelot of transformational community mediation" was widely held in the mediation community by mediation theorists, practitioners, and foundation funders, and even believed in the "reformist" mediation camps. This captivating image and the entrepreneurial energy of Director Shonholtz largely explain SFCB's many successes. It grew rapidly, opening six mediation centers in the San Francisco area. It trained thousands of mediators in San Francisco and across the nation, attracted millions of dollars in funding primarily from large private foundations like Ford and Hewlett, and it was the model for many other "grass-roots" transformational mediation programs. As the SFCB's fame spread around the nation and around the world, many mediation centers adopted the rhetoric of empowerment and social transformation as a symbolic resource even when they did not adopt SFCB mediation practices or attempt to resist close linkages to the courts for referrals and funding as did the SFCB.

In short, SFCB has for nearly twenty years been the "shining beacon" of transformational community mediation and the primary representative of the personal empowerment and social transformational ideological projects identified by Harrington and Merry (1988). However, as Becker astutely observed nearly ten years ago, "There is sparse data to prove any assertion concerning the success of the unique Community Board program. Considering the difficulties in getting and processing cases at the community level, the time span necessary to accomplish such lofty social and political goals (developing community awareness and educating the public in democratic organizational principles), and the difficulty of rigorously measuring this kind of success empirically, such data will be difficult to derive" (Becker 1986, 121).

Such data is now available from a recently published major evaluation on the SFCB, which begins to distinguish "the rhetoric from the reality" of the SFCB. A major two-year program evaluation of the SFCB was begun in 1980 funded by the Hewlett Foundation and the Ford Foundation. Given the large amounts of funding that had been given to the SFCB and its growing fame, there was considerable interest in determining whether the program was accomplishing the lofty goals it espoused. The major evaluation research was conducted between 1981 and 1983 when SFCB was enjoying great financial success and its fame was generating nationwide interest in community mediation. The project director was Fredric L. DuBow. DuBow and several researchers developed a detailed history and description of the program's operation. The researchers collected and analyzed data on caseloads, types of cases, and characteristics of the volunteers, and conducted ethnographic research on the SFCB mediation process. Data were derived from program case records; surveys of interviews with volunteer mediators, program staff, disputants, and community members; and observation of mediation hearings and other program activities. The evaluation research was finally finished in 1985, but unfortunately the research director, DuBow, died before the final written report was completed.

In about 1989, Sally Engle Merry, Neal Milner, and other mediation theorists recovered the SFCB evaluation data and used it as the basis for a case study to assess *The possibility of popular justice* (Merry and Milner, 1993). DuBow's evaluation of SFCB and the theoretical analysis provided by Merry, Milner, and the other theorists regarding the possibility of popular justice, speaks directly to the future of community mediation and the concerns of reformers and transformationalists.

To begin with, these theorists acknowledge SFCB's uniqueness and the major contributions made to the community mediation movement by this bold experiment in popular justice. As Merry and Milner point out, the SFCB's ideological "vision captured the attention of idealistic program developers, foundations, government policy makers, and countless eager volunteers. It has inspired numerous programs and training models. SFCB continues to stand for a grass-roots vision of mediation when other wings of the field are becoming more technocratic, more closely annexed to the courts" (1993, 11; see also DuBow and McEwen 1993; Thomson and DuBow 1993). However, despite SFCB's image and important contributions, Merry and Milner and associates also contend that in many important ways the practice and performance of SFCB has not been consistent with its own vision, image, and rhetoric and that in recent years, the early mission and program focus have shifted significantly.

In brief, the most important findings of this study indicate that there are a number of substantial contradictions and misunderstandings about SFCB. First, for example, they point out that while SFCB was rhetorically committed to the democratic empowerment of citizens and widespread participation by volunteers in internal governance, the SFCB had significant organizational conflicts about the director's autocratic leadership style. Major policy decisions were made by the Director, not by a democratic process (Thomson and DuBow 1993, 120). Second, the SFCB mediation hearings were not really used as forums to politically educate the disputants and the community. Disputants were not educated about the root causes of conflict. Third, the focus of the SFCB mediation process was on narrowing the dispute to deal with communication problems and the disputants personal feelings about the conflict. Fourth, the emphasis of the mediation process was on restoring "harmony" to the neighborhood, instead of mobilizing the neighborhood to change inequitable power relations that generated community conflict and violence.

In other words, according to Merry and Milner (1993), in SFCB mediation hearings, disputes were narrowed and privatized instead of being broadened and politicized to reveal the economic, social, and political structural roots of community conflict. Based on her research and lengthy observations of SFCB hearings, Judy H. Rothschild concluded that "the SFCB approaches conflict from an apolitical perspective: . . . a political perspective about social change and social control is absent, if not antithetical to the normative framework that informs the SFCB approach to conflict resolution" (1993, 320).

Similarly, Laura Nader (1993) agrees that SFCB de-emphasizes the possible linkages between individual disputes and their larger political context. She argues that the SFCB "ideology of harmony" actually suppresses conflict and discourages the open expression of rights or interests under the guise of therapeutic consciousness and a commitment to community harmony. Nader contends that the SFCB should be recognized "as part of a broader strategy of minimizing conflict and maximizing order by managing interpersonal conflicts—rather than root causes—in specific locales." Nader argues that "An opposing strategy requires, in addition to dealing with conflict, an examination of root causes of social problems and an address of those causes as central to the strategy of preventing social conflict" (1993, 435).

Barbara Yngvesson suggests that SFCB's discourse on building community blurs the distinction between two kinds of community—the "internal community," which consists of SFCB volunteer mediators and staff, and the "external community," which consists of the disputants and other local neighborhood residents. She argues that there is a clear conflict between these two communities, and suggests "that far from creating communities in which local people are empowered, the SFCB program empowers mediators at the expense of the parties to conflict, producing forms of community that *exclude* the parties to conflict, while generating relationships of control that expand (rather than undermine) diffuse mechanisms of power in the modern state" (1993, 381).

By studying the history of SFCB and interviewing early participants, Douglas R. Thomson and Fredric L. DuBow identified different stages of organizational development beginning in 1976 and ending in 1989. As the SFCB grew in size and evolved ideologically it underwent significant changes in mission, organizational culture, and strategy. In the earliest period, SFCB tended to align itself with the All People's Coalition (APC), a Saul Alinsky-based community organization involved in organizing advocacy and political action. After a brief period of collaboration SFCB shifted away from organizing advocacy to community social service (1993, 174–175). At this juncture, the SFCB rejected confrontation and collective action as possibilities and began to emphasize empowerment and the centrality of training for community building and empowerment. This ideological development evolved through several phases. According to Thomson and DuBow, the "SFCB began by emphasizing democratic governance for the community but shifted to internal democratic governance as a way of modeling community and building capability. When that effort failed, SFCB shifted again to empowerment. Now, however it emphasized microempowerment, which dovetailed with conflict-resolution services and thus brought SFCB full circle" (1993, 184).

However, Thomson and DuBow argue that by 1983 SFCB's empowerment mission was essentially abandoned. "Empowerment has vanished completely from the picture, and governance was subordinated to service" (1993, 193). They explain that many factors caused the organizational shift to service or "the civic work," including the conventional process of institutionalization that most social movement organizations undergo, the need for resources when private foundation funding declined, and the real attraction of doing mediation work for SFCB staff and volunteer mediators. SFCB has now established much closer ties to the formal legal system. It now receives referrals from public agencies, and provides feedback to social-control organizations like the police when disputants referred by the police use SFCB's services.

Thomson and DuBow contend that SFCB's legacy differs significantly from its original vision. They argue that while the original mission and ideological rhetoric generated the enthusiastic community support and foundation funding that enabled the early successes, they were a trap in that SFCB promised more than they could deliver. Thomson and DuBow conclude somewhat disappointedly:

If we must assess what SFCB was and has meant, the conclusion lacks splendor. SFCB was a symbol of hope, an innocuous effort in itself, expensive but promising and inspiring. Yet, it did not transform San Francisco or even any of its neighborhoods, and it did not achieve the success in political empowerment enjoyed by its contemporaries in the new populism. But neither did it do any great harm. . . . Ultimately, then, SFCB was neither colonization nor empowerment; it was deprofessionalized and quasi-indigenous initiative in "civic work" that became institutionalized as a more conventional social-service agency. (1993, 196)

Finally, in a rejoinder chapter in the Merry and Milner volume, the originator and first director of the SFCB, Raymond Shonholtz, responds to his critics and clarifies his view of the ideology and developmental history of SFCB. Shonholtz argues that the central theme of SFCB ideology was "citizen power and the important role of citizens in dispute settlement" (1993, 209). The mediation hearing panels were designed to express "the civic quality of community life" and to present "a model for the exercise of democratic power and responsibility by the disputants themselves" (212). Shonholtz contends that "SFCB staff and volunteers were not primarily about the business of building community" and perhaps even more significantly for transformationalists that "SFCB never took as its mission the direct restructuring of political power, economic relationships, or issues of social conditions (poverty, bad housing, racism, illiteracy, etc.). Nor has SFCB sought to build an internal community through voluntarism and empowerment of individuals" (216). Shonholtz points out that after 1979, SFCB "explicitly moved away from any form of traditional community organizing and adhered to a service organizing model that promoted the community's capacity to hear and resolve its own disputes" (216). At this juncture, SFCB left the larger social dimensions of community conflict and political action to other local advocacy organizations like ACORN (see Harrington 1993).

Based on these comments by Shonholtz and the other mediation theorists who have closely evaluated and studied SFCB, it seems clear that the fame and image of SFCB as the exemplar of the social transformational ideological project in community mediation has been mistaken, misinterpreted, or confused. These theorists suggest that SFCB initially expressed a grandiose mission of social transformation that it could not fulfill, or perhaps never really expected to be able to fulfill, and that this mission has shifted over time to the dual objectives of citizen empowerment and conflict resolution service delivery. Therefore, several of these theorists suggest that SFCB's legacy with regard to the social transformation project is disappointing. They argue that SFCB might have advanced the cause of social transformation and the goals of popular justice by aligning itself with political activists and neo-populist organizations in the San Francisco area, such as ACORN and Citizen Action (see Harrington 1993 and Thomson and DuBow 1993), but SFCB moved away from advocacy to service delivery and the opportunity was lost.

According to Shonholtz, the true mission of SFCB was citizen empowerment, the "civic work" of conflict resolution, and the development of a community capacity for dispute resolution independent of the formal court system. It was not social transformation in the sense of community building, political education about the root causes of conflict, or advocating structural transformation. Regardless of which interpretation is correct, it seems clear that the widely held view of SFCB as a true model of the social transformational project in community mediation must be re-assessed.

So, at this juncture, what appears to be the probable future of community mediation and the implications for personal and political empowerment? Based on this analysis of other historical and contemporary social movements, the strong and perhaps inevitable tendency toward institutionalism, professionalization, and co-optation by the political system seems clear. This tendency toward co-optation is apparent whether we look at alternative dispute resolution movements in other cultures or in American history. Finally, an examination of the recent successes of the reformist movement in community mediation on the one hand and the recent evaluation of the shortcomings of the SFCB, the exemplar for transformationalist community mediation movement on the other hand, all point consistently toward the probable success of the reform movement and the demise or further diminution of the social transformational project.

Transformationalists may be disappointed at this probable future scenario for community mediation and at the apparent loss of hope and promise for community mediation as a vehicle for personal and political transformation. Other community mediation theorists, however, see some positive aspects to the probable success of the reform movement. Sally Engle Merry, for example, argues:

Paradoxically, because of the process of colonization and domestication of more radical forms of popular justice, the potential for social transformation is greater for reformist popular justice operating within the hegemonic liberal legal order than anarchic popular justice pursuing more revolutionary objectives.

Most importantly, however, popular justice introduces a new ideology of conflict resolution based on nonviolence and opposition to the violence of law. Most forms of popular justice . . . share a commitment to consensual amicable resolution of conflicts. Whatever its impact on transforming power relations, popular justice is ideologically powerful in its capacity to imagine the nonviolent ideology of managing conflict. (1993, 62)

It should be remembered that under the reform agenda, personal empowerment of mediators and disputants is still a possible although a less probable ideological project, and that personal empowerment may directly or indirectly support social transformation, as discussed earlier.

Alternative Futures for Community Mediation

Although the most "probable" future for the community mediation movement appears to be the success of the reform agenda over the transformational agenda, the increased growth of the court adjunct model and community social service agencies with close ties to the formal legal system, and therefore the service delivery project over the social transformational project, are there other "possible" futures for community mediation?

One possible future is the loss of interest in, and the declining importance of, community mediation. As Peter Adler suggests, in attempting to discern the future of ADR, "Mediation might also be viewed as nothing more than a modest innovation that has captured temporary attention because of its novelty but that carries no other intrinsic or extrinsic value" (1993, 81–82).

A second possibility is that instead of the future of community mediation being a choice between either the reform agenda or the transformation agenda, we could end up with a both/and, or a balance, emerging between the two conflicting perspectives. A few theorists have not yet given up hope for the transformationalist agenda. Some theorists see the possibilities of the pendulum of alternative dispute resolution swinging back, or a reaction to legal co-optation restoring a balance to the transformationalist agenda (see Hermann 1993). Other theorists see the possibility of an alliance of transformationalist models of community mediation with community advocacy organizations. This alliance would bring together the capacity for community conflict resolution with the capacity for political education and advocacy, and for organizing political action to bring about meaningful structural transformation to eliminate the "deep-rooted" causes of community conflict and social violence. Others speculate on the possibility for a major rebirth of the transformational political cycle based on major social and political forces that will also benefit and support the possibilities for transformational community mediation.

For example, in Becker's article, "Conflict and paradox in the new American mediator movement: Status quo and social transformation," he suggests that while the trends of domination of the American mediation movement by the legal system may appear to be inevitable there is still hope. Becker argues, "Trends . . . are not inexorable. . . . [T]he fact that there is still the semblance of life in . . . community-based transformational mediation means that alterations in near future environments can produce changes in its growth patterns as well. Given a sudden wind, embers can produce forest fires. Indeed, there is sufficient evidence to reveal that recent American history of the twentieth century may illustrate cycles or spirals as well as trends" (Becker 1986, 129). Becker briefly describes a series of fifteen-year cycles beginning with the Progressive Movement, which flourished at the turn of the century and which was followed about fifteen years later by the "Red Scare" of the early 1920s and then successively by liberal and conservative movements, including the New Deal and welfare capitalism, then McCarthyism, followed by the counter-culture movement of the 1960s and the Reagan era of the 1980s. Becker is cautiously optimistic that Reagan conservatism may again be followed by a more progressive or transformational movement. He suggests, "This does not mean that the late 1990's, at the threshold of the Third Millennium, will witness a new anti-establishment movement reaching a new peak. But it may. If a transformation-rooted political wave were cresting then, it would not be un-likely that community mediation programs might be the rage. Such a develop-ment might also cause the legal embrace of mediation to loosen substantially. This possibility is not a prediction" (Becker 1986, 129).

Writing more recently about the future of community mediation and the potential impact of larger political cycles, Peter Adler speculates about thirty-year cycles and also sees the possibilities for a new populist movement, but seems to draw the opposite conclusions to Becker about its desirability and implications for the future of community mediation. He argues that in the process of assessing mediation's future, "we should also ask if mediation . . . would continue to be credible if a new wave of rights-acquisition movements emerges. In fact, such a scenario seems quite plausible. . . . The 1990's are upon us. Scholars . . . have shown that significant economic, political, and social transformation seems to occur in American society in thirty-year cycles. In many ways, the coming decade is likely to echo much of the social turmoil of the 1960's" (Adler 1993, 84).

Unlike Becker, Adler does not appear to believe that new progressive movements would be good for community mediation. "It does not take a great deal of predictive imagination to see the reemergence of rights-oriented thinking by populist and grass-roots movements, to see a resurgence of shrill new demands for substantive justice and political participation. . . . In this context mediation may . . . be viewed as a quaint but archaic remnant of a by gone era" (Adler 1993, 84). So while Becker and Adler both appear to agree on the possibility of a new transformational or populist movement emerging in the 1990s, they have very different views of the kind of impact such a political cycle would have on the future of community mediation.

While Becker and Adler have speculated on what "could" happen with the future of community mediation, other theorists have suggested what "should" happen to achieve a more balanced agenda, to provide more alternative dispute resolution options, more social justice, or more effective conflict resolution mechanisms that would deal with "deeply rooted" social conflict.

Laura Nader suggests both what should and could happen with the future direction of community mediation. She argues, "There should be a backlash in the alternative dispute-resolution movement, for the same reason that there was a backlash on the judicial system: ADR is not relevant to most people's substantive concerns. In addition, it promises what it cannot deliver. The dispute resolution movement is not providing the kind of alternative justice systems that originally motivated the public-interest community's critique" (1993, 448). Nader also believes that it is not too late for community mediation. She contends, "There could be an effort from within the movement to reform the goals, the organization, and the professional spirit that presently governs dispute resolution, one that moves in the direction of prevention. . . . I mean macro prevention, where you find out where the number and seriousness of disputes occur in society in order to look for some kind of structural organizational, or productive means of preventing those disputes" (1993, 448). Nader's view of the need to get at the "root causes" of conflict and the need for structural transformation has many similarities to John Burton's analysis of "deeply rooted" conflict and the need for a "problem-solving" approach to conflict resolution that deals directly with the structural causes of most serious societal conflicts (see Burton 1990a).

Yet another perspective on mediation is set forth in a provocative new book, *The promise of mediation* (Bush and Folger 1994). This book appears to bring together some elements of both the "reformist" and "transformationalist" perspectives on community mediation. Bush and Folger argue that the mediation movement is losing sight of the goal of transformation by focusing on disputants' satisfaction and the settlement of disputes. Their suggested "transformative approach to mediation" emphasizes the primary objectives of achieving both empowerment of the disputants as well as mutual recognition. They argue that neither empowerment alone nor recognition alone is sufficient—they must be achieved together. Therefore, they define "successful" mediation in terms of achieving empowerment and recognition, not in terms of whether or not a settlement is reached.

On the one hand, Bush and Folger resemble the transformationalists with their emphasis on empowerment and social transformation as the main objectives of mediation and their references to the growing importance of the "relational" or "communitarian" movement. On the other hand, they seem to agree with the "reformers' " view that professionalization of mediation along with intensive mediator training is necessary to develop the sophisticated skills essential for an adept and accountable mediator.

If the future of community mediation is to continue to focus on the desirability and possibility of the personal empowerment as well as the social transformation ideological projects and other aspects of the transformational agenda, I would suggest that an important contributing factor would be continued research on empowerment to advance theoretical elaboration and the development of more effective empowerment training, interventions, and settings.

Even as some programs become increasingly institutionalized and focused on service delivery, the ideology of empowerment remains a valuable symbolic resource for the community mediation movement. Empowerment ideology serves a variety of important functions. First, it helps to legitimize and promote the mediation movement to the general public and to potential funders. Empowerment is a concept with strong popular appeal today that is embraced by liberals, conservatives, and moderates. Second, empowerment ideology has a strong appeal to potential citizen volunteers who hope to empower themselves through mediation participation as well as to empower the individuals who seek assistance from the community mediation center. Thus, empowerment rhetoric provides a powerful tool that can be used to recruit and motivate volunteer mediators. Community mediators involved in the programs that stress personal growth and social transformation, say that their belief in the value of mediation for individual and community empowerment is a primary motivation for the core mediators who mediate most often (see Harrington and Merry 1988).

Despite the obvious symbolic value of empowerment, its complexity and the lack of understanding about what empowerment is are barriers to increasing empowerment in community mediation programs. Therefore, research on the empowerment concept would further enhance its value as a program objective for program staff and leaders. While empowerment has clear ideological appeal, it has not been included in program evaluations as a success measure for mediation, in part because of its complexity. If mediation practitioners and policy-makers understood how empowerment benefits individuals involved in the mediation process, and the local community, and how it impacts mediation service delivery, its practical use as a measurable program objective might be encouraged—at least in programs that promote the ideology of individual and community empowerment.

The primary focus of this book is on the development of empowerment theory, and to a large degree on conflict resolution, and community mediation as a setting with potential for citizen empowerment and political transformation. As I have discussed, the potential of community mediation as a vehicle for empowerment and transformation depends on many factors, both internal and external to the movement, and on its future development and direction. But empowerment as a general social theory, as a guide to public policy formulation, and as a paradigm for the Post-Modern Era also has importance to many other settings, and social movements, in addition to community mediation. Now it is time to move beyond community mediation, and to consider the development of empowerment in other social movements, and its pivotal importance to transformational politics. Therefore, the central questions addressed in the final chapter are: What have we learned about empowerment? What more do we need to know about empowerment? And, what is the future of empowerment in other settings and social movements relevant to transformational politics?

8

The Future of Empowerment and Transformational Politics

This final chapter returns to many of the issues and questions considered in chapter 1 about the future of the Post–Cold War or Post-Modern world and its major trends and transformations. It therefore represents a shift from the micro or community level back to the macro level of analysis. Chapter 1 also introduced the new field of Transformational Politics and its concern with conflict resolution and empowerment at all levels. It should be noted that all three phenomena of interest to this project—empowerment, mediation, and Transformational Politics—are inherently multilevel processes or movements. As discussed, empowerment is relevant to individuals, groups, organizations, communities, and larger collectivities. Mediation can be used for conflict resolution at the interpersonal, community, and international levels. Transformationalists debate whether they should focus their analysis and strategies at the individual or system levels. A popular saying among political activists counsels to "Think Globally, and Act Locally."

Indeed, the Post-Modern world is increasingly interdependent and multilevel with growing economic, political, and telecommunication linkages. Tourists, refugee flows, and transnational problems, such as population growth and global pollution, provide other linkages, and require research that links different levels of analysis, and multilevel political strategies.

After introducing these issues in chapter 1, I focused on developing a multilevel theory of empowerment in the context of the American community mediation movement. The conceptual and empirical analysis was grounded in a case study of an urban community mediation center. After discussing the empirical findings and their implication for citizen empowerment and community mediation, I offered an analysis of the "probable" and "possible" futures of the American community mediation movement.

Now the time has come to explore the future of empowerment as a social movement, and as a theory relevant to Transformational Politics, and to discuss what transformationalists might do to help shape a kinder, and more just future.

THE FUTURE OF EMPOWERMENT: THEORY, POLICY, PRAXIS, AND PARADIGM

Possible Futures for Empowerment

There are at least three possible scenarios for the future of empowerment, including its declining attraction as a new age "buzzword," a critical reaction to empowerment theory, or its increasing importance and development as a social theory and a social movement. First, will empowerment become passé? It is possible that the term empowerment has simply become a pop culture buzzword, and like all fads it will lose its popular appeal in a short time. Until recently, the term empowerment was not widely known or used. During the 1960s the concept of empowerment was primarily used by political activists, some educators, and social workers. During the 1970s and 1980s empowerment became even more widely used. In the 1980s the term became a core concept for leading community psychologists, such as Julian Rappaport, who suggested it as a central theory or paradigm for the discipline. Its use spread rapidly through the social science and educational journals and it soon appeared in the business journals as well. In business the primary emphasis is on the value of empowering workers and managers in order to increase productivity and profitability. Politicians on both the left and the political right soon discovered the term empowerment, and have embraced it as a value that is central to both the liberal and the conservative agenda.

By the early 1990s the term empowerment has become familiar to many Americans, and it is now widely used in the popular media. Empowerment has become the "in thing" to do, and being empowered has become the "in thing to be." Empowerment is now in fashion. But fashions come and go. Many of the people who are presently enamored with empowerment will eventually become bored with it and move on to some other term, or trend, that comes into vogue. Most Americans who use the term empowerment in everyday language or in their business brochures have only a vague idea about its meaning. They know that it is positively regarded, "a good thing" to be and do. However, it is possible that in the next few years many people will lose interest in the notion of empowerment and it will be displaced in the popular culture by a new concept.

A second possible scenario is a critical backlash to empowerment as a theory or social movement. Thus far, this term has uniformly positive connotations for theorists, educators, business people, and the American public. A survey of the professional and popular literature on empowerment reveals an almost uncritical acceptance of empowerment as a positive phenomenon with few apparent problems, drawbacks, or undesirable side effects. But most important theories or movements usually have both critics as well as advocates.

For example, the related concept of power has strong negative connotations for many people. Few people will openly acknowledge the desire to acquire power or to wield power over others. Power is often viewed as a necessary evil. The development of the power concept has been difficult and controversial. But because power is such a central concept, especially to political scientists, we have retained it and have continuously labored to refine it, elaborate the theory, and empirically operationalize and test it in a variety of settings and situations. Despite these labors, the concept remains somewhat problematic, and much work remains to be done to understand the varieties and vagaries of power.

As a relatively new concept, empowerment will also require a lot of critical scrutiny and theoretical elaboration before it can become useful for practitioners and policy-makers beyond its symbolic value. In this regard, a few scattered critiques of empowerment have begun to emerge (Clarke and Stewart 1992; Riger 1993). But so far these are friendly critics who support the development of empowerment as a theory, practice, or policy, and they have pointed out some theoretical gaps, inconsistencies, or apparent conflicts that should be addressed. If empowerment theory is to continue to develop, much more of this kind of critical analysis of the concept is needed. Just as power theory has benefited from both proponents and critics, so too will empowerment theory.

Finally, I would contend that the most probable future for empowerment theory as we move into the third millennium is that it will become increasingly central to our social and political concerns about the present world and the future world. I base this assertion on several trends. First, powerlessness is an important problem in the world today, both because of the immediate human suffering involved and also because it creates many social dilemmas with long-term consequences. Second, in this information age, a widespread awareness of the existence and detrimental effects of powerlessness is growing. Third, many of the political leaders, theorists, and populist social movements in America and around the world believe that empowerment is a vital key to solving these human dilemmas. Fourth, we are beginning to make theoretical and practical progress that will enable us to design empowerment systems and interventions more effectively to address social and political problems.

To begin with, the problems of powerlessness, disempowerment, and alienation, in the world today are even more widespread and pervasive than is commonly believed. Unless these problems are recognized, acknowledged, and addressed, they will worsen in the years to come. When we consider the disempowered people of the world, images come to mind of people living in poverty in third world villages, or in first world ghettos, or dying of hunger in Ethiopia, or of violence and hatred in Bosnia or Rwanda. These indeed represent some of the extreme depths of powerlessness and human misery in the world today, however, there are other significant kinds and degrees of powerlessness that create pain and social problems in every society.

Many perceptive observers agree that we are in a period of dramatic turmoil, turbulence, and transformation, and that widespread and pervasive powerlessness is one of the greatest problems we face now and in the foreseeable future. First, many development theorists have poignantly described the powerlessness of traditionally oppressed people in the *third* world (Freire 1970; Kent 1988; Friedmann 1992). Second, social theorists and social workers have amply documented the powerlessness of traditionally oppressed people in the *first* world, including African-Americans (Solomon 1976), Hispanics (Abalos 1993), and women (Gutierrez 1988).

In addition to the powerlessness of the traditionally oppressed people, some theorists argue that most children and adults in American society (and most likely other western societies) are crippled by "surplus powerlessness" that makes them believe they are powerless victims, and they cannot trans-form themselves or society (Lerner 1979). Confirmation of this view comes from recent Harris polls (1989, 1994), which reported a growing sense of powerlessness in America. According to *The Harris poll: Alienation index*, "the near record high of public alienation has not been affected . . . by the first year of the Clinton presidency." Alienation includes feelings of eco-nomic inequity ("the rich get richer and the poor get poorer"), feelings of disdain for "people with power" and "the people running the country," and feelings of powerlessness—being "left out of things" and "not counting very much" (Harris 1994, 2).

This widespread and pervasive sense of personal and political powerlessness is exacerbated by the far-reaching economic, political, and environmental changes that are occurring with greater rapidity in the world today. Futurists and other concerned scholars talk about the "world problematique," the global problems caused by the complex interaction of myriad, seemingly overwhelm-ing problems and challenges occurring at local, national, and international levels, including the population explosion, widespread global environmental pollution, the "greenhouse effect," the widespread rain forest destruction that continues at a frightening pace, the threat of nuclear proliferation and the specter of nuclear winter, and the other potent threats that confront mankind with overwhelming and seemingly intractable dilemmas.

At this time, momentous political changes are sweeping across Eastern Europe, the former Soviet Union, and South Africa. The failure of communism has left a political and economic void in what we called the "second world," and many scholars doubt that the capitalist free market paradigm presents a viable alternative model for most of the formerly communist world, or for many third world countries (Stauffer 1990). There was initially some understandable euphoria about these dramatic political and economic changes and the opportunities they represented for increasingly greater advances in political freedom, human dignity, and economic prosperity. But lacking a clear vision of the future, the path of transformation to a more democratic and equitable world will be both difficult and dangerous.

Because of this pervasive and growing sense of powerlessness in all societies and the global turmoil that further exacerbates it, many of those who seek a general theory or new paradigm for personal and political transformation see great promise in the vision of personal and community empowerment. Empowerment is solidly grounded in positive values, such as self-sufficiency, personal competence, mass political participation, community involvement, social responsibility, human freedom and dignity, and cultural diversity. It has widespread intuitive appeal to both those of the political left and the political right in America. Empowerment is a complex, multilevel concept that has powerful meaning for individuals, groups, organizations, communities, and larger social collectivities. As Julian Rappaport (1987, 142) has eloquently expressed, "Empowerment is a term that cuts across all levels of analysis, expresses our world view, and our commitment to a diverse society. Empowerment suggests a belief in the power of people to be both masters of their own fate and involved in the life of their several communities."

The empowerment ethos is the underlying philosophy of the growing self-help movement that emphasizes the importance of people gaining control over their lives (Rappaport 1984). Empowerment is the central value in the new populism that is beginning to affect grass roots politics (Boyte and Reissman 1986). Empowerment is the core of the ideology that underlies the Green political movement and its vision of democracy (Slaton and Becker 1990).

Given the seemingly overwhelming challenges of the world population explosion and other aspects of the "world problematique," the problem of world powerlessness is likely to be exacerbated in the future. Because these beliefs regarding powerlessness are widely shared among most of the social movements in the Western and non-Western world, empowerment is widely regarded as a key to survival and transformation to a better world. Therefore, the interest in empowerment theory, and in ways of increasing empowerment at all levels of society, is quite likely to grow for the foreseeable future.

Thus we return to the questions posed earlier: What have we learned about empowerment? What do we need to do to enhance empowerment's value to theorists, practitioners, and policy-makers? At this juncture it is useful to consider what we have learned about empowerment from both the conceptual analysis and empirical analysis findings of this study. These insights, questions, and propositions about empowerment warrant further analysis and refinement. I list these insights below in order to summarize some of the findings of this study, to identify gaps in our knowledge, and to suggest the next steps in empowerment research, practice, and policy formulation.

The Empowerment Inventory

I. Perspectives

1. Empowerment is difficult to define. It is a complex concept with many meanings, many components, and many levels of analysis.

2. Empowerment is sometimes defined as the antonym of terms such as disempowerment, powerlessness, alienation, and normlessness.

3. The levels of empowerment include the individual (micro level), the group or organization (mediating level), the community, and larger macro levels and social collectivities.

4. Most of the empirical research and theory development has thus far focused on the individual level, with relatively little attention given to empowered organizations or communities.

5. The individual level of empowerment has at least eight components, including self-esteem, self-efficacy, knowledge and skills, political awareness, social participation, political participation, resources (material and nonmaterial), and rights and responsibilities.

6. The components of individual empowerment are the basis for three types of personal empowerment: psychological empowerment (self-esteem and self-efficacy), social empowerment (psychological empowerment plus development of knowledge and skills relevant to personal competencies and participation in collective behavior), and political empowerment (social empowerment plus political awareness). Political awareness enables an individual to take effective political action and either work within the political system, or to work against the political system for political change.

7. Different individuals may be empowered in different ways and to different degrees. A partially empowered individual would have at least some of these characteristics. For example, a socially or politically apathetic individual with relatively high levels of self-esteem and self-efficacy might be considered "psychologically" empowered. He/she might be mentally healthy and happy and be capable of functioning creatively as an artist or writer but have little interest in social or political participation.

8. There may be different sequences of development in the empowerment process. For example, it might be optimal for some individuals to progress on several different empowerment components simultaneously, such as developing both self-esteem and political awareness concurrently. For other individuals, developing to some "take off" level of "psychological" empowerment might be a necessary precondition for successful social and political participation. Conversely, for others active social and political participation may be an effective strategy for developing self-esteem and self-efficacy as well as social skills.

9. There are different approaches to empowerment. Certain paths may be optimal for different types of people to develop different types of empowerment. For example, introverted or contemplative individuals might achieve some aspects of empowerment autonomously by studying the great books, through meditation, or through writing. These solitary pursuits of human development and creativity are honored in both the Western and non-Western cultures.

10. Another path to empowerment is provided by social participation, which includes many types of activities, groups, and opportunities for personal empowerment, such as community mediation, self-help mutual assistance groups, churches, and social service clubs. Through this kind of participation, individuals can derive a variety of empowerment benefits, including growth in self-esteem and self-efficacy, increased knowledge and skills, and access to material and nonmaterial resources.

11. The political participation path includes many types and levels of political action, including local and state politics and national and international politics. I have differentiated four categories of politics, including "politics as usual" or normal politics, reform politics, transformational politics, and radical revolutionary politics. Participation in different types of politics may empower the same individual somewhat differently by impacting their empowerment attitudes and capabilities as well as the empowerment outcomes. For example, participation in "politics as usual" will likely shape an individual's political awareness somewhat differently than participating in radical revolutionary politics. Also, access to resources, such as wealth, power, or professional career opportunities will vary somewhat with the level and type of political participation. Of course the same individual could be simultaneously involved in different types of political activity.

12. The different autonomous and collective paths to empowerment can also be traveled simultaneously. An individual may be involved, for example, in writing a book on transformational politics, training community mediators, and campaigning for political office as a Green's party candidate.

13. Individual empowerment can be simply defined as the process of gaining mastery over one's self and one's environment in order to fulfill human needs.

14. The empowerment process links individual attitudes (i.e., self-esteem and self-efficacy) and capabilities (i.e., knowledge and skills and political awareness) to enable efficacious individual and collaborative actions (i.e., social and political participation) in order to attain personal and collective sociopolitical goals (i.e., political rights, responsibilities, and resources).

15. The empowerment components can be organized in a theoretical framework that illuminates their interrelationships and suggests various models and research designs that can guide and inform empirical research or praxis.

16. The empowerment concept may be conceived of in different ways. It might be most simply represented as a continuum running from complete disem-

powerment/powerlessness at one end of the scale to complete empowerment at the other end.

17. Or empowerment might be represented by a personal empowerment profile with different levels of individual development on each of the empowerment components. For example, one individual might rank highly on self-esteem and social participation but relatively lower on the other empowerment components. Another person may rank highly on self-efficacy, knowledge and skills, and political awareness, but low on social and political participation.

18. An empowerment profile might be based on the three factor dimensions that emerged in the empirical analysis, including Mastery, Political Awareness/Participation, and Leadership. An individual's factor scores on these types of dimensions might be useful in constructing empowerment/personality scales and in additional empirical analysis.

19. While these kinds of empowerment continuums and profiles may be useful theoretically and empirically, they are also somewhat arbitrary. Empowerment, like the related concept of power, is a relative concept. There is no absolute standard or bench mark for empowerment. Whether or not an individual is judged to be empowered or disempowered is somewhat problematic. The assessment may be made by a comparison of that individual with some reference group or cultural standard, or perhaps to themselves at various life stages. For example, an individual in a wealthy developed nation may be considered disempowered compared to societal norms or quality of life indicators for that nation, but the same individual might be viewed as relatively empowered by the quality of life standards in a much poorer developing nation.

20. Empowerment is not only relative to different standards and situations, but also it varies or runs in cycles within the life of each individual. Empowerment is not unidirectional; there are periods of progress and there are often periods of regress. The average individual, for example, is relatively powerless and dependent as a child, generally becomes more empowered as an adult, and probably becomes less empowered in the senior years, although it is not clear that this must be an inevitable progression. Individuals may become increasingly empowered with age, at least on some of the empowerment components, such as political awareness.

21. There may be other kinds of empowerment cycles. For example, an adult might become temporarily or permanently disempowered by a traumatic event or crisis, such as the loss of a loved one or destruction of a valued reputation or career. We need to learn how to increase empowerment, maintain desirable levels of empowerment, and restore empowerment when it declines. The processes may not be the same in each case.

22. No one ever becomes completely empowered. Empowerment is a journey with hills and valleys but no final destination.

23. Empowerment is related to, but not synonymous with, power. Empowerment is a process by which people gain greater control over their lives and

create alternatives to domination. Power is often associated with domination, coercion, and dependency. Powerful people are not necessarily empowered, nor are empowered people always powerful. Only integrative power, or power *with* (not over) is truly empowering.

24. Significant empowerment requires access to *both* political rights and resources. In capitalist democratic countries, individuals may have the right to vote but continue to live in abject poverty. In authoritarian countries, basic material needs may be met, but human freedoms are severely constrained. Neither political-economic system maximizes the opportunities for personal and political empowerment.

25. The empowerment literature focuses on the importance of rights and resources and usually neglects the importance of responsibility. This emphasis is understandable because being powerless for most people in the world usually means not having adequate resources to meet their needs or not being able to exercise political rights. But responsibilities and rights are linked, and being an empowered individual is associated with being a responsible citizen. Generally speaking the more one becomes empowered, the more one should feel willing and able to be responsible for one's self, responsible for others, and responsible for the environment. Being responsible and taking social and political action to achieve individual and collective goals is the hallmark of highly developed citizen empowerment.

26. Leadership is not mentioned prominently in the mediation or social science empowerment literature. Leadership is traditionally more closely associated with the use of power, especially power *over* others, than with empowerment. But leadership is associated with the empowerment of *self* and *others* in several ways: First, as demonstrated in Kieffer's (1984) study of grassroots leaders, political leadership can be the path to personal empowerment for ordinary people with little prior leadership experience. In order to efficaciously accomplish collective goals, leaders must acquire the necessary skills, self-efficacy, and political awareness to operate successfully in their political environment. Operating successfully as a leader enhances the individual's self-confidence and motivates ongoing social and political participation, which increases personal empowerment still further. Second, certain types of leaders may use power *with* in a conscious attempt to empower their followers. James MacGregor Burns (1978) uses Gandhi as a positive example of "transforming leadership." This is the type of leadership role that a good teacher or mentor plays (Freire 1970). In this symbiotic process, the empowerment of the self and the *other* becomes reciprocal. Thus, empowering leaders are transformed in the process of empowering others, and empowering teachers learn from their students and are empowered by them.

27. There are both internal and external barriers to personal empowerment. Internal barriers would include physical and mental factors such as malnutrition, serious sickness, fatigue, passivity, learned helplessness, mental illness, fear of success, or fear of failure. External barriers would include lack of support or resources, or active resistance to empowerment within

the family, organization, community, or society. Those in power usually attempt to maintain control and oppose those who struggle to restructure inequitable power imbalances.

28. These barriers to empowerment imply that the process of personal and political empowerment is likely to cause or exacerbate both internal and external conflicts. The probability of increased conflict must be expected and contended with by those who seek to become empowered.

29. Conversely, disempowerment or powerlessness can be seen as the deep-rooted causes of some types of personal and social conflict and violence. The powerless, by definition cannot satisfy their basic needs, and are therefore frustrated and often angry. When the conditions are favorable, these deep-seated grievances may erupt in violence against the self and others.

30. Empowerment may be viewed from many perspectives. First, it may be viewed as a *state* or condition of possessing empowerment. Second, empowerment may be considered as a *way of being* in the world. Third, it may appear as a *vision* for personal or political transformation or as self-transcendence. Fourth, it may be conceived as a lifelong, often arduous, individual *process* of becoming. Fifth, empowerment may be seen as the collective *human evolution* toward optimal functioning, and the actualization of each individual's potential.

These thirty propositions suggest some of the insights and concerns relevant to empowerment that have been derived from this study. Most are concerned with individual empowerment rather than with empowerment at other levels or the possible interrelationships between levels of empowerment. Most of these propositional statements could also be usefully restated as research questions. I will list just a few questions about other aspects of empowerment before we discuss the possible work agenda for advancing the elaboration of empowerment theory and practice.

II. Questions

1. How does the type of political system affect the possibilities for empowerment? For example, can you empower citizens in an authoritarian system? Or, can you transform an authoritarian system without empowered citizens?

2. Whom should we empower? Should everyone be empowered? Should only those likely to be good citizens be empowered? Who should be empowered first, the most oppressed, for example, or those most easily empowered?

3. If we only empower some individuals or groups, will they have an unfair advantage or dominate others?

4. How does culture impact the empowerment process?

5. How is individual empowerment related to collective empowerment?

6. Should we attempt to empower individuals first and then work for structural transformation? Or should we begin with structural transformation?

7. Will empowered individuals support structural change if they are able to act effectively in the present system and are personally successful?

8. Should transformationalists be willing to use power *over* against those who oppose or resist individual empowerment and structural transformation?

9. What is an empowered organization? What is community empowerment? What are the characteristics of each and how would we measure them?

10. How do organizations and communities empower individuals? How do individuals empower organizations and communities? In what way are these different micro and macro levels interrelated?

These ten questions and the prior thirty propositions provide a plethora of ideas and tasks for those wishing to move ahead with a future agenda for empowerment.

Agenda for Empowerment

Earlier I made suggestions for future research, advancements in practice, and policy formulation specific to the linkage between citizen empowerment and community mediation. At this point, I am focusing on the future of empowerment as a theory, and as a possible social movement. This discussion builds on but moves beyond the suggestions made with regard to community mediation.

Empowerment Theory. The theory development and empirical findings presented here provide a foundation for further conceptual and empirical research on empowerment. The research goal should be the development of a general scientific theory of empowerment. For researchers, such a theory would provide direction and a focus of attention for the interdisciplinary research necessary to understand this complex concept. A good theory would explain, predict, and enable understanding of individual, group, and community empowerment in various settings and multicultural contexts. For reflective practitioners, an empowerment theory would provide guidance for thinking about and designing empowering settings that would maximize the opportunities for participating in decision making, encouraging diversity, and promoting individual freedom and social justice.

A general theory of empowerment should have both theoretical breadth as well as intuitive appeal. A good empowerment theory should go beyond attempting to understand reality. It should help to transform present political and social structures and to create a new social reality that is more empowering for all citizens. Future reality is at least somewhat indeterminate. What happens in the future depends partially on the theories and values held by social actors about how the world works, and how it should work. This is what I have called political awareness, and it is a key component of personal empowerment. Therefore, empowering theories about empowerment can have real-world consequences. A general theory of empowerment would provide a vision for the future, and the foundation for a new "politics of empowerment and transformation."

Empowerment Praxis. Just as research on empowerment is at an early stage of development, so it is with doing empowerment work. There are few cases to study, few guidelines to follow. Most of the empirical studies on empowerment have examined case studies of community settings or educational settings where it was believed individual empowerment was occurring. These organizations or settings have been designed for purposes and missions either unrelated to empowerment, or where empowerment has been of secondary concern to the primary mission, such as mediation, health services, or education. Few settings have been designed specifically for the purpose of enhancing personal empowerment.

One way to proceed is to identify and study those settings or programs, or the types of participation that are the most effective at increasing personal empowerment. In this study, the training aspect of the mediation experience was most powerful, at least in increasing self-esteem and self-efficacy as well as knowledge and skills. We could, for example, do a comparative study of training in different community mediation programs and other types of training, such as group facilitation, presentation skills, and management. Different kinds of training are likely to affect personal empowerment in different ways because training modules are usually carefully designed to achieve specific outcomes that are relevant to the empowerment components identified here.

In addition to training, which has objectives related to the development of skills and specialized knowledge, other educational settings are relevant for empowerment. In his *Pedagogy of the oppressed*, Paulo Freire (1970) contrasts traditional disempowering models of education with the models he designed for teaching and empowering illiterates in Brazil. Freire's theory of education and transformational methods were specifically designed to help these oppressed people to come to a new awareness of selfhood, to look critically at the social situation in which they find themselves, and to take the initiative in acting to transform the society that has denied them this opportunity of participation. Research and design work is also being done on various modes of experiential learning and the kind and degree of empowerment that results. In this regard, academics who view themselves as transformationalists and who teach in traditional University settings might examine their own teaching methods to determine if they are using approaches that are empowering for their students.

Reflective practitioners who regard themselves as transformationalists might study their own organizations and determine what could be done to make them more empowering organizations. For example, many social service voluntary organizations are hierarchically organized and autocratically governed, and consequently are less empowering than they might be. It might be possible to transform the organizational culture and leadership styles to institute a more democratic management approach that is more conducive to personal and organizational empowerment. Democratic management implies developing systems where the organizational members can design, implement, and control processes and structures to achieve members' goals. The goal of democratic management is to create an organization that reflects the goals of the members, where they control or at least influence the design and implementation of these processes and structures within the confines of internal and external opportunities and constraints.

How can we create more empowering communities? There are at least two approaches. One focuses on individual transformation; the other on collective or structural transformation. One variant of the first approach is the strategy used by the San Francisco Community Boards in attempting to build community by training community members in conflict resolution skills. According to SFCB ideology, the "civic work" constituted a form of democratic participation in which members transferred conflict resolution skills to other community members, and the community developed a conflict resolution capacity independent from the formal legal system. Thus they were empowered by taking ownership and control of their own disputes.

Another strategy for community empowerment focuses on facilitating collective empowerment through mobilizing existing networks. These networks are the "mediating agencies" discussed earlier. They are often based on ties of kinship, friendship, and neighborhood. In some indigenous or religious communities, individual identity is less important than the identity established through the family, church, or cultural association. Networks play an important social support function in linking individuals to other people they trust and who can provide assistance. In the social network approach, community leaders are recruited and trained to promote increased community participation and social mobilization that develops community competence and facilitates structural transformation and empowerment.

In many urban communities that may lack viable social networks, advocacy organizations like ACORN in San Francisco use community organizing models to empower people to take political action. Two different models are commonly used. One model uses Paulo Freire's idea that by teaching people how to think, they will determine how to organize. Education leading to critical consciousness is among the most radical of transformational approaches to empowerment. For Freire, reflection comes prior to action. Freire's model is particularly appropriate in authoritarian situations where knowledge is being controlled because it helps people transcend the restrictions of official knowledge. It sensitizes them to the struggle over knowledge as an important part of the empowerment process. According to Freire's view, both reflection and action are essential to being empowered.

The second and most widely used community action strategy in the United States is based on the thinking of Saul Alinsky, the leading American political activist thinker and organizer. In the Alinsky model, people are organized around a specific community issue, such as welfare entitlements or dealing with threats to the community. They are mobilized to participate in social action, and through their participation they may learn how to think about issues and political structures and thus develop a critical consciousness. Thus, as opposed to Freire's approach, in Alinsky's approach reflection develops as a result of political participation. Critics of Alinsky's approach point out that people are not likely to become truly empowered just because they walked a picket line or handed out pamphlets advocating the installation of a school crossing light. Critics of Freire's approach point out that it is possible to develop critical consciousness without having the resources, skills, or political knowledge needed to take effective action. The inability to act, or failure resulting from inept social action, may actually contribute to increased disempowerment.

On the other hand, if you only do skills training without providing the political education necessary to develop critical consciousness, as happens with community mediation programs, you produce citizens with enhanced personal competence who are unlikely to become agents for social transformation. What is needed then in order to empower those who are willing and able to work for social transformation is a combination of both the critical education to develop political awareness or critical consciousness, along with skills training to develop political competencies.

In summary, there is much to be learned and much to be done in the area of empowerment praxis. Some of the questions we must consider include: who should be empowered? How should they be empowered (e.g., strategy and tactics)? What are the desired empowerment objectives or outcomes? In other words, empowerment for what (e.g., mental health, personal competence, increased rights or resources, structural transformation)? What is the role of the empowerment practitioner? Does the practitioner provide services, set the agenda, provide expertise and resources, or function primarily as a helper or collaborator? Is there a preferred approach to empowerment, or are there many different models? If there are many empowerment models or strategies, which do we use in a given situation?

Empowerment Policy and Democracy. Empowering public policy is intrinsic to democratic systems, and empowerment has important implications for enhancing citizen participation and democratization. Empowered citizens are essential to the successful functioning of a democratic system. A democratic society presumes the existence of an educated electorate and relatively high levels of citizen participation. Citizens must have the basic skills and knowledge and the political awareness that are vital elements of political competence. Citizens must possess sufficient levels of self-esteem and self-efficacy to participate in the political system and to believe that they are capable of political actions that will influence the political system and bring about transformational changes to improve functioning of the system. They must be willing and able to take responsibility and to act individually, as well as collaboratively with others, in order to achieve democratic values, such as freedom, equality, and social justice. The empowering benefits of citizen participation demonstrated in many studies suggest that high levels of political participation are vital to the health and happiness of the individual, and to the vitality and quality of life in the society.

What kind of citizen participation is the most empowering and supportive of democratization? Earlier, I distinguished between social and political participation. I classified community mediation as a form of social participation because for most of the community mediation programs, the mission of the organization is the delivery of dispute resolution services or personal growth, not a political critique or political action associated with social or political transformation. But the kind of personal empowerment that individuals can develop through involvement in types of social participation may have political relevance. When people have developed the capabilities needed to deal with some aspects of their lives in a competent fashion, the skills and positive feelings they acquire as a result may spread to other areas of their lives or to other settings, and thus empower them to deal with these other aspects of their lives more efficaciously. In other words, the competencies they have developed through social participation may be applied to political activities and issues. Many of the major social movements that have arisen in the past decades are essentially movements for empowerment, and of empowerment, including the various consumer movements: the environmental movement, the self-help movement, the Greens movement, the nuclear freeze movement, and the community mediation movement.

Berger and Neuhaus (1977) have argued that "mediating agencies," such as community mediation centers, provide the opportunities for voluntarism that are vital to a successful democratic society. According to Berger and Neuhaus, mediation agencies serve as schools for democracy and facilitate the fulfillment of public policy. While many kinds of social and political participation provide the opportunities to develop empowering skills and knowledge, it would seem that the kinds of communication, problem solving, and conflict resolution skills that are learned by community mediators may be especially useful for participating effectively in the democratic process.

One aspect of democratic process that is central to the peaceful political evolution preferred by most transformationalists is the process of public policy formulation. One indicator of the widespread strong public attraction to the concept of empowerment is that both liberal and conservative policy-makers have recently embraced the language and symbolism, if not the substance, of empowerment. This shift is reflected in numerous public statements and the titles of new programs and organizations such as Clinton's Community Empowerment Zones, and the conservative republican organization, Empower America. Policy-makers at all levels of government have been influenced by

David Osborne and Ted Gaebler's (1992) ideas in *Reinventing government*. Subtitled, *How the entrepreneurial spirit is transforming the public sector, from schoolhouse to statehouse, city hall to the Pentagon*, this influential book is an interesting mix of reformist and potentially transformational suggestions for improving and restructuring public institutions at all levels of government.

Osborne and Gaebler contend that government is inefficient and ineffectual. Their analysis suggests that "the people who work in government are not the problem; the systems in which they work are the problem" (1992, xviii). Their prescriptive focus is on system transformation and using resources in new ways to maximize productivity and effectiveness. Their reform principles emphasize the importance of empowering individuals, organizations, and communities. Osborne and Gaebler point out, "We all know that people act more responsibly when they control their own environment than when they are under the control of others. . . . It stands to reason that when communities are empowered to solve their own problems, they function better than communities that depend on service provided by outsiders" (1992, 51).

Osborne and Gaebler contend that there is now an emerging reaction to control by professionals, bureaucrats, and the mega-institutions of our society: big business, big government, and big labor. They claim that government at all levels has begun to respond and is beginning to "push ownership and control of public services out of the hands of bureaucrats and professionals, into communities" (1992, 53).

In the area of criminal justice, they laud the San Francisco Community Boards as an innovative program that uses volunteer mediators "to resolve the kinds of everyday conflicts that often erupt into violence" and in the process builds "a sense of empowerment, a sense that people working together in neighborhoods can solve their own problems" (1992, 56). In the area of empowering education policy, they praise former Arkansas Governor Bill Clinton's sponsorship of programs like the Home Instruction Program for Pre-School Youngsters (HIPPY), that encourages people to teach their own children (1992, 55–56). In discussion of government programs that are "managing the transition from service to empowerment," Osborne and Gaebler laud Jack Kemp's empowerment initiatives, as secretary of housing and urban development (HUD) (1992, 71). Kemp, who may be a Republican candidate for president in the next election, has been one of the most vocal champions of empowerment programs on the Republican side. Along with William Bennett, another potential Republican presidential candidate, Kemp has formed the Empower America organization, which is housed in the Heritage Institute, a conservative "think-tank" in Washington, DC.

The present Democratic administration has also launched several recent public policy initiatives that use empowerment as a central theme. For example, Vice-President Gore has recently released the results of the Gore report, "Reinventing government," and the Clinton administration's Community Empowerment Zone program has begun awarding multimillion-dollar grants to ten urban communities. At this time, a Clinton administration committee is preparing a program on "sustainable development" based on empowerment initiatives, which should be released in 1995. The underlying philosophy, and sometimes the specific program objectives of these recent public policies is "to empower people and communities." Since these are new programs, it is far too early to evaluate outcomes, but at least the rhetoric is promising for those who favor the transformation of public institutions and political structures.

Empowerment as a Paradigm for Transformational Politics. Given empowerment's potential as an interdisciplinary theory, and its value as a guide for reflective practitioners and innovative policy-makers, I would suggest that it has great potential as a unifying theory or paradigm for Transformational Politics. As the old curse proclaims, "May you live in interesting times." The twenty-first century promises to be quite an interesting time, full of crises, challenges, dangers, and opportunities. Turbulent times call for courage and creativity. We will need a vision powerful enough to hold us together, and a moral compass to chart our course and to guide our steps down new paths. Empowerment is a leading candidate for this essential transformational paradigm. Empowerment theory naturally focuses on the future. It poses the right questions: What will be? What should be? How do we get there from here?

TRANSFORMATIONAL POLITICS AND THE FUTURE

What are our probable and possible futures? What are the most important trends and transformations? What are the areas of change and of continuity? How can Transformational Politics contribute to shaping a better future for more people? Since the beginning of human existence the future has been an important concern. During times of war, pestilence, and famine, the future has seemed dark and dangerous. At other times during the eras of peace, prosperity, and intellectual enlightenment the future has seemed full of potential, at least for those fortunate enough to enjoy the benefits of the times.

After World War I, often called "the war to end all wars," there was for some time a feeling of optimism and idealism. The future to many in the Western developed nations, especially in the United States, seemed bright and full of promise and progress.

But the Great Depression and the horrible carnage of World War II ended the era of idealism and optimism. After World War II, and with the onset of the Cold War, the mood was more realistic and pessimistic. As the Cold War alliances formed, the future to many in the West appeared to be a death struggle between the "godless communists" lurking and plotting behind the "iron curtain" and the democratic defenders of the bastion of free democracies. The specter of nuclear war forced us to "think about the unthinkable," and across America school children were taught to "duck and cover" during frequent civil defense drills to prepare for nuclear attack. As the super power nuclear arms races continued to escalate out of control, we used metaphors like "two scorpions in a bottle," or "two men with flaming matches standing knee deep in gasoline," to describe the seeming futility of the future, the looming possibility of a world-wide nuclear catastrophe, and the possible onset of "nuclear winter." In the background lurked the North-South conflict between the rich nations and poor nations, and the "world problematique" generated by overwhelming global problems, such as the population explosion, resource depletion, and environmental pollution.

Then, almost overnight the world experienced an incredible and unpredicted transformation. Communist, authoritarian governments throughout Eastern Europe capitulated, and with only a few exceptions these fundamental political transformations were accomplished rapidly and without bloodshed. The foreign policy pundits and CIA super spies armed with high-tech information-gathering devices and moles in the enemy camp, were confused and dumbfounded by the unexpected turn of events. Soon, even the Berlin Wall, the most powerful symbol of the Cold War, had fallen, and in 1991 the powerful Soviet Union fragmented into the amorphous Commonwealth of Independent States.

A wave of optimism and euphoria spread around the Western world as one scholar proclaimed the "End of History" (i.e., the end of ideological struggle) and the triumph of Western liberal democracies. There was hopeful debate about the best way to spend the multibillion-dollar "peace dividend" that would be available now that we could halt the nuclear arms race, dismantle the missiles on both sides, and withdraw our troops from the many military bases around the world that implemented our Cold War foreign policy of containment. It was anticipated that the large peace dividend might enable us to get our economic house in order, to rebuild our crumbling domestic infrastructure, to pay back our crippling debt burdens, and to move forward into a lengthy period of peace and prosperity. It was suggested that the peace dividend might also enable us financially to aid our new friends in the former Soviet Union and Eastern Europe to make the difficult transition from totalitarianism to freedom, from their failed planned economics to our prosperous free market economies.

But this optimistic mood passed quickly as the difficulty and dangers of these political and economic transformations have become apparent, and as the peace dividend faded away like a mirage. Some pessimistic scholars now suggest that we may come to reflect on the Cold War years with nostalgia. It was after all, they point out, a time of relative political stability and certainty. We knew who our enemies were, and we knew who President Reagan meant when he talked about "the evil empire." Despite our nuclear fears, during the Cold War there was a long period of peace between the most powerful nations with no major wars for over forty-five years. The United States had a well-articulated foreign policy called "containment," which provided a coherent strategy for dealing with our only major enemy, and we had developed a nuclear deterrence strategy, with well-thought-out safeguards to prevent accidental nuclear war.

Future Trends and Transformations

Whether we will truly come to miss the Cold War is a matter for conjecture, but most foreign policy experts agree that the Cold War is over, at least for the immediate future. The future is now beginning to appear less sanguine, however. There now seems to be less stability and certainty in the world, and we are beginning to perceive new threats from nuclear proliferation (partially resulting from the demise of the Soviet Union), and the rebirth and salience of nationalism, fascism, tribalism, Islamic fundamentalism, and racism. A prominent political scientist has recently predicted that frequent and serious future conflicts will result from the coming "clash of civilizations." The world is again beginning to look very dangerous, but now we are far less certain about the face of the enemy. Now the policy of containment is outdated in the Post–Cold War world, but we have not yet developed a new foreign policy, or vision to guide us as we stumble from one emerging crisis to another.

In addition to political-military problems, we face worsening domestic economic challenges that the peace dividend might have lessened. We also face grave social and environmental challenges as the world population continues to explode at a geometric rate, and exacerbates other components of the "world problematique," such as environmental pollution, global warming, and the rapid spread of AIDS throughout the world. Thus it seems that we have not yet arrived at the "End of History," but instead we are entering a new era of history, a major turning point. The Post–Cold War future may lead to the devastating disasters that pessimists have warned of, or perhaps it may be a transformational opportunity to shape a better world, perhaps even leading to a new stage of human evolution envisioned by some optimistic thinkers.

Optimists versus Pessimists. Who should we believe about our prospects for the future—the optimists or the pessimists? What are the consequences of adopting each position? What position should transformationalists take, and what should we do about the future? The future is difficult to predict because change is happening at an ever-increasing pace. In this "information age" it is difficult not to be overwhelmed by the prodigious amount of information available. It is difficult to differentiate the forces of change from the forces of continuity, major changes from minor changes, and long-term trends from short-term fads. In recent years, a major "futurist industry" of scholars, seers, and charlatans has developed to meet our needs to understand the future, to anticipate the dangers and opportunities, to plan, to budget, and to strategize.

Generally, the futurist theorists and consultants can be divided into "optimist" and "pessimist" camps. The optimists emphasize the positive social, economic, and political trends, and seem oblivious to serious problems, whereas the pessimists call attention to the seemingly intractable problems. In many cases, optimists and pessimists focus on the same issue or trend but come to opposite conclusions. For example, some pessimists have warned that the high-tech products like computers and telecommunications, may be tools used by "Big Brother" or other sinister forces to control and manipulate people and centralize power. Conversely, optimists like John Naisbitt (1994) argue that advances in telecommunications and computers will facilitate the global spread of democracy, and decentralize power to the people.

As we look around the world at emerging domestic and international trends and issues, there are many challenges that will affect individuals and political communities at every level of the global system. How serious these challenges are and whether they will constitute major crises is a matter of debate between optimists and pessimists. One cluster of problems that generates major debate centers on the larger demographic forces that will shape national and international politics and economics for decades to come and will generate ecological crisis. The causes and implications of continued population growth, environmental deterioration, the transnational movement of environmental refugees and economic refugees (mostly from the underdeveloped South to the more developed North), and the competition for scarce resources, require explanation as well as assessments of appropriate responses by state and non-state actors. On one side of the debate on many of these issues are the "growth pessimists" whose arguments are informed by the "tragedy of the commons metaphor," and whose primary concern is generally the "population explosion," which is viewed as the primary engine driving most ecological crises. On the other side are the "growth optimists," many of whom are economists who argue that markets will effectively maintain a balance among population growth, resources depletion, and environmental pollution. They also argue that scientific and technological advances in resource generating (i.e., the "green revolution"), or resource saving (recycling) innovations, occur in response to the various shortages or temporary crises generated by population growth. Therefore, population growth can be viewed as a positive stimulus to scientific and economic advancement.

This debate involves complex social and scientific issues that are difficult to disentangle and understand. Each of these opposing positions represents very different values and perspectives on reality and leads to very different policy prescriptions. The problems are further exacerbated because they are transnational in nature, which means that they impact more than one nation, and their seriousness and economic, social, and political consequences vary widely from one nation-state to another. Therefore, their solutions will require international coordination and cooperation. As complicated as this may seem, we must remember that ecological crises are not the only problems that face us as citizens of a nation, and members of a global society.

Another major problem emerging in the aftermath of the Cold War is the widespread occurrence of ethno-political conflict. During the Cold War period, the two Superpowers permitted and sometimes even encouraged violence and wars on the periphery of their worlds, if it served their ideological purposes. However, they also kept the peace within their borders and generally within their respective alliances and "spheres of influence." Now, however, "Pandora's box" has been opened and long-festering hostilities and animosities have reemerged. Militant nationalistic, ethnic, and religious movements are generating new conflicts and reviving old conflicts within and between states. These conflicts pose major theoretical, social, economic, and political challenges. They necessitate research on developing conflict early warning systems, the design of transnational conflict intervention strategies, and continued and coordinated efforts to respond in concerted humanitarian efforts to prevent bloodshed and minimize human suffering.

Human rights have moved higher on the agenda, especially for some of the Western developed nations like the United States. Two obvious examples of critical humanitarian crises that appear to be increasing are the massive refugee flows within Asia, Africa, and Latin America, and from South to North, and the gross human rights violations that have sparked debate about United States-China trade policy and the viability of sovereignty. In some political systems there are persistent threats to disadvantaged groups, such as children, women, and ethnic minorities. These issues impact ethical and legal, as well as political, considerations.

In a related problem, economic disparities and material inequalities within nations and between nations are increasing. The economic gap, already too wide, is growing between the nations of the underdeveloped South and the highly developed North. The economic gap is also growing between minorities and dominant groups, and among the economic classes in advanced industrial societies (including the United States, where real income for the average American has declined over the last twenty years by about fifteen percent), and between rural and urban populations. Research is needed on the causes of these growing disparities as well as their consequences for increasing conflict within and between nations. What are the possibilities for reducing global inequities and promoting sustainable development?

Another related cluster of problems arises from growing military spending, especially in the undeveloped nations that can least afford it, and the threat of nuclear proliferation, which has increased with the end of the Cold War. Massive military spending undermines economic development, exacerbates economic disparities, and generates additional conflict within and between nations. Nuclear proliferation increases the likelihood that one or more states will choose to use nuclear weapons, that terrorists will have access to nuclear weapons, or that an accident or miscalculations will lead to a human and ecological catastrophe.

A new cluster of problems has been generated by the internationalization of crime. Local and national politics are being corrupted by the availability of significant wealth gained from international drug dealing, illegal banking operations, illicit arms shipments, and other illegal activities. For example, the Latin American drug lords have for years influenced the economics, politics, and criminal world of the United States. Now, strong, organized criminal groups that have prospered with the end of communism in the former Soviet Union are also penetrating the United States and setting up major operations here. In an ironic twist the Russian government has invited the F.B.I. to set up an office in Moscow to advise them and train them to deal with the new threat from organized crime.

One of the most hopeful trends in recent years has been the spread of democracies around the world. A recent survey by Freedom House, a private organization that monitors world progress toward democracy estimates that as of 1994, 114 out of 191 countries, or about 60%, are classified as democratic. During the height of the Cold War it seemed for a long time that international communism was on the march and that country after country was being overwhelmed by this aggressive ideology. It was widely believed in the West that once a country became communist there was little or no chance that it could ever be liberated, and that each country that became communist would increase the probability of the same fate for others in the region. Thus developed the powerful "domino theory" metaphor, which provided the justification for U.S. involvement in Vietnam and other diplomatic and military interventions throughout the world.

Now some scholars see this as "a democratic moment" in history and suggest that the promotion of global democracy should be a keystone of U.S. Post–Cold War foreign policy (see Diamond 1994). Most international relations theorists, as a result of major research findings, now believe that democracy is a force for peace because democracies seldom, if ever, fight each other. Logically, as democracies spread, there should be less warfare (see Ray 1995). One prominent scholar, R. J. Rummel (in press), contends that democracy is the solution to war, violence, genocide, and poverty. He argues that "were the world to become wholly democratic, then war would be completely eliminated for the human species, lesser political violence would be minimized, and poverty and inequality would be sharply reduced" (1992, 1).

Other scholars caution that this is the "third wave" of democracy to sweep the world, and that many of the new democracies are quite fragile and could easily regress to more authoritarian systems (see Huntington 1991). Therefore, much more research is needed on the factors that may lead to successful and enduring democracies, on strategies for making the transition from authoritarian to democratic systems, and the most democratic and efficacious ways in which the existing democratic states might facilitate the transition to global democracy.

Considering this brief overview of emerging domestic and international trends, should we be optimists or pessimists about the future prospects for humanity? Certainly there seems to be ample cause for pessimism when one contemplates the number, scope, and complexity of threats and challenges discussed above. The world is in chaos, and the problems seem to be intractable. There is a lack of world leadership, and the barriers to positive transformation are formidable and multiple.

Some of these barriers to transformation are internal. They reside within ourselves in the form of negative emotions, such as fear and passivity. Other barriers, located within transformational social movements. They are caused by factors such as internal dissension and unwillingness to collaborate with other groups. Many of the barriers to political transformation are external, such as the resistance and oppression of the power elite in all states, and the rivalry between nation-states that prevents the cooperation needed to deal with transnational problems.

There are also intellectual barriers that inhibit cooperation on solving complex problems. There are for example, traditional intellectual boundaries between the natural sciences and the social sciences and humanities, and between those who work at the micro level and those who work at the macro level. Even within the social sciences, disciplinary boundaries provide significant intellectual barriers to the kind of multilevel, multidisciplinary collaboration that is essential to dealing with complex problems in an increasingly interdependent world.

There is also a good argument to be made for being overly cautious, for generating worst-case scenarios, and preparing for catastrophe. Many of the problems facing us today may only get worse, and if we err on the side of taking them too lightly and letting them resolve themselves, they may get totally out of control. Then, the long-run costs of dealing with them will be greater than we can afford, or it may be too late to prevent disasters. War and the technology of war have evolved with increasing civilization, but we have now reached a juncture where the evolution of war technology has moved beyond the evolution of civilization. There is now a possibility that nuclear technology might destroy the world before civilization evolves sufficiently to control or destroy these terrible weapons.

In summary, there is clearly ample cause for pessimism when one considers the immensity of the challenges and the elusiveness of viable solutions. However, the pessimistic position is problematic. Pessimism breeds despair. Pessimism can result in passivity, depression, frustration, alienation, or even social violence. Studies have shown that pessimistic individuals have more physical and mental health problems, less success in life, and shorter lives than optimists (see Seligman 1991). Pessimism can result in a self-fulfilling prophecy if it discourages individual or collective actions to cope with or solve problems. Even if action is taken, pessimism can result in self-sabotage, half-hearted efforts, or discouragement and disengagement when inevitable resistance is encountered. Pessimism in short, is a *disempowering* attitude or perspective.

But what about optimism? Optimism can also be problematic. Like pessimists, optimists may also be unwilling to take needed actions, but for very different reasons. Pessimists may be stultified by fear or fatalistic feelings of despair that immobilize them. Optimists on the other hand, may have an unrealistic lack of regard for the very real dangers that exist and may totally underestimate the challenges they face. Their complacency may lead them to believe that no matter how serious the threat appears to be, there is no need for great concern because the problem will solve itself. Or, optimists may believe that those who are concerned are merely being alarmists, or that the evidence of a threat is exaggerated. "Technological" optimists, for example, tend to believe that science will find an answer to environmental problems in time. "Religious" optimists tend to believe that either God will intervene to save the day (the escape fantasy), or that "true believers" will go to salvation when the world ends.

When viewing the future, pessimists focus on the risks and danger, and fail to see the potential opportunities for growth, wealth, or transformation. Pessimists serve a useful function for society by alerting us to dangers at an early stage while there is time to deal with them efficaciously, but they tend to get locked into a vision of the future that excludes hope. If their analyses are mistaken, or if they exaggerate the risks like the boy who cries wolf, they may lose credibility. Pessimists may also have difficulty communicating their concerns because people generally don't enjoy dwelling on "gloom and doom" messages, or with regard to nuclear deterrence, "thinking the unthinkable."

Optimists, on the other hand, focus on the opportunities and believe that the risks are inflated. Optimists think that things usually turn out for the best. In short, optimists and pessimists represent two different ways of looking at life, or two explanatory styles—hope versus despair. Both are right, and both are wrong. In some situations where the consequences of being wrong are great, perhaps fatal, where a realistic appreciation of risk may be essential to survival, pessimism may be the most rational approach. In other situations where persistence and perseverance are needed to continue in the face of adversity, optimism may be essential for success.

We cannot know the future, although we must try to comprehend it as best we can. The world could end tomorrow, or we could be on the verge of a great human leap forward. The political events that occurred in Eastern Europe and the Soviet Union between 1989 and 1991, demonstrated quite dramatically how rapidly and unexpectedly major personal and political transformation can occur. While we cannot choose the future, we can choose whether we want to approach it optimistically or pessimistically. While wide-eyed optimism has its potential dangers, it has many advantages over pessimism. Studies of optimists have consistently demonstrated that they are happier, healthier, and wealthier than pessimists (see Seligman 1991). An optimistic vision of the future offers a "politics of hope" that has the power to mobilize that is lacking in a pessimistic "politics of despair." Recall the public reaction to Reagan's optimistic view of America's future, and rejection of Carter's gloomy vision. As mentioned above, pessimism is primarily problematic because it is a "disempowering" attitude. Optimism, despite its drawbacks, is primarily "empowering."

Therefore, because we really can choose how to look at life and the future, I would suggest that optimism is the preferred attitude for transformationalist theorists and practitioners. More specifically, we should adopt an attitude of *realistic optimism*—flexibly combining the advantages of both optimism and pessimism. Realistic optimism suggests that we look clearly at the risks and dangers; that we attempt to fully understand the odds against success and the difficulties we will face in attempting to cope with or solve the ecological, economic, and political crises we face now and in the foreseeable future, and that we face the fear—and do it anyway. Being realists, we will try to understand the deep-rooted causes and complexity of the challenges facing us. Being optimists, we will forge ahead and do whatever must be done to survive and succeed.

If transformationalists are to succeed, they must develop, integrate, and incorporate the components of empowerment discussed above, such as self-efficacy, knowledge and skills, political awareness, and resources. While these are necessary factors for success, they are not sufficient. What is essential in addition, is the will to action. What is required is the combination of personal and collective empowerment, along with *the power of commitment*. Because, as W. H. Murray (1951), the intrepid Scottish mountaineer proclaimed,

Until one is committed there is hesitancy, the chance to draw back, always ineffectiveness. Concerning all acts of initiative (and creation), there is one elementary truth, the ignorance of which kills countless ideas and splendid plans: that the moment one definitely commits oneself, then Providence moves too. All sorts of things occur to help one that would never otherwise have occurred. A whole stream of events issues from the decision, raising in one's favor all manner of unforeseen incidents and meetings and material assistance, which no man could have dreamt would have come his way. I have learned a deep respect for one of Goethe's couplets:

"Whatever you can do, or dream you can, begin it.
Boldness has genius, power, and magic in it."

Agenda for Transformational Politics

Using the power of commitment combined with personal and political empowerment, individuals and groups aligned with Transformational Politics, such as the greens, feminists, neo-populists, and communitarians, can take action, and make important contributions to the shape of the future. Many of these contributions have been discussed with regard to empowerment theory but I will briefly summarize them here and add other suggestions specific to the Transformational Politics agenda.

First, transformationalists and others who critique the existing sociopolitical systems in the Western developed world, as well as authoritarian systems in other nations, contribute to the understanding of the social inequities and economic disparities that exist in all governments, and the underlying structural causes of serious social conflict and violence. This kind of critical analysis partially answers the two related political awareness questions: What is the nature of power relations and social justice in the existing system? and What will be the future if power relations are not transformed?

Second, in addition to providing a critique of the existing system, transformationalists should set forth, and advocate for, and organize for, positive social and political alternatives. In some situations these positive alternatives may take the form of designing specific community programs that empower individuals, groups, and the community, and in other cases advocating and lobbying for transformational public policies.

Perhaps even more importantly, transformationalists need to formulate a vision or paradigm that has the cogency, appeal, and power to bring together the diverse groups gathered under the transformational banner, and to excite and attract other individuals and groups to join together to work for transformational goals. Earlier, I suggested that empowerment theory had the potential to contribute to the transformationalist agenda at many levels, including the design of community empowerment programs, and progressive public policies, and as a major theory or paradigm for Transformational Politics.

The fourth area of contribution is the transformational research agenda. Many specific suggestions for future research can be found in the empowerment inventory set forth earlier in this chapter, and in the discussion of theory and future research related to community mediation and other social movements. A major research task is a need for more theoretical elaboration of empowerment. The theory framework formulated in chapter 4 is suggestive of the interrelationships between empowerment components, and linkages to needs theory, conflict theory, and theories of participatory democracy. However, there is much work to do in order to develop empowerment theory, and to clarify linkages to other theories. Along with theory development we need to do more empirical analysis to test theoretical propositions, and suggest which social programs and public policies might impact personal and political empowerment. Again, many of the knowledge gaps and ideas for empirical analysis can be culled from the list of empowerment propositions and statements. Whenever possible, empowering approaches like action research and participatory research should be used (see Yeich and Levine 1992).

Fifth, transformationalists must also be willing and able to do the difficult "nitty gritty" tasks of developing transition strategies and alliances with individuals and groups that might collaborate in at least part of the transformationalist agenda. This task is essential for several reasons. First, even if a powerful transformational vision is created, it is difficult to mobilize support and persuade others to participate if there is no viable set of strategies or tactics for "getting there from here." History is full of failed utopian plans that had strong ideological appeal but lacked a viable transition plan. Advocates of world federation, for example, have advanced some cogent arguments for the desirability of such a plan, but even many of those attracted to world federation do not believe that it is doable. How can we move from the present anarchic state system to a world society even if we wanted to? Second, it is not easy to obtain the necessary resources for implementing transformation projects that are by nature anti-status quo. The power elite controls most of the available resources. As discussed with regard to the development of community mediation and other social movements, it is difficult to survive much less thrive in opposition to established power. Some theorists fear that, in addition to the problem of accessing scarce resources, time is short. Those concerned with the population explosion or nuclear proliferation, for example, argue that we must take effective action now.

For these reasons, transformationalists must plan, strategize, mobilize, coordinate and collaborate, and make difficult decisions about priorities. Some of these decisions have to do with strategic and theoretical issues, such as where we should focus our empowerment efforts. For example, should we concentrate on empowering individuals, or groups, or communities, or focus on structural transformation? Or should we try to support and promote empowerment at all levels simultaneously? Another strategic decision is about whether to support reform movements like community mediation, or to oppose projects that are not clearly transformational. Some types of piecemeal reform may be clearly supportive of status quo maintenance, while others may be more ambiguous. Does the "reinventing government" movement, for example, represent a clearly reformist approach, or does it have transformational potential? Sometimes the advocates of reform movements may intend to implement only minor changes, but then they lose control, and major unintended transformations can occur. When Gorbachev, for example, set glasnost and perestroika in motion, he never intended to destroy the Communist Party or dissolve the Soviet Union.

Developing viable transformational transition strategies requires more clarity about transformational values, strategies, and goals, as well as better communication and cooperation among the transformationalist groups and movements.

With regard to enhancing communication, we might revive and implement a suggestion made by Marilyn Ferguson (1980) in her book on "personal and social transformation in the 1980s." She suggested that networks are a powerful tool of transformation. Ferguson argued, "Amplified by electronic communication . . . the network is the antidote to alienation. It generates power enough to remake society. It offers the individual, emotional, intellectual, spiritual, and economic support. It is . . . a powerful means of altering the course of institutions, especially government. . . . [T]he function of most of these networks is mutual support and enrichment, empowerment of the individual, and cooperation to effect change. Most aim for a more humane, hospitable world" (213–214).

Ferguson alludes to using "electronic communications" to network, but when her book was published in 1980, computers and telecommunications were difficult to use and not readily accessible, especially to grass-roots groups and indigenous peoples. Both are now much more "user friendly" and widely accessible. In most universities E-mail is readily available to faculty, students, and staff; there are numerous private companies offering on-line services. Those without computers can often get free access in public libraries. A world-wide computer network that could be used to facilitate teledemocracy and other transformational projects is now in place. Most of the items on the transformational agenda, such as research, advocacy, and political action, would be facilitated by the development of a transformational network.

Just because such a network was created, however, does not ensure cooperation and coordination. There are many conflicts and communication problems within and between transformational groups and movements. For example, Slaton (1992) has documented the squabbles and rivalries that cripple most of the Greens party organizations at the local and national level. Zisk (1992) has described the reluctance of related social movement groups like the environmental and the peace organizations to work together and pool their resources. Transformational movements must also remain alert, and struggle to resist efforts by those who would co-opt them (see Kothari 1993).

Transformational Politics can make a difference and can contribute to a better world in the future. The mission is daunting; the path will be difficult. Empowerment, courage, and commitment are essential. But the greater the challenge, the more empowering the struggle. What other choice can we make as responsible citizens, but to work together and do what must be done?

Over thirty years ago a charismatic young American President addressed the U.N. General Assembly during a major international crisis. As we move ahead into the uncertainty, chaos, and challenges of the future we might do well to reflect on his inspirational words:

however close we sometimes seem to that dark and final abyss, let no man of peace and freedom despair. For he does not stand alone. If we all can persevere, if we can in every land . . . look beyond our own shores and ambitions, then surely the age will dawn in which the strong are just and the weak secure and the peace preserved.

. . . the decision is ours. Never have the nations of the world had so much to lose, or so much to gain. Together we shall save our planet, or together we shall perish in its flames. Save it we can—and save it we must—and then shall we earn the eternal thanks of mankind and, as peacemakers, the eternal blessing of God. (President John Fitzgerald Kennedy, 1961, *Public papers of the presidents of the United States*)

References

Abalos, D. T. 1993. *The Latino family and the politics of transformation.* Praeger Series in Transformational Politics and Political Science. Westport, CT: Praeger.

Abel, R. L., ed. 1982. *The politics of informal justice.* New York: Academic Press.

Adler, P. 1987. Is ADR a social movement? *Negotiation Journal* 3:59–71.

Adler, P. S. 1993. The future of alternative dispute resolution: Reflections on ADR as a social movement. In *The possibility of popular justice: A case study of community mediation in the United States,* edited by S. E. Merry and N. Milner. Ann Arbor: University of Michigan Press.

Adler, P., K. Lovaas, and N. Milner. 1988. The ideologies of mediation. *Law and Policy* 10:317–399.

ADR report. 1988. The Bureau of National Affairs, Inc. Washington, DC. 2:424–427.

Ajzen, I. 1988. *Attitudes, personality and behavior.* Chicago: Dorsey Press.

Alinsky, S. D. 1971. *Rules for radicals: A practical primer for realistic radicals.* New York: Random House.

American Bar Association. 1986. *Dispute resolution directory.* Washington, DC: American Bar Association.

American political dictionary. 1972. 3d ed. Hinsdale, IL: Dryden Press.

Arterton, C. F. 1987. *Teledemocracy: Can technology protect democracy?* Newbury Park, CA: Sage.

Auerbach, J. 1983. *Justice without law.* New York: Oxford.

Babbie, E. A. 1973. *Survey research methods.* Belmont, CA: Wadsworth.

Bachrach, P., and A. Botwinick. 1992. *Power and empowerment: A radical theory of participatory democracy.* Philadelphia: Temple University Press.

Bandura, A. 1986. *Social foundations of thought and action: A social cognitive theory.* Englewood Cliffs, NJ: Prentice-Hall.

Barber, B. 1984. *Strong democracy.* Berkeley: University of California Press.

Barber, B. R. 1992. *An aristocracy of everyone.* New York: Ballantine Books.

Barnes, B. E., and P. S. Adler. 1983. Mediation and lawyers: The Pacific way: A view from Hawaii. *Hawaii Bar Journal* 28:37–52.

Becker, T. 1986. Conflict and paradox in the new American mediation movement: Status quo and social transformation. *Missouri Journal of Dispute Resolution* 1986:109–129.

Becker, T. L., and C. D. Slaton. 1991. Sources of resistance to political transformation. Paper presented at the American Political Science Association meeting in Washington, DC.

Becker, T. L., ed. 1991. *Quantum politics: Applying quantum theory to political phenomena.* New York: Praeger.

Beer, J. E. 1986. *Peacemaking in your neighborhood.* Philadelphia: New Society Publishers.

Bellah, R. N., R. Madsen, W. M. Sullivan, A. Swidler, and S. M. Tipton. 1985. *Habits of the heart.* Berkeley: University of California Press.

Bem, D. J. 1970. *Belief, attitudes and human affairs.* Belmont, CA: Brooks/Cole.

Berger, P., and R. Neuhaus. 1977. *To empower people.* Washington, DC: American Enterprise Institute.

Berkowitz, L., and E. Donnerstein. 1982. External validity is more than skin deep: Some answers to criticisms of laboratory experiments. *American Psychologist* 37:245–257.

Biegel, D. E. 1984. Help seeking and receiving in urban ethnic neighborhoods: Strategies for empowerment. *Prevention in Human Services* 3:119–143.

Biehl, J. 1991. *Rethinking ecofeminist politics.* Boston: South End Press.

Blalock, H. M. 1984. *Basic dilemmas in the social sciences.* Beverly Hills, CA: Sage.

Block, P. 1987. *The empowered manager.* San Francisco: Jossey-Bass.

Bobo, L., and F. D. Gilliam, Jr. 1990. Race, sociopolitical participation and Black empowerment. *American Political Science Review* 84:377–393.

Bookchin, M. 1986. *The modern crisis.* Philadelphia: New Society Publishers.

Bookman, A., and S. Morgen. 1988. *Women and the politics of empowerment.* Philadelphia: Temple University Press.

Borg, W., and M. Gall. 1971. *Educational research.* 2d ed. New York: David McKay.

Boulding, K. E. 1989. *Three faces of power.* Newbury Park, CA: Sage.

Boyte, H. C., 1980. *The backyard revolution: Understanding the new citizen movement.* Philadelphia: Temple University Press.

Boyte, H. C., and F. Reissman, eds. 1986. *The new populism: The politics of empowerment.* Philadelphia: Temple University Press.

Burger, J. M., and H. M. Cooper. 1979. The desirability of control. *Motivation and Emotion* 3:381–393.

Burns, J. M. 1978. *Leadership.* New York: Harper and Row.

Burton, J. W. 1988. Conflict resolution as a political system. Working paper 1. Center for Conflict Analysis and Resolution. George Mason University.

Burton, J. 1990a. *Conflict resolution and prevention.* New York: St. Martin's Press.

Burton, J., ed. 1990b. *Conflict: Human needs theory.* New York: St. Martin's Press.

Burton, J., and F. Dukes. 1990. *Conflict: Practices in management, settlement, and resolution.* New York: St. Martin's Press.

Bush, B. 1989. Efficiency and protection, or empowerment and recognition? The mediator's role and ethical standards in mediation. *Florida Law Review* 41:252.

Bush, R.A.B., and J. F. Folger. 1994. *The promise of mediation.* San Francisco: Jossey-Bass.

Buss, A. H., and R. Plomin. 1975. *A temperament theory of personality.* New York: Wiley.

Campbell, D., and J. Stanley. 1963. *Experimental and quasi-experimental designs for research.* Chicago: Rand-McNally.

Carmines, E. G. 1978. Psychological origins of adolescent political attitudes: Self-esteem, political salience, and political involvement. *American Politics Quarterly* 6:167–186.

Caulder, B. J., L. W. Phillips, and A. M. Tybout. 1981. Designing research for application. *Journal of Consumer Research* 8:197–207.

Checkaway, B., and A. Norsman. 1986. Empowering citizens with disabilities. *Community Development Journal* 21:270–277.

Chesler, M. A., and B. K. Chesney. 1988. Self-help groups: Empowerment attitudes and behaviors of disabled or chronically ill persons. In *Attitudes toward persons with disabilities*, edited by H. E. Yuker. 230–245. New York: Springer.

Clark, M. 1993. Symptoms of cultural pathologies: A hypothesis. In *Conflict resolution theory and practice*, edited by D.J.D. Sandole and H. van der Merwe. Manchester: Manchester University Press.

Clarke, M., and J. Stewart. 1992. Empowerment: A theme for the 1990s. *Local Government Studies* 18:18–26.

Cohen, J. A. 1977. Criminal law: Reflections on the criminal process in China. *Journal of Criminal Law and Criminology* 68:323–353.

Cohen, J. W. 1962. *Statistical power analysis for the behavioral sciences*. rev. ed. Orlando, FL: Academic Press.

Compact edition of the Oxford English dictionary. 1971. London: Oxford University Press.

Concise encyclopedia of psychology. 1987. New York: John Wiley and Sons.

Cook, T. D., L. C. Leviton, and W. R. Shadish. 1985. Program evaluation. In 3d ed., Vol. 1. *Handbook of social psychology*, edited by G. Lindzey and E. Aronson. 699–777. New York: Random House.

Coser, L. 1967. *Continuities in the study of social conflict*. New York: Free Press.

Couto, R. A. 1993. The transformation of "transforming leadership" reclaiming a lost theoretical term. Paper presented at the American Political Science Association meeting in Washington, DC.

Couto, R. A. 1994. Teaching democracy through experiential education: Bringing the community into the classroom. Paper presented at the American Political Science Association meeting in New York.

Craig, J., and M. Craig. 1979. *Synergic power: Beyond domination and permissiveness*. 2d ed. Berkeley, CA: Proactive Press.

Craig, S. C., and M. Magiotto. 1982. Measuring political efficacy. *Political Methodology* 3:85–109.

Cronbach, L. J. 1982. *Designing evaluations of educational and social programs*. San Francisco: Jossey-Bass.

Dahl, R. A. 1957. The concept of power. *Behavioral Science* 2:201–215.

Danzig, R. 1973. Towards the creation of a complementary decentralized system of criminal justice. *Stanford Law Review* 26:1–54.

Davis, A. M., and R. A. Salem. 1984. Dealing with power imbalances in the mediation of interpersonal disputes. *Mediation Quarterly* 6:17–27.

Dean, D. G. 1961. Alienation: Its meaning and measurement. *American Sociological Review* 26:753–758.

Dean, D. G., ed. 1969. *Dynamic social psychology*. New York: Random House.

Deutchman, I. E. 1991. The politics of empowerment. *Women and Politics* 11:1–17.

Diamond, L. 1994. The global imperative: Building a democratic world order. *Current History*. 93:1–7.

Dictionary of key words in psychology. 1986. London: Routledge and Kegan Paul.

Dictionary of philosophy. 1976. London: Routledge and Kegan Paul.

Dictionary of the social sciences. 1964. New York: The Free Press.

Dispute Resolution Forum. 1988. How community justice centers are faring, 7–14. Washington, DC: National Institute for Dispute Resolution.

Du Bow, F. 1986. Preliminary findings: Study of the San Francisco Community Board program. Unpublished manuscript.

Du Bow, F. 1987. Conflicts and community: A study of the San Francisco Community Boards. Unpublished manuscript.

DuBow, F. L., with E. Currie. 1993. Police and "Nonstranger" conflicts in a San Francisco neighborhood: Notes on mediation and intimate violence. In *The possibility of popular justice: A case study of community mediation in the United States*, edited by S. E. Merry and N. Milner. Ann Arbor: University of Michigan Press.

DuBow, F. L., and C. McEwen. 1993. Community boards: An analytic profile. In *The possibility of popular justice: A case study of community mediation in the United States*, edited by S. E. Merry and N. Milner. Ann Arbor: University of Michigan Press.

Duffy, K. G., J. W. Grosch, and P. W. Olczak, eds. 1991. Community mediation. New York: Guldford Press.

Ehrlich, P. R., and A. H. Ehrlich. 1990. *The population explosion*. New York: Simon & Schuster.

Encyclopedia of education. 1971. New York: Macmillan.

Encyclopedia of philosophy. 1967. New York: Macmillan.

Etzioni, A. 1993a. Teledemocracy: The electronic town meeting. *Current* February:26–29.

Etzioni, A. 1993b. *The spirit of community*. New York: Crown Publishers.

Fawcett, S. B., T. Seekins, P. L. Whang, C. Muiu, and Y. Suarez de Balcazar. 1984. Creating and using social technologies for community empowerment. *Prevention in Human Services* 3:145–171.

Ferguson, M. 1980. *The aquarian conspiracy: Personal and social transformation in the 1980s*. Los Angeles: J. P. Tarcher.

Fishbein, M., and I. Ajzen. 1974. Attitudes toward objects as predictive of single and multiple behavioral criteria. *Psychological Review* 81:59–74.

Fishbein, M., ed. 1967. *Readings in attitude theory and measurement*. New York: Wiley.

Fishell, J. 1992. Leadership for social change. *Political Psychology* 13:663–692.

Fitzpatrick, P. 1993. The impossibility of popular justice. In *The possibility of popular justice: A case study of community mediation in the United States*, edited by S. E. Merry and N. Milner. Ann Arbor: University of Michigan Press.

Florin, P., and A. Wandersman. 1984. Cognitive social learning and participation in community development. *American Journal of Community Psychology* 12:689–708.

Folberg, J., and A. Taylor. 1984. *Mediation: A comprehensive guide to resolving conflicts without litigation*. San Francisco: Jossey-Bass.

Folger, J. P., and T. S. Jones, eds. 1994. *New directions in mediation*. Thousand Oaks, CA: Sage.

Fowler's Dictionary of modern English usage. 1950. London: Oxford University Press.

Freire, P. 1970. *Pedagogy of the oppressed*. New York: Herder and Herder.

Friedmann, J. 1992. *Empowerment: The politics of alternative development*. Cambridge, MA: Blackwell.

Fromkin, H. L., and S. Streufert. 1976. Laboratory experimentation. In *Handbook of industrial and organizational psychology*, edited by M. D. Dunnette. 415–465. Chicago: Rand-McNally.

Fukuyama, F. 1989. The end of history? *The National Interest* 16:3–18.

Garrett, R. D. 1994. Mediation in Native America. *Dispute Resolution Journal* March:38–45.

Gaventa, J. 1980. *Power and powerlessness*. Chicago: University of Illinois Press.

Gaventa, J. 1985. The powerful, the powerless and the experts: Knowledge struggles in an information age. In *Participatory research in America*, edited by P. Park, B. L. Hall, and T. Jackson. Westport, CT: Bergin & Garvey.

Gentry, D. B. 1994. The certification movement: Past, present, and future. *Mediation Quarterly* 1:285–291.

Gilbert, J. P., R. J. Light, and F. Mosteller. 1977. Assessing social innovations: An empirical base for policy. In *Statistics and public policy*, edited by W. B. Fairley and F. Mosteller. Reading, MA: Addison-Wesley.

Glasser, W. 1984. *Take effective control of your life*. New York: Harper and Row Publishers.

Gold, D. 1969. Statistical tests and substantive significance. *The American Sociologist* 4:42–46.

Goldberg, S. B., E. D. Green, and F.E.A. Sander, ed. 1985. *Dispute resolution*. Boston: Little, Brown.

Goldstein, S. B., and D. B. Chandler. 1988. PCR data base project report. Honolulu, HI: University of Hawaii Program on Conflict Resolution.

Gordon, M. E., L. A. Slade, and N. Schmitt. 1986. The "science of the sophomore" revisited: From conjecture to empiricism. *Academy of Management Review* 11:191–207.

Gordon, M. E., L. A. Slade, and N. Schmitt. 1987. Student guinea pigs: Porcine predictors and particularistic phenomena. *Academy of Management Review* 12:160–163.

Gore, A. 1993. *The Gore report on reinventing government: Creating a government that works better and costs less*. N.p.: Times Books.

Greenberg, J. 1987. The college sophomore as guinea pig: Setting the record straight. *Academy of Management Review* 12:157–159.

Gruber, J., and E. J. Trichett. 1987. Can we empower others? The paradox of empowerment in an alternative public high school. *American Journal of Community Psychology* 15:353–372.

Gutierrez, L. M. 1988. Working with women of color: An empowerment perspective. Unpublished paper.

Hagood, M. J. 1969. *Statistics for sociologists*. New York: Reynal and Hitchcock.

Halpern, M. 1991. Why are most of us partial selves? Why do partial selves enter the road into defamation? 1991. Paper presented at the American Political Science Association meeting in Washington, DC.

Hanks, L. J. 1987. *The struggle for black political empowerment in three Georgia counties*. Knoxville: University of Tennessee Press.

Harper dictionary of modern thought. 1977. New York: Harper and Row.

Harrington, C. B. 1993. Community organizing through conflict resolution. In *The possibility of popular justice: A case study of community mediation in the United States*, edited by S. E. Merry and N. Milner. Ann Arbor: University of Michigan Press.

Harrington, C. B., and S. E. Merry. 1988. Ideological production: The making of community psychology. *Law and Society Review* 22:709–734.

Harris, L. 1989. A growing sense of powerlessness. *Midweek*, November 15, B–9.

Harris, L. 1994. *The Harris poll: Alienation index*. New York: Louis Harris and Associates.

Heller, K., R. Price, S. Reinharz, S. Riger, and A. Wandersman. 1984. *Psychology and community change: Challenges of the future*. 2d ed. Homewood, IL: Dorsey.

Hellinger, D., and D. R. Judd. 1994. *The democratic facade*. 2d ed. Belmont, CA: Wadsworth Publishing.

Henry, S. 1983. *Private justice*. Boston: Routledge and Kegan Paul.

Hermann, M. S. 1993. On balance: Promoting integrity under conflicted mandates. *Mediation Quarterly* 11:123–138.

Hess, R. 1984. Thoughts on empowerment. *Prevention in Human Services* 3:227–230.

Hitt, W. D. 1988. *The leader-manager*. Columbus, OH: Battelle Press.

Honolulu Neighborhood Justice Center Annual Report. 1986–87. 1988. Honolulu: Honolulu Neighborhood Justice.

Honolulu Neighborhood Justice Center Annual Report. 1987–88. 1989. Honolulu: Honolulu Neighborhood Justice.

Huntington, S. P. 1991. *The third wave: Democratization in the late twentieth century.* Norman, OK: University of Oklahoma Press.

Huntington, S. P. 1993. The clash of civilizations. *Foreign Affairs* Summer 72:22–49.

International encyclopedia of the social sciences. 1968. New York: Macmillan.

International relations dictionary. 1969. New York: Holt, Rinehart and Winston.

Israel, B. A., S. J. Schurman, and J. S. House. 1989. Action research on occupational stress: Involving workers as researchers. *International Journal of Health Services* 19:135–155.

Ito, K. 1985. Ho'oponopono, to make right: A Hawaiian conflict resolution and metaphor in the construction of a family therapy. *Culture, Medicine and Psychiatry* 9:201–217.

Jackson, D. N. 1967. *Personality research form manual.* Goshen, NY: Research Psychologists Press.

Johnny, N. 1987. The relationship between traditional and institutionalized dispute resolution in the Federated States of Micronesia. Program on Conflict Resolution. Occasional Paper 1987–3. Honolulu: University of Hawaii at Manoa.

Jones, E. E. 1985. Major developments in social psychology during the past five decades. In 3d ed., Vol. 1. *Handbook of social psychology,* edited by G. Lindzey and E. Aronson. 47–107. New York: Random House.

Katz, R. 1984. Empowerment and synergy. *Prevention in Human Services* 3:201–226.

Keilitz, S., G. Gallas, and R. Hansen. 1988. State adoption of alternative dispute resolution. *State Court Journal* 12:4–13.

Kelly, P. 1983. *Fighting for hope.* Boston: South End Press.

Kelly, P. 1989. Foreword. In *Healing the wounds: The promise of ecofeminism,* edited by J. Plant. ix–xi. Philadelphia: New Society Publishers.

Kelso, W. A., and B. E. Swanson. 1994. Empowering the urban poor: Contending perspectives from left and right. Paper presented at the Florida Political Science Association meeting.

Kent, G. 1988. Empowerment for children's survival. Unpublished paper.

Kent, G. 1990. *Politics of children's survival.* New York: Praeger.

Kerlinger, F. 1973. *Foundations of behavioral research.* 2d ed. New York: Holt, Rinehart and Winston.

Kieffer, C. 1984. Citizen empowerment: A development perspective. *Prevention in Human Services* 3:9–36.

Kindervatter, S. 1979. *Nonformal education as an empowering process.* Amherst: University of Massachusetts.

Knebel, F. S., and G. S. Clay. 1987. *Before you sue.* New York: William Morrow and Company.

Kolb, D. M. 1983. *The mediators.* Cambridge, MA: MIT Press.

Kothari, R. 1993. The yawning vacuum: A world without alternatives. *Alternatives* 18:119–139.

Kressel, K. 1986. Research on divorce mediation: A summary and critique of the literature. Unpublished paper.

Kressel, K., and D. G. Pruitt. 1985. Themes in the mediation of social conflict. *Journal of Social Issues* 41:179–198.

Kressel, K., D. G. Pruitt, and associates. 1989. *Mediation research.* San Francisco: Jossey-Bass.

Kuhn, T. S. 1970. *The structure of scientific revolutions.* 2d ed. Chicago: University of Chicago Press.

Lappe, F. M. 1989. *Rediscovering America's values.* New York: Ballantine Books.

Laue, J. H. 1982. Ethical considerations in choosing intervention roles. *Peace and Change* 8:29–41.

Lederach, J. P., and R. Kraybill. 1993. The paradox of popular justice: A practitioner's view. In *The possibility of popular justice: A case study of community mediation in the United States,* edited by S. E. Merry and N. Milner. Ann Arbor: University of Michigan Press.

Lerner, M. 1979. Surplus powerlessness. *Social Policy* 9:18–27.

Levenson, H. 1974. Activism and powerful others: Distinctions within the concept of internal-external control. *Journal of Personality Assessment* 38:377–383.

Li, V. H. 1978. *Law without lawyers: A comparative view of law in China and the United States.* Boulder, CO: Westview Press.

Lipset, S., M. Trow, and J. Coleman. 1956. Statistical problems. Appendix 1–B. In *Union democracy*. 427–432. Glencoe, IL: Free Press.

Locke, E. A., ed. 1986. *Generalizing from laboratory to field settings.* Lexington, MA: Lexington Books.

Lockhart, D. C., ed. 1984. *Making effective use of mailed questionnaires.* San Francisco: Jossey-Bass.

Lowry, K. 1993. Evaluation of community-justice programs. In *The possibility of popular justice: A case study of community mediation in the United States*, edited by S. E. Merry and N. Milner. Ann Arbor: University of Michigan Press.

McClelland, D. C. 1975. *Power: The inner experience.* New York: John Wiley and Sons.

McGillis, D. 1986. *Community dispute resolution programs and public policy.* Washington, DC: National Institute of Justice.

McGillis, D., and J. Mullen. 1977. Neighborhood justice centers: An analysis of potential models. Washington, DC: U.S. Government Printing Office.

McLaughlin, C., and G. Davidson. 1994. *Spiritual politics.* New York: Ballantine Books.

Mansbridge, J. J. 1983. *Beyond adversary democracy.* Chicago: University of Chicago Press.

Marks, J. B., E. Johnson, Jr., and P. Szanton. 1984. *Dispute resolution in America: Processes in evolution.* Washington, DC: National Institute for Dispute Resolution.

Marsella, A. J., and A. Dash-Scheurer. 1988. Coping, culture, and healthy human development. In *Health, and cross-cultural psychology*, edited by P. R. Dasen, J. W. Berry, and N. Sartorius. London: Sage.

Maslow, A. 1962. *Toward a psychology of being.* Princeton, NJ: D. Van Norstrand.

Maton, K. I., and J. Rappaport. 1984. Empowerment in a religious setting. *Prevention in Human Services* 3:37–72.

May, R. 1972. *Power and innocence.* New York: W. W. Norton.

Mearsheimer, J. J. 1990. Back to the future: Instability in Europe after the cold war. *International Security* 15:5–56.

Merry, S. E. 1982. Defining success in the neighborhood justice movement. In *Neighborhood justice: Assessement of an emerging idea*, edited by R. Tomasic and M. Feeley. New York: Longman.

Merry, S. E. 1987. Disputing without culture. *Harvard Law Review* 100:2057–2073.

Merry, S. E. 1990. *Getting justice and getting even.* Chicago: University of Chicago Press.

Merry, S. E. 1993. Sorting out popular justice. In *The possibility of popular justice: A case study of community mediation in the United States*, edited by S. E. Merry and N. Milner. Ann Arbor: University of Michigan Press.

Merry, S. E., and N. Milner. 1993. Introduction. In *The possibility of popular justice: A case study of community mediation in the United States*, edited by S. E. Merry and N. Milner. Ann Arbor: University of Michigan Press.

Merry, S. E., and N. Milner, eds. 1993. *The possibility of popular justice: A case study of community mediation in the United States.* Ann Arbor: University of Michigan Press.

Merton, R. K. 1958. *Social theory and social structure.* New York: Free Press.

Michels, R. 1962. *Political parties.* New York: Collier Books.

Milbrath, L. W. 1989. *Envisioning a sustainable society: Learning our way out.* SUNY Series in Environmental Public Policy. Albany: State University of New York Press.

Milbrath, L. W., and M. L. Goel. 1977. *Political participation: How and why do people get involved in politics.* 2d ed. Chicago: Rand-McNally.

Milner, N., K. Lovaas, and P. Adler. 1987. The public and the private in mediation ideology. Paper presented at meeting of Law and Society Association. Washington, DC, June 14.

Miyazawa, S. 1987. Taking Kawashima seriously: A review of Japanese research on Japanese legal consciousness and disputing behavior. *Law and Society Review* 21:219–223.

Moore, C. W. 1986. *The mediation process: Practical strategies for resolving conflict.* San Francisco: Jossey-Bass.

Morrison, D., and R. Herkel, eds. 1970. *The significance test controversy: A reader.* Chicago: Aldine-Atherton.

Mueller, D. J. 1986. *Measuring social attitudes: A handbook for researchers and practitioners.* New York: Teachers College Press, Columbia University.

Mueller, J. 1989. *Retreat from doomsday: The obsolescence of major war.* New York: Basic Books.

Murray, W. H. 1951. *The Scottish Himalayan expedition.* London: J. M. Dent & Sons Ltd.

Nader, L. 1993. When is popular justice popular? In *The possibility of popular justice: A case study of community mediation in the United States,* edited by S. E. Merry and N. Milner. Ann Arbor: University of Michigan Press.

Naisbitt, J. 1994. *Global paradox.* New York: William Morrow and Company.

Neubauer, D., and M. Shapiro. 1985. The new politics of mediation: disclosing silences. Presented to the 13th World Congress of the International Political Science Association, Paris, France, July 15–20, 1985.

Oakes, M. 1986. *Statistical inference: A commentary for the social and behavioral sciences.* New York: John Wiley and Sons.

O'Connell, B. 1983. *America's voluntary spirit: A book of readings.* New York: Foundation Center.

Ondrusek, D. 1993. The mediators role in national conflicts in post-communist Central Europe. *Mediation Quarterly* 10:243–248.

Ornstein, R., and P. Ehrlich. 1989. *New world new mind: Moving toward conscious evolution.* New York: Doubleday.

Osborne, D., and T. Gaebler. 1992. *Reinventing government.* New York: Addison-Wesley.

O'Sullivan, M. J., N. Waugh, and W. Espeland. The Fort McDowell Yavapai: From pawns to powerbrokers. *Prevention in Human Services* 3:73–97.

Paehlke, R. C. 1989. *Environmentalism and the future of progressive politics.* New Haven: Yale University Press.

Parenti, M. 1995. *Democracy for the few.* 6th ed. New York: St. Martin's Press.

Parsons, R. J. 1989. Empowerment for role alternatives for low income minority girls: A group work approach. In Vol. 11, *Group work with the poor and oppressed,* edited by J. A. Lee. 27–47. New York: Haworth Press.

Pe, C. L., and A. F. Tadiar. 1979. *Kararungang pambarangay: Dynamics of compulsory conciliation.* Manka: UST Press.

Pruitt, D. G., and K. Kressel. 1985. The mediation of social conflict: An introduction. *Journal of Social Issues* 41:1–10.

Public papers of the presidents of the United States. 1962. Washington, DC: U.S. Government Printing Office.

Random House dictionary of the American language. 1966. New York: Random House.

Rappaport, J. 1984. Studies in empowerment: Introduction to the issue. In *Studies in empowerment: Steps toward understanding and action,* edited by J. Rappaport, C. Swift, and R. Hess. New York: Haworth Press.

Rappaport, J. 1985. The power of empowerment language. *Social Policy* 16:15–21.

Rappaport, J. 1987. Terms of empowerment/exemplars of prevention: Toward a theory of community psychology. *American Journal of Community Psychology* 15:127–148.

Ray, J. L. 1989. The abolition of slavery and the end of international war. *International Organization* 43:405–440.

Ray, J. L. 1995. *Democracy and international conflict: An evaluation of the democratic peace proposition.* Columbia: University of South Carolina Press.

Reissman, F. 1986. The new populism and the empowerment ethos. In *The new populism: The politics of empowerment,* edited by H. C. Boyte and F. Reissman. Philadelphia: Temple University Press.

Rensenbrink, J. 1992. *The Greens and the politics of transformation.* San Pedro, CA: R and E Miles.

Rifkin, J. 1991. *Biosphere politics: A new consciousness for a new century.* New York: Crown Publishers.

Riger, S. 1984. Vehicles for empowerment: The case of feminist movement organizations. *Prevention in Human Services* 3:99–118.

Riger, S. 1993. What's wrong with empowerment? *American Journal of Community Psychology* 21:279–292.

Riggs, F. W. 1988. Interdisciplinary tower of Babel. Unpublished paper.

Rivera, F. 1989. A definition of empowerment. Unpublished paper.

Robbins, A. 1986. *Unlimited power.* New York: Simon and Schuster.

Rogers, S. J., S. Kanrich, and I. Steinhauser. 1989. Understanding our community justice volunteers. Unpublished paper.

Rokeach, M. 1973. *The nature of human values.* New York: Free Press.

Rose, S., and B. Black. 1985. *Advocacy and empowerment: Mental health care in the community.* London: Routledge and Kegan Paul.

Rosenberg, M. 1988. Hypersensitivity and political participation. In *Surveying social life: Papers in honor of Herbert H. Hyman,* edited by H. J. O'Gorman. 236–251. Middletown, CT: Wesleyan University Press.

Rossi, P. H., and H. E. Freeman. 1985. *Evaluation: A systematic approach.* Beverly Hills, CA: Sage.

Rothschild, J. H. 1986. Mediation as social control: A study of neighborhood justice. Unpublished Ph.D. dissertation, University of California, Berkeley.

Rothschild, J. H. 1993. Dispute transformation, the influence of a communication paradigm of disputing, and the San Francisco community boards program. In *The possibility of popular justice: A case study of community mediation in the United States,* edited by S. E. Merry and N. Milner. Ann Arbor: University of Michigan Press.

Rotter, J. 1966. Generalized expectancies for internal versus external control of reinforcement. In *Psychological monographs* 80:1. Washington, DC: American Psychological Association.

Rummel, R. J. 1976. *Understanding conflict and war: The conflict helix.* Beverly Hills, CA: Sage.

Rummel, R. J. In press. *The miracle that is freedom: The solution to war, violence, genocide, and poverty.*

Sander, F.E.A. 1982. Alternatives to courts. Presented at the Conference on the Lawyer's changing role in dispute resolution. Harvard Law School, Cambridge, MA, October 15.

Sandole, D.J.D. 1985. Training and teaching in a field whose time has come: A post graduate program in conflict management. In *Elements of good practice in dispute resolution,* edited by C. Cutrona. Proceedings of the 12th Annual SPIDR conference. Washington, DC: SPIDR.

Sandole, D.J.D. 1988. Paradigms, movements, and shifts: Indication of a social invention. In *New approaches to international mediation*, edited by C. R. Mitchell and K. Webb. Westport, CT: Greenwood Press.

Sandole, D.J.D., and I. Sandole-Staroste, eds. 1987. *Conflict management and problem-solving: Interpersonal to international applications*. London: Francis Pinter.

Sarat, A. 1988. The "new formalism" in disputing and dispute processing. *Law and Society Review* 21:695–715.

Sartori, G., ed. 1984. *Social science concepts*. Beverly Hills, CA: Sage.

Satin, M. 1979. *New age politics: Healing self and society*. New York: Delta.

Scheibe, K. E. 1970. *Beliefs and values*. New York: Holt, Rinehart and Winston.

Schuler, M. 1986. *Empowerment and the law: Strategies of third world women*. Washington, DC: OEF International.

Schwerin, E. W. 1992. Models of transformational teaching. Paper presented at the American Political Science Association meeting in Chicago.

Scimecca, J. A. 1987. Conflict resolution: The basis for social control or social change. In *Conflict management and problem-solving: Interpersonal to international applications*, edited by D.J.D. Sandole and I. Sandole-Staroste. 30–33. London: Francis Pinter.

Seligman, M. 1975. *Helplessness*. San Francisco: Freeman.

Seligman, M. 1991. *Learned optimism*. New York: Alfred A. Knopf.

Selltiz, C. 1964. *Research methods in social relations*. New York: Holt, Rinehart and Winston.

Serrano-Garcia, I. 1984. The illusion of empowerment: Community development within a colonial context. *Prevention in Human Services* 3:173–200.

Shailor, J. G. 1994. *Empowerment in dispute mediation*. Westport, CT: Praeger.

Shonholtz, R. 1984. Neighborhood justice systems: Work, structure, and guiding principles. *Mediation Quarterly* 5:3–30.

Shonholtz, R. 1987. The citizen's role in justice: Building a primary justice and prevention system at the neighborhood level. *Annuals of the American Academy of Political and Social Sciences* 494:42–52.

Shonholtz, R. 1993a. Justice from another perspective: The ideology and developmental history of the community boards program. In *The possibility of popular justice: A case study of community mediation in the United States*, edited by S. E. Merry and N. Milner. Ann Arbor: University of Michigan Press.

Shonholtz, R. 1993b. The role of minorities in establishing mediating norms and institutions in the new democracies. *Mediation Quarterly* 10:231–242.

Shook, V. 1985. *Ho'oponopono: Contemporary uses of a Hawaiian problem-solving process*. Honolulu: University of Hawaii Press.

Shook, V., and N. Milner. 1993. What mediation training says—or doesn't say—about the ideology and culture of north American community-justice programs. In *The possibility of popular justice: A case study of community mediation in the United States*, edited by S. E. Merry and N. Milner. Ann Arbor: University of Michigan Press.

Silbey, S. S., and S. E. Merry. 1986. Mediator settlement strategies. *Law and Policy* 8:7–32.

Slaton, C. D. 1992. *Televote: Expanding citizen participation in the quantum age*. Westport, CT: Praeger.

Slaton, C., and T. Becker. 1981. Hawaii's community mediation service: The university-based model of neighborhood justice center. Presented at the 1981 National Convention of the American Psychological Association, Los Angeles, CA.

Slaton, C., and T. Becker. 1990. A tale of two movements: ADR and the greens. In *Conflict: Readings in Management and Resolution*, edited by J. Burton and F. Dukes. New York: St. Martin's Press.

Sniderman, P. M. 1975. *Personality and democratic politics.* Berkeley: University of California Press.

Solomon, B. B. 1976. *Black empowerment: Social work in oppressed communities.* New York: Columbia University Press.

Spangler, D. 1988. *The new age.* Issaquah, WA: Morningtown Press.

Spretnak, C. 1986. *The spiritual dimension of green politics.* Santa Fe, NM: Bear & Company.

Spretnak, C., and F. Capra. 1986. *Green politics.* Rev. ed. Santa Fe, NM: Bear & Company.

Starhawk. 1987. *Truth or dare: Encounters with power, authority, and mystery.* San Francisco: Harper & Row.

State of Hawaii Data Book. 1988. Honolulu, HI: Department of Business and Economic Development.

Stauffer, R. 1990. Capitalism, development, the decline of the socialist option, and the search for critical alternatives. *Occasional Papers in Political Science* 3:29–53. Honolulu: University of Hawaii.

Stulberg, J. B. 1987. *Taking charge/managing conflict.* Lexington, MA: D. C. Heath and Company.

Stulberg, J. B. 1993. Cultural diversity and democratic institutions: What role for negotiations? *Mediation Quarterly* 10:249–264.

The Center Letter. 1988. Fall/Winter. Honolulu, HI: Honolulu Neighborhood Justice Center.

The Center Letter. 1988. Spring. Honolulu, HI: Honolulu Neighborhood Justice Center.

Theobald, R. 1987. *The rapids of change: Social entrepreneurship in turbulent times.* Indianapolis: Knowledge Systems.

Thomson, Sir G. 1961. *The inspiration of science.* London: Oxford University Press.

Thompson, W. I. 1985. *Pacific shift.* San Francisco: Sierra Club Books.

Thomson, D. R., and F. L. DuBow. 1993. Organizing for community mediation: The legacy of community boards of San Francisco as a social-movement organization. In *The possibility of popular justice: A case study of community mediation in the United States,* edited by S. E. Merry and N. Milner. Ann Arbor: University of Michigan Press.

Tipton, R., and E. Worthington. 1984. The measurement of generalized self-efficacy: A study of construct validity. *Journal of Personality Assessment* 48:545–548.

Tirucheluam, N. 1984. *The ideology of popular justice in Sri Lanka: A socio-legal inquiry.* New Delhi, India: Vikas Publishing House.

Tomasic, R., and M. Feeley. 1982. *Neighborhood justice: Assessment of an emerging idea.* New York: Longman.

Torre, D. 1986. Empowerment: Structured conceptualization and instrument development. Unpublished Ph.D. dissertation. Cornell University, Cornell, NY.

Vogt, J. F., and K. L. Murrell. 1990. *Empowerment in organizations.* San Diego: University Associates.

Volkema, R. J. 1986. Training disputants: Theory and practice. *Mediation Quarterly* Fall:27–35.

Wahrhaftig, P. 1984. Non-professional conflict resolution. *Villanova Law Review.* Presented at National Conference in Peacemaking and Conflict Resolution, St. Louis, September 20–23.

Walbek, N. V. 1988. *Saving the planet: The politics of hope.* Winona, MN: Northland Press.

Walkey, F. 1979. Internal control, powerful others, and chance: A confirmation of Levenson's factor structure. *Journal of Personality Assessment* 43:532–540.

Wall, J. A., Jr. 1981. Mediation: An analysis review and proposed research. *Journal of Conflict Resolution* 25:157–180.

Wall, J. A., and A. Lynn. 1993. Mediation: A current review. *Journal of Conflict Resolution* 37:160–194.

Warren, M. 1992. Democratic theory and self-transformation. *American Political Science Review* 86:8–23.

Weber, M. 1946. Politics as a vocation. In *From Max Weber*, edited by H. Gerth and G. W. Mills. New York: Oxford University Press.

Webster's new world dictionary of the American language. 1966. New York: World Publishing.

Wildau, S. T., C. W. Moore, and B. S. Mayer. 1993. Developing democratic decision-making and dispute resolution procedures abroad. *Mediation Quarterly* 10:303–320.

Winter, D. G. 1973. *The power motive.* New York: The Free Press.

Wolff, B. 1983. The best interest of the divorcing family-mediation, not litigation. *Loyola Law Review* 29:55–90.

Wolff, T. 1987. Community psychology and empowerment: An activist's insights. *American Journal of Community Psychology* 15:151–166.

Wrong, D. 1979. *Power: Its forms, bases, and uses.* New York: Harper and Row.

Yeich, S., and R. Levine. 1992. Participatory research's contribution to conceptualization of empowerment. *Journal of Applied Social Psychology* 22:1894–1908.

Yngvesson, B. 1993. Local people, local problems, and neighborhood justice: The discourse of "community" in San Francisco community boards. In *The possibility of popular justice: A case study of community mediation in the United States*, edited by S. E. Merry and N. Milner. Ann Arbor: University of Michigan Press.

Zimmerman, M. A. 1990. Taking aim on empowerment research: On the distinction between psychological and individual conceptions. *American Journal of Community Psychology* 18:169–177.

Zimmerman, M. A., and J. Rappaport. 1988. Citizen participation, perceived control, and psychological empowerment. *American Journal of Community Psychology* 16:725–750.

Zisk, B. H. 1992. *The politics of transformation: Local activism in the peace and environmental movements.* Westport, CT: Praeger.

Zukav, G. 1989. *The seat of the soul.* New York: Simon and Schuster.

Zurcher, L. A. 1970. The poverty board: Some consequences of Maximum Feasible Participation. *Journal of Social Issues* 26:85–107.

Index